Theology and the University

Theology and the University

Essays in Honor of John B. Cobb, Jr.

David Ray Griffin and Joseph C. Hough, Jr.,
Editors

STATE UNIVERSITY OF NEW YORK PRESS

Published by
State University of New York Press, Albany

For information, address State University of New York
Press, State University Plaza, Albany, N.Y., 12246

Production by E. Moore
Marketing by Theresa A. Swierzowski

Library of Congress Cataloging in Publication Data

Theology and the university : essays in honor of John B. Cobb, Jr. /
   David Ray Griffin and Joseph C. Hough, Jr., editors.
      p.   cm.
   Includes bibliographical references and index.
   ISBN 0-7914-0592-3 (alk. paper). — ISBN 0-7914-0593-1 (pbk. :
alk. paper)
   1. Education (Christian theology)   2. Theology—Study and teaching
(Higher)   3. Theology—Study and teaching (Graduate)   4. Church and
college.   I. Cobb, John B.   II. Griffin, David Ray, 1939–
III. Hough, Joseph C.
   BT738.17.T43   1991
   230'.071'1—dc20   90-36908
                                                            CIP

10   9   8   7   6   5   4   3   2   1

Contents

III. HISTORICAL-DESCRIPTIVE ANALYSES

IV. APPENDICES

Preface

John Cobb is, as Thomas Altizer points out herein, a university theologian. He received his theological education at the Divinity School of the University of Chicago. He has taught in university settings: after a brief stint at Emory University (1953–1955), his teaching career has been at Claremont, where he has from the outset taught at Claremont Graduate School of the Claremont University Center as well as at the School of Theology. Since 1973, besides continuing as Ingraham Professor of Theology at the School of Theology, he has been Avery Professor of Religion at Claremont Graduate School, a position he will continue to hold for a few years after his retirement in 1990 from the School of Theology. More important, Cobb practices the kind of theology that is described as appropriate within a university by several of the contributors to this volume: a critical rather than an authoritarian theology. And he has addressed issues that are, or at least should be, central in the university's thinking, issues such as the nature of life, the intrinsic value and rights of nonhuman species, a sustainable economic order, the falsity and destructiveness of modern individualism, the possibility of affirming pluralism without relativism, and the way in which the disciplinary ordering of knowledge, research, and teaching defeats the central aim of the university: to educate for the common good.

Because Cobb is a university theologian in all these senses, we decided, when asked by the faculty of the School of Theology at Claremont to edit a *Festschrift* for Cobb upon the occasion of his retirement from this faculty, that the theme should be "theology and the university." Our aim was to produce a volume that would not only nominally be composed of "essays in honor of John B. Cobb, Jr.," but would actually honor him by being an important book on a topic at the center of his concerns.

Most of the essays herein were written specifically for this volume, and all of them are published here for the first time. Contributors were invited to write on any topic of their choice under the general theme of "theology and the university." Three of the essays speak to the question of the way in which theology can help the university better contribute to the common good, which is especially appropriate in the light of the fact that one of Cobb's recent books is entitled *For the Common Good*. Three of the essays are grouped under the unexciting heading "Historical-Descriptive Analyses," but readers should find each of these essays stimulating as well as illuminating. Five of the essays address the question of "the place of theology in the university," especially the question of whether theology, at least theology of a particular sort, is appropriate within a secular university. This question is in fact the central issue of the volume: the essays under the other headings speak to this question, even if not as centrally as do the essays in the first section. The volume as a whole, then, challenges the widespread assumption that theology is out of place in the contemporary university. The combined message is that theology, at least theology of a particular sort, is not only appropriate in the university, but vital.

Those interested in Cobb's own thinking may turn to Marjorie Suchocki's essay (Chapter 8), which deals with certain aspects of his theology, and to Appendix A, which is a slightly revised reprint of an essay originally published in *A Handbook of Christian Theologians*, edited by Dean G. Peerman and Martin E. Marty (Nashville: Abingdon, 1984). Those who want to pursue discussions of Cobb's theology in more depth may turn to *John Cobb's Theology in Process*, edited by David Ray Griffin and Thomas J. J. Altizer (Philadelphia: Westminster, 1977; the book is out of print, but can be obtained from the Center for Process Studies, 1325 North College, Claremont, CA 91711). Appendix B offers an updated (through the first half of 1990) bibliography of Cobb's writings.

We give thanks to the School of Theology at Claremont for supporting this volume, to William Eastman of the State University of New York Press, to the various authors for taking time from their busy schedules to contribute, and most of all to John Cobb for inspiring us all.

D. R. G. AND J. C. H., JR.

I. THE PLACE OF THEOLOGY IN THE UNIVERSITY

DAVID RAY GRIFFIN

1

Professing Theology in the State University

Teachers in colleges and universities (henceforth I use "universities" inclusively to cover colleges as well as universities) are called "professors," which indicates that they profess what they believe. Much that goes on under the rubric of teaching does not, to be sure, involve that conveyance of personal belief implied by the word "profess." Nonetheless, because teachers are "professors," for them to explain and defend their own beliefs about the subject matter as an integral part of their teaching is entirely appropriate. I ask here whether this appropriateness obtains when the subject matter is theology, and especially when the university is supported by the state. I divide this question of appropriateness into two questions: *Can* theology (legally, constitutionally) be taught in the state university in the United States? *Should* it be taught?

This dual question is, of course, part of the larger question about the teaching of religion in public schools. A consensus has been growing, thanks in large part to some Supreme Court rulings, with regard to both aspects of the question. This consensus depends upon distinguishing some meanings of "teaching religion" from others. If teaching religion means leading religious activities (such as saying prayers or reading the Bible devotionally) or attempting to inculcate a religious creed, then religion cannot be taught without violating the First and Fourteenth Amendments to the Constitution (the Fourteenth Amendment made the Bill of Rights applicable to individual states). But if teaching religion means teaching *about* religion, and this teaching is done "objectively" as part of a "secular" program of education (hence primarily for educational purposes rather than to advance or inhibit religion), and this teaching does not entail undue "entanglement" between the state's agencies and religious bodies, then teaching religion in state-supported schools is entirely legal.[1] A consensus is also growing that the teaching of religion in this sense *should* be part of the curriculum. This objective study of religion is advocated on the grounds, for example, that it is necessary for understanding history, human nature, and important differences between cultures.

The teaching of theology is, in one sense, already included in this growing consensus about the teaching of religion. To learn about Judaism, Christianity, Islam, Hinduism, Buddhism, African religions, and Native American religions includes learning about their sets of beliefs, including those highly developed systems produced by thinkers such as Maimonides, Augustine, Śankara, and Nagarjuna. So, whether one uses the term "theology" broadly to cover any set of religious beliefs or reserves it for highly articulated systems, the study of theology in one sense is an integral part of the objective study of religion.

In this essay, however, I ask about teaching theology in a different sense. I ask not simply about examining the theological beliefs of various groups but also about questioning their truth in the context of professing one's own theological perspective. This might well be done while teaching about a wide variety of theological perspectives, but the point is that one would explain and give supporting reasons for one's own theological convictions. Could this be done? At first glance it might seem that this is precisely what is ruled out by the distinction between the teaching of religion and teaching *about* it, and by the stipulation that the teaching be objective. I argue, however, that this is not necessarily the case. The phrase "professing theology" can, to be sure, suggest several things that could not be practiced in a state university. But, just as distinctions between possible meanings of "teaching religion" opened the way for clarifying what is and is not possible, distinctions between possible meanings of "professing theology" might open the way for seeing that at least one form of this activity would be possible.

If the profession of theological perspectives in any sense were permissible in a state university, the further question would be whether it is desirable. If we can do it, should we? I will suggest that we both can and should.

Before entering into this twofold question, I should say what I mean by "theology" in the sense of a "theological perspective." Two characteristics are crucial. First, in a theological portrayal of the world or some part or aspect of it (such as human experience), some reality, or dimension of reality, is explicitly portrayed as holy, divine, worthy of ultimate concern and commitment, perhaps of worship. This portrayed holy reality might be a distinct being, thought in some sense to be the creator of the universe and continually active in it (which is what the term "God" or "theos" usually connotes in bibically based religious traditions and several others besides). A position need not be theistic in this sense to be called theological, as I am using the term. But I stress the theistic possibility because a position that is theological in this sense raises questions that are not raised by theologies that do not speak of God, or that equate God with the world or some undeniable aspect thereof.

Second, such a portrayal is theological if it includes a recognition that it is significantly based upon some "community of faith." I am here employing a feature of John Cobb's definition of theology (which is meant, among other things, to distinguish "theology" from constructive "philosophy of religion").[2] What distinguishes theology from metaphysical philosophy and scientific cosmology is not that it is in fact based on a "faith" that is more brought to the data than derived from them, or that this "faith" is derived from participation in and socialization into a particular community, such as the scientific community in general, or the physics community in particular. The discussion of "paradigms" and the resulting rejection of an idealized "empiricism" in the quarter-century since Cobb proffered his definition have confirmed these two points. What distinguishes a perspective as theological (besides the fact that it explicitly affirms something as holy) is that it *explicitly recognizes and affirms* its dependence upon a community of faith.

Given this understanding of theology, then, should professors in a state university be allowed and even encouraged by the university to profess a theological, perhaps theistic, perspective? If so, could they do so consistently with the U.S. Constitution?

I. SHOULD THEOLOGY BE PROFESSED
IN THE UNIVERSITY?

With regard to the question of legality, the difference between private and state universities is crucial: private universities can teach theology however they wish; they can even require chapel attendance and other religious practices. But with regard to the question of whether theology should be professed in the university (assuming the legality of doing so), the difference between public and private universities has been diminishing. Many private universities, of course, were historically founded by churches, and the teaching of theology, indeed a particular form of theology, was an integral part, often a required part, of the curriculum. The churches' control of most of these universities, however, has long been a thing of the past, and in recent decades their departments of religion or theology have tended to become dapartments of "religious studies," indistinguishable from such departments at state universities. The sense of what is appropriate to teach in these schools is increasingly shaped by sensibilities pervasive of the academy in general and the religious academy in particular. The result is that the profession of a theological position is increasingly thought to be no more appropriate in a private than in a state univerity. Indeed, already in 1936 in *The Higher Learning in America*, Robert Hutchins said: "Theology is banned by law from some institutions. It might as well be from the rest."[3] (This sensibility is so pervasive that the appropriateness of theology, in distinction from historical, sociological, psychological, and phenomenological studies of religion, is even questioned by some professors in theological seminaries.) Accordingly, although the question of whether theology can legally be professed applies only to state universities, the present question of whether it should be professed can be discussed in relation to universities in general.

My threefold argument for the appropriateness of professing theology in the university is that, with regard to at least one meaning of "professing theology," (A) there is no good reason to exclude it, (B) it would be arbitrary to exclude it, and (C) there is good reason to include it.

A. There is no good reason to exclude theology. One common objection to professing a theological perspective in the university is that theology is dogmatic or authoritarian, being based on faith in revelation, whereas the other disciplines that intend to describe the nature of reality—philosophy, the natural sciences, and the social sciences—are based upon objective evidence and reason. Theology simply announces the "truth," which it claims to have been given in an earlier age, while the university is committed to the gradual discovery of truth. Philosophy and the sciences suggest hypotheses that are to be tested in terms of their illuminating power (called "predictive success" by the natural sciences), but the alleged truths announced by theology are to be accepted not on the basis of any objective criteria but solely on the basis of the claim that they were revealed by God (a claim, incidentally, that does not stand up well under scrutiny, such as the historical-critical study of the Bible). Theology is therefore out of place in the university.

But this objection equates theology as such with a particular form of theology—a form that is rejected by many theologians. For these theologians, such as John Cobb, the old idea that theology is "faith seeking understanding" is interpreted to mean that the method of theology is not formally different from that of constructive philosophical and scientific thinking.[4] Biblically based ideas are not assumed to be products of infallible revelation, but are treated as hypotheses to be tested. They are tested by seeing whether they can lead to an interpretation of reality that is superior (or at least equal) to other positions based on different starting points in terms of the normal criteria for rational-empirical thought. That is, is the position more self-consistent, more adequate to all the relevant data of experience, and more illuminating of those data? To the extent that these criteria are fulfilled, the hypotheses, initially taken on faith, are verified.

Seeing that this approach is not formally different from philosophical and scientific thinking depends upon recognizing that the old idea of a purely empirical approach is unrealistic. It is now widely recognized that no constructive thinking is empirical in the sense of first gathering data and only secondarily formulating a hypothesis to account for them. Rather, *all* thinking, including philosophical and scientific thinking, is influenced from the outset by various intuitions, insights, or hunches. These intuitions are not so much taken from the data of experience inductively—they certainly are not initially justified by the data—as brought to them as hypotheses to be tested. These hypotheses must temporarily be taken on faith. This "faith" is not an alternative approach to knowledge from that based on reason and experience, but is a necessary ingredient in the rational-empirical method, whatever the subject matter. Given the growing acceptance of the idea that this is how scientific as well as philosophical thought works, there is no reason to exclude this type of theology from the university on methodological grounds. Theology differs from these other approaches in this respect only by being more self-conscious of the source of its faith-perspective.

To be sure, the term "hypothesis" can be quite misleading. It suggests that thinkers characteristically hold their unproven ideas with a tentativeness that allows them to let go of these ideas readily in the face of disconfirming evidence. In reality, the term "conviction"[5] would be more descriptive. But this is as true of philosophers and scientists as it is of theologians. They may be as committed to, say, a materialistic worldview as a theologian is to the existence of an omnipotent creator. The fact that many theologians hold to their hypotheses tenaciously, therefore, does not differentiate them from many philosophers and scientists. Furthermore, to say that the hypotheses are really convictions is to speak of the person's psychological attitude, not of the method he or she has agreed to stand by. The method is as I have described it as long as the person agrees that the initial idea can be defended as true not on the basis of its alleged mode of origination (namely, through "revelation"), but only in terms of its ability to account for the relevant facts of experience in a comprehensive, self-consistent way.

A second common objection to including theology in the university curriculum is the ontological correlate to the previous methodological objection: The university now presupposes a naturalistic worldview, whereas theology speaks of the supernatural. Although the various sciences in the seventeenth and eighteenth centuries continued to presuppose God as the external creator of the world, and some scientists, including Isaac Newton, even believed that God continued to intervene now and then in the world after its original creation, the scientific community has long since left behind this supernaturalistic context. Historians do not speak of God as a causal factor in history, but seek to explain all events on naturalistic terms. The same is true for psychologists and sociologists. The idea that the web of natural causes is never broken is the assumption of natural scientists, social scientists, and historians. Theology, with its supernaturalism, may not have been out of place in the universities in earlier centuries, but it would be out of place in the university of our time.

The main problem with this objection is that it assumes that a theological worldview is necessarily supernaturalistic. But if "supernaturalism" involves the belief that the web of natural causation can be interrupted by a divine being, many of the leading theologies of the twentieth century have not been supernaturalistic. Some theologians have avoided supernaturalism by rejecting theism, that is, by denying that the term "God" refers to a divine being. It is taken to refer instead to being itself (Paul Tillich), a cluster of ideals (John Dewey, Donald Cupitt), creative interchange (Henry Nelson Wieman), the linguisticality of human existence (Gerhard Ebeling),[6] or some other feature or dimension of reality. Other theologians have developed a naturalistic theism. According to the version of naturalistic theism (or pan-en-theism) developed by Alfred North Whitehead, Charles Hartshorne, and the process theologians inspired by them (such as John Cobb), God and a world exist with equal necessity (not our particular world, but some world or other of finite existents). God did not create the world *ex nihilo*, therefore, if that means out of absolute nothingness. Rejecting *creatio ex nihilo* in this sense means rejecting the idea that there has been, or could have been, a time (or a pretemporal situation) in which God alone existed. God and a world necessarily coexist. Inherent in this necessary coexistence is a set of metaphysical principles that exists with equal necessity and cannot be changed, canceled, or interrupted. Included is the principle that all finite existents have inherent causal power, and that this power can never be interrupted. God, therefore, cannot interrupt the normal causal relationships of the world any more than God could make a round square. The feature of many forms of theism that makes them incompatible with the naturalism presupposed by the contemporary university is therefore ruled out in principle. These many examples show that to have a theological perspective, perhaps even a theistic theological perspective, is not necessarily to believe in supernaturalism.

A third objection is that theology has simply been shown to be superfluous. A fully adequate explanation of reality in general and human experience in particular is in principle possible without reference to anything that could meaningfully be called God, divine, or holy (unless some generally accepted feature of reality, such as energy, or the whole universe, be called divine). Any theological perspective on reality either contradicts our best understanding of reality or fails to add anything significant to it.

But this objection begs the question. If some nontheological perspective *is* superior to every theological perspective, that superiority should be established intellectually, through debate about the respective positions' adequacy, self-consistency, and illuminating power, not decreed *a priori* by the administration or by faculty committees acting politically. It may be true that many theological positions have been shown to be false or superfluous beyond a reasonable doubt. It may well be that this is true of all the theological positions known to most university administrators and faculty members. But that consensus should not settle the issue, especially in this age of specialization, in which awareness of developments outside one's own discipline is usually minimal. Even in less specialized ages the consensus of the majority was far from infallible. In any case, the falseness or superfluity of a theological perspective on human beings and the universe in general should be settled not by fiat but by debate.

The customary objections to including theology within the university, I conclude, provide no good reason for excluding theology of every sort from the university. Saying this, however, does not establish that there is any good reason for including theology in the contemporary university curriculum. This is the task of the next two points.

B. To exclude theology would be arbitrary. Although "theology" as conceived here includes positions that do not speak of a divine being distinct[7] from the world and exercising causal efficacy in it, it also includes positions in which this twofold affirmation *is* made. My argument in this section is that given a number of other professions of belief that are regularly made as a natural part of university teaching, it would be arbitrary to exclude in principle professions of belief in the existence and causal efficacy of a being who would in our tradition most naturally be called "God."

With regard to the question of existence: physicists, for example, are free to profess their belief in the real existence of electrons, neutrinos, quarks, gravitons, and black holes. These entities are not directly observed; their existence is based on inference. In the case of black holes and gravitons, in particular, the reasons for postulating their existence are highly speculative, depending upon chains of inferential reasoning within a very complex framework that could well be overthrown as theoretical physics proceeds. And the physics community is not unanimous on these points. Some physicists, for defensible reasons, have doubts about the dominant viewpoints, and publish alternative interpretations of the relevant data. They also may express their opinions in the course of their teaching.

Many theologians believe that there are data that point to the existence of a being who created (or is creating) the world. One argument is from the order of the world. Other arguments are from religious, moral, and aesthetic experience, from novelty, and from the presupposition of truth.[8] These theologians argue that the existence of a divine being with certain attributes is the most reasonable inference from these data.

Why is it legitimate for physicists to profess their belief in the real existence of electrons, neutrinos, quarks, black holes, gravitons, and so on, but not legitimate for theologians to profess their belief, and the reasons therefor, in the real existence of a creator of the universe? The convention is that professors in religious studies should limit themselves to discussing the beliefs professed by the adherents of particular religious points of view, and that they should not engage in the discussion of the truth of these beliefs. This is usually understood to be entailed by the "objective" study of religion. Religion professors can discuss truth in one sense, to be sure: they can argue about what the beliefs of various individuals and groups truly were. But the truth they can discuss is thereby limited to historical, psychological, and sociological truth; they are enjoined from discussing philosophical or theological truth. They can report the ideas others have expressed about deity; they cannot themselves discuss the truth of these ideas. If physicists were so constrained, physics departments would become departments in the psychology, history, anthropology, and sociology of physicists. Professors of physics would report what physicists (working outside the university structure, of course) had said about the real existence of electrons, neutrinos, and so on, but the professors would not raise the question of the truth of these claims. They certainly would not venture their own inferences from the relevant data. Students would be encouraged to enter these cosmological debates only indirectly, insofar as exposure to these speculative ideas could be expected to lure some of them into thinking through their own beliefs about these matters. But if that type of thinking about real existence occurred, it would have to occur on the students' own time. In the classroom, and in their papers, they would limit themselves to purely "objective" approaches. Their real object of study would be physicists, not nature.

Such an approach to physics in the university would, of course, be absurd. It would mean that the university would cease to be a locus of progress for the understanding of the universe. Any progress would have to occur outside the university in private institutes and companies, which would generally mean in settings in which the pursuit of the truth about the nature of the universe is not enshrined, even nominally, as the chief purpose.

The question of whether the universe has a purposeful creator is arguably as least as important as the question of the various entities and laws constituting the universe. Why should the
university exclude itself from informed, disciplined, and sustained
consideration of this question? Why should the injunction that
religious studies be "objective" mean that religion professors can
only study religious devotees, not the putative reality that evoked
their devotion? We also expect that the teaching of physics, chemistry, and biology will be "objective," but we do not take this to
mean that the teaching will be limited to exploring the beliefs and
practices of the natives of the physics, chemistry, and biological
communities. Objective teaching takes into consideration the various reasonable points of view (although considerable subjectivity
is involved in deciding which points of view are "reasonable") and
seeks to conform reasonably well (another caveat is needed) to the
standard criteria of objectivity: adequacy to the facts, self-
consistency, and illuminating power. The injunction that teaching
must be objective does not, in general, mean that it will exclude
all assertions about the nature of reality. Why must religious studies alone bracket all questions about the nature of reality itself in
order to be objective? Why should the university thereby exclude
itself from the possibility of contributing to progress on one of
the most important questions faced by human beings, arguably *the*
most important one? To do so is arbitrary, and cannot be justified
on the basis of the fully appropriate judgment that religious studies should be objective.

A similar conclusion can be reached if we approach the issue
in terms of causality. The issue of divine causality was already implicit in the previous point about divine existence, because most of
the inferential arguments for this existence are based on features
of the universe, including human experience, taken to be instances
of divine causation, past and/or present. But the question of divine
causation also comes up more explicitly in the discussions of the
most adequate framework for interpreting various phenomena.
With respect to theistic and nontheistic worldviews, the fundamental question is: Can explanations of all phenomena apart from
the catagory of divine causation be in principle sufficient with regard to all features of our world? For example, can the direction of
evolution be explained without this category? Can the existence of
moral and religious beliefs be explained without it?

The convention in late modern thought has been to exclude
all reference to divine causation in explaining the various phenomena of experience. This late modern thought evolved out of early

modern thought and then deism. In early modern thought, which was supernaturalistic and dualistic, the necessity for employing the category of divine causation was allowed for, even insisted upon. Divine causation was needed to account for the original creation of the universe, some subsequent natural phenomena (Newton's appeal to God to adjust planetary orbits is well known), miracles, revelation, religious experience, and the mind-body relation. In the transitional form of modern thought generally known as deism, God was still employed to account for the original creation of the universe (even Charles Darwin retained this view)[9] and for the implantation of moral and religious principles in the human mind (Thomas Jefferson).[10] But in late modern thought, it is generally accepted that the category of divine causation is not to be used to explain any phenomena, even if the person offering the explanation believes in God. This is true in all fields. Divine causation is not to be used by astrophysicists to explain the origin of the universe (although astrophysicists, being among the most prestigious and therefore most secure of the scientists, often feel free to use God-language—as does Stephen Hawking in *A Brief History of Time*), by evolutionary biologists to explain the direction of the evolutionary process, or by historians or psychologists to explain any features of human experience or behavior, including moral and religious convictions. Psychologists and historians can, of course, infer that so-and-so did such-and-such because he or she *believed* that he or she had been influenced by God; but psychologists and historians cannot, as part of their explanatory account, say that the person in question had in fact been causally influenced by God.

This exclusion, insofar as it is an exclusion in principle, is arbitrary. Virtually every other conceivable type of causal influence is allowable in explanatory accounts taught in the university. Physicists speak of the four forces of physics, and many of them say rather openly, and reductionistically, that these four forces (electromagnetism, gravity, and the weak and strong forces within the nucleus of the atom) account for all the phenomena of the universe—including the behavior of the physicist in reaching this conclusion. Biological evolutionists discuss the true causes of evolution, and neo-Darwinians, propounders of the current orthodoxy, insist that these causes are limited to purely random mutations (at least some of which are caused by cosmic rays) and natural selection. They emphatically insist that other types of causes, such as divine guidance and the inheritance of acquired characteristics, do not occur.[11] Psychologists debate whether genetic or environmental factors are more important in causing human behavior. Some psychologists allow self-determination to be a contributing cause. Freudians and other depth psychologists discuss the relative causal power of conscious and unconscious factors, and which kinds of unconscious influences are decisive. Various thinkers debate whether economic, psychodynamic, or genetic causes are more important, and all of these types of causes are used to explain social phenomena, including religion. Seemingly the only kind of conceivable causal influence that is ruled out *a priori* is divine influence. Is such an exclusion not arbitrary?

One can, of course, explain historically, at least to some extent, how this exclusion came about. One factor is the aforementioned point that divine causation has generally been, at least in previous centuries, understood as supernatural causation, whereas natural scientists decided, properly, to limit their investigation to natural causes. Social scientists, understandably, followed suit.

Another important historical factor in accounting for the exclusion of divine causation in intellectual explanations was that the relation between divine and natural causation was traditionally formulated in terms of primary and secondary causation. In this schema, God was the primary cause of every event, but every event also had a set of necessary and sufficient natural or secondary causes: sufficient, that is, to account for everything except the existence of the whole chain of causes and effects; only God as the primary cause could account for this. In this schema, accordingly, divine causation was different in kind from natural causation; it operated on a different level. Natural causation accounted for the "whatness" of things, divine causation for their "isness." God, therefore, was not one cause among others, but was a cause of a categorically different kind. Reference to divine causation answered a different kind of question. As long as one asked only why particular things are as they are, and did not ask this different question (namely, "Why does anything finite exist at all?"), one did not need to refer to God—with one exception. Some events were said by some theologians to have no natural causes, at least no sufficient ones. These events, known as "miracles," were caused by God directly, without the mediation of secondary causes. For these events, divine causation directly accounted for the whatness as well as the isness of the events, being the sufficient cause of both. Only for these rare events did one need to speak of divine causation to account for the whatness of things. To be sure, God as the primary cause of all things was the sufficient cause of the whatness as well as the isness of all events, miraculous and ordinary. But ordinary events had a set of secondary causes that were also sufficient to account for them (that is, for their whatness). Ordinary events had two sufficient causes: the divine causes, and the set of secondary causes. This position was said not to be self-contradictory because the two sufficient causes operated on different levels. In any case, this position fostered the expectation that most events could be completely explained, as long as one stayed away from ultimate questions, without reference to the category of divine causation. This expectation was extended to all events when the category of miraculous events was rejected. Through this process the notion of divine causation came to seem superfluous at best.[12]

Other factors also played a role in shaping the sensibility of late modern intellectuals. One such factor is the problem of evil: To introduce any talk of divine causation raises the problem of why, if God is active in the world, the world contains so much evil.[13] Another factor is that the notion of divine causation has been most prominently associated with now-discredited ideas. It has been associated in the popular mind not only with miracles, understood as supernatural interruptions of the normal cause–effect relations, but also with infallible inspiration of the Bible (which would involve the same kind of interruption) and natural catastrophes (still called "acts of God" by insurance companies). Divine causation has also been associated with temporary gaps in our understanding of the natural (in the sense of finite) causes of certain events. The practice of using such gaps for theological apologetics gave rise to the widespread conviction that any attempt to employ divine causation for explanatory purposes constitutes an appeal to a "God of the gaps."

For these and other reasons, modern intellectuals have become nervous about, even adamant against, employing any notion of divine causation.[14] Included among these intellectuals are religion scholars and even many theologians. Indeed, it is often students of religion who are most programmatic in excluding the category of divine causation from intellectual explanations, because they are often the ones who have thought through most thoroughly the implications of the modern worldviews for this question and who are most conversant with the problems inherent in the traditional ways of speaking of divine causation.

We can see then that the exclusion of the category of divine causation from university intellectual life is not totally arbitrary; there are historical reasons for it that make it quite understandable. But in one sense it *is* arbitrary, at least if there are ways of thinking about divine causation other than those that led to the problems. I have already pointed out the existence of theistic naturalisms, or naturalistic theisms, according to which divine causation involves no interruption of the normal causal processes. Belief in divine causation in this sense is therefore not necessarily contradicted by the vast evils of our world, or by naturalistic explanations of natural catastrophes, extraordinary (so-called miraculous) events, and the composition of sacred scriptures. At the same time, the schema of primary and secondary causation is not the only way to understand the relation between divine and nondivine causes. God is portrayed in some versions of naturalistic theism as in one sense "a cause among other causes," yet not in such a way as to fill a gap in our knowledge that could in principle be filled by some finite cause.[15]

My argument, in short, is that although the exclusion in principle of the category of divine causation from university intellectual life may be historically understandable, it is philosophically indefensible. If this exclusion *is* thought defensible, it should be actually defended, not simply presupposed without discussion. And it should be defended in debate with those who believe that the category of divine causation is necessary if our explanations of some (or perhaps all) phenomena are to be in principle adequate. This means that those with this latter belief should be allowed, and even encouraged, by the university to make the case for their position. It is philosophically arbitrary to exclude this position from being professed in the university, especially when positions that more or less explicitly reject the necessity for the category of divine causation, and perhaps even its intelligibility, are professed.

One way to overcome the arbitrariness involved in the exclusion of discussions of divine existence and causation from the university's academic life would be to propose that all science (including science-based philosophy) should become purely positivistic, phenomenological, or behavioristic. Although these terms have different connotations, I am using them all to mean the claim that science should limit itself to describing phenomena and correlations (e.g., David Hume's "sense-data" and "constant conjunctions"), systematically eschewing all talk of causality (in the non-Humean sense of real influence). Included in this positivistic program would be the rejection of any (causal) inferences from observed phenomena to unobserved entities. This would mean not only the rejection, with behaviorists and materialists, of any talk of mind and of all unconscious processes, but also the rejection of all talk of entities such as quarks, neutrinos, and black holes, and all talk of the four forces of physics as real causes. It would also mean, unfortunately for historians and futurists, that one could not talk about the past or the future. All debates between Marxists and non-Marxists about the true causes of historical developments would have to cease; the same for all debates between Freudians and other depth psychologists about the true causes of human behavior. Ecologists would have to cease discussing the true causes of ozone depletion, global warming, and pollution in gereral. And on and on. Although this positivistic, phenomenological, behavioristic approach has had its advocates, it has not been widely practiced and is not consistently practiced even by its advocates. Indeed, anything approaching a complete implementation of this program would bring to an end all intellectual progress, which has been based on the sustained effort to distinguish reality from appearance, and true from spurious causal connections. Because the academy (rightly) continues this quest, the continued *a priori* exclusion of the arguments for the existence and causal efficacy of a divine being will continue arbitrarily to exclude a possible source of a more complete understanding of the universe and therefore ourselves.

A possible rebuttal would be to claim that the discussion of true existence and causality in the sciences is justified, while the discussion of divine existence and causality is not, because the sciences, dealing with empirical questions that are in principle falsifiable, are able to reach consensus, whereas theology, dealing with speculative issues, is not. Although this contrast is often drawn, it is largely overdrawn. On the one hand, falsification can and does occur in theology. For example, the problem of evil has falsified, at least for a large percentage of intellectuals, the traditional concepts of God, and the historical-critical study of the Bible has falsified traditional understandings of divine inspiration. On the other hand, some issues classified as scientific are highly speculative, such as the origin of the universe, the nature of gravitation (is it real attraction or the result of the curvature of space?), the possibility of particles going backward in time, and the causes of evolutionary change. And consensus is not so complete on many issues as conventional textbooks about science often suggest. For example, there are many different views about the correct interpretation of quantum theory, and neo-Darwinism is simultaneously being staunchly (even dogmatically) defended and widely questioned—and Lamarckism is making a comeback. When we get into psychology and sociology, the range of speculation is even greater. "Crucial experiments" are increasingly difficult to devise, and the number of theories with substantial following is, accordingly, even larger. Of course, one may reply that the so-called social sciences are not really sciences just for this reason. But this reply would be irrelevant to the point at hand, which is that professors of these subjects regularly profess their beliefs about these highly speculative matters upon which consensus is difficult to obtain. The difference between all these disciplines and theology is at most a difference of degree. This difference could not provide a justification for ruling theological discussion out of the university.

I conclude that no nonarbitrary reason for excluding theology as such from the university can be derived from considering the nature of theology in relation to the nature of the university. I move now from this negative point to the positive point that the nature of the university implies that theology *should* be taught.

C. There is good reason to include theology in the university. Although several reasons for including theology in the university could be given, I limit my discussion here to one: By allowing nontheological and even antitheological views of reality to be professed, while not allowing theological views, the university implicitly gives support to antitheological worldviews. For example, neo-Darwinisn is an explicitly antitheological view, maintaining that random mutations and natural selection are the causes, and the only causes, of evolution. Neo-Darwinism explicitly excludes the possibility of theistic guidance. (Even if some of the textbooks have been cleaned up, under pressure from the creationists, so that this point is not so explicit, the fact remains that this account of the origin of the species is not neutral with respect to theism.) Likewise, the widely taught reductionistic idea that the four forces of physics account for all developments in the world rules out all "downward causation" and thereby both human freedom and divine providence of even the subtlest sort. Psychobiology, sociobiology, and behaviorism are three examples of reductionistic theories that rule out human freedom and divine influence.[16] Freudian psychology and Marxian sociology are explicitly atheistic. Most of these schools of thought offer explanations of the existence of religion that presuppose the absence of divine influence on human exeperience. If it allowed these theories to be taught, but not theological theories that would counter them, the university would not remain neutral about theology. It would allow students to be exposed not only to nontheological and antitheological theories but, more importantly, to living advocates of those theories, while it would not allow students, as part of their academic life, to be exposed to living advocates of theological understandings of reality. The university's policy would therefore legitimate nontheological and antitheological theories while withholding legitimacy from theological theories. The university would thereby not be fulfilling its duty to be neutral, encouraging the free exchange of opinions among advocates of all reasonable points of view. If one retorts that a theological point of view is not a reasonable one, that returns us to a point discussed earlier. If no theological point of view can hold its own in rational debate with its competitors, this will become obvious in the debate. But this point should be decided by debate, not *a priori*.

We may conclude that, if only the nature of theology and the nature of the university are considered, the university should include theology. But this discussion has prescinded from what many people consider to be the main reason for excluding theology from the state university in the United States: the idea that the U.S. Constitution, as interpreted by the Supreme Court, prohibits the profession of religious viewpoints within state-supported schools.

II. CAN THEOLOGY BE PROFESSED IN THE STATE UNIVERSITY?

I contend that for professors in a state university to profess their theological position, in the sense of both stating it and giving reasons for considering it superior to other theological and antitheological positions, would not necessarily conflict with either the establishment clause or the free exercise clause of the First Amendment to the U.S. Constitution. It would not necessarily involve the state in the establishment of religion, and it would not necessarily include the state in preventing the free exercise of religion, at least no more than does the teaching of a number of other subjects whose constitutionality is generally accepted.

A. Professing theology and the establishment clause. The First Amendment to the U.S. Constitution begins: "Congress shall make no law respecting an establishment of religion, or prohibiting the free exercise thereof." In our system of government, what exactly this means with respect to teaching religion in state-supported schools is determined by rulings of the Supreme Court. Probably the most common way of summarizing the import of the various rulings of the Supreme Court relevant to this issue is to say that there can be teaching *about* religion, but not *of* religion, and that religion must be taught objectively, as part of a secular program of education, as opposed to being taught with a religious purpose to indoctrinate or to elicit commitment. It is widely thought that the Supreme Court rulings, thus interpreted and summarized, prohibit any consideration of the truth of religious doctrines, such as the existence of God. The teacher can report that the adherents of a particular religion believe in a divine being with certain attributes, but the teacher cannot reflect out loud about the truth of this belief. For example, Frederick Olafson, in an essay titled "Teaching *About* Religion," begins with the premise "that the teaching of religion in the public schools is unconstitutional." By the teaching of religion he means "straightforward indoctrination." What *is* constitutional, he says, is "the historical and sociological study of religion [which] treats religion simply as one aspect of human culture without any presuppositions as to the validity of the epistemic claims it typically makes." Truth of one kind is to be sought, to be sure: Religious studies are to be pursued "with a high degree of that scholarly objectivity that cleaves unflinchingly to the truth." But the truth he has in mind is historical and sociological truth, not theological or metaphysical truth. We can have in public schools only a "treatment of religion that bypasses the ultimate issues of the truth or validity of the claims about man and the world made by religions."[17] In this interpretation, the only two possibilities seem to be indoctrination, on the one hand, and a study of religion that completely brackets the question of the truth of religious views about human beings and the rest of the universe, on the other. There seems to be no middle ground. Olafson is, to be sure, speaking primarily about elementary and secondary schools. But because he is speaking about what is and is not constitutional, his remarks would seemingly apply to the state-supported university as well. Although physics courses in the university can presuppose or consider evidence for the existence of quarks, no religion course could presuppose or consider evidence for the existence of God as believed by Christians, Moslems, or Hindus. This position is widely accepted in the university community in general and the academic religious community in particular.

I believe that this position involves an overinterpretation of Supreme Court rulings about the establishment clause. (Chief Justice Warren Burger once remarked that, when the Supreme Court speaks, "a whisper becomes a shout.") Most of the relevant rulings have been occasioned by lawsuits involving religious practices, especially prayers (*Engel v. Vitale* [1962]) and Bible reading (*Abington v. Schempp* [1963]). There should be no doubt by now that all such practices are prohibited. There should also be no doubt about any teaching that could reasonably be classified as religious propaganda and indoctrination. What is not so clear is whether the idea that all teaching of religious subjects must be "objective" means that the question of the truth of religious beliefs must always be avoided. Could not this question be approached objectively? Professors of physics, biology, astronomy, and psychology are not denied the right, and are even encouraged, to explore the truth about the universe and human nature and to teach their students the ideas that they and their colleagues consider to be most probably true. The idea that questions about religion should be explored objectively should not automatically be taken to mean that the truth of various religious beliefs about the universe cannot be explored.

The primary basis for the notion that religion can be studied in public schools if, and only if, it is "objective" is a paragraph near the end of the opinion delivered by Justice Clark, writing for the Court, in *Abington v. Schempp*. After replying to one anticipated objection to the Court's ruling, Clark stated another possible reaction: "In addition, it might well be said that one's education is not complete without a study of comparative religion or the history of religion and its relationship to the advancement of civilization." Clark's response has been repeated countless times: "It certainly may be said that the Bible is worthy of study for its literary and historic qualities. Nothing we have said here indicates that such study of the Bible or religion, when presented objectively as part of a secular program of education, may not be effected consistent with the First Amendment."[18] This statement has been used since its utterance in 1963 as the basis for starting courses in secondary schools on comparative religion, history of religion, and "The Bible as Literature," and for starting or expanding departments of religious studies in state universities. This has been all to the good, and is fully justified by the Court's opinion. But this statement has also been used to say that *only* courses of the type mentioned are permissible, and that courses in which the truth of religious beliefs is considered would in all cases be impermissible. That conclusion is not justified by Justice Clark's statement.

First, the ruling was not treating the topic of religion in the public schools in general, but the very specific question, involved in *Abington v. Schempp*, of the constitutionality of a Pennsylvania law requiring that "at least ten verses from the Holy Bible shall be read, without comment, at the opening of each public school on each school day."[19] The decision, accordingly, was focused on the question of the way in which the Bible could and could not be read in the schools. The Court was not asked to rule on every possible question about the study of religion that might be raised. Second, Justice Clark's statement, insofar as it did deal with questions broader than that of the study of the Bible, was given in response to an anticipated objection that "one's education is not complete without a study of comparative religion or the history of religion and its relationship to the advancement of civilization." His oft-quoted response is a response to that particular objection; it is not a general discourse on the one and only type of study of religion that might be permissible. The Supreme Court has not been asked that question, and it accordingly has not spoken on it. Indeed, the Court is never asked that kind of open question; its rulings are always in response to specific suits. We should, therefore, disabuse ourselves of the idea that the Court has provided some complete prescription as to what is and is not permissible. To say that x is permissible is not necessarily to say that y and z are not. The Court will not rule on y and z until it is asked.

In his concurring opinion in *Abington v. Schempp*, Justice Goldberg maintained that "the teaching *about* religion" should be "distinguished from the teaching *of* religion in the public schools."[20] The same desiderata mentioned above are applicable here as well. This statement, furthermore, is found in the concurring opinion of one judge (whereas the opinion of Justice Clark was delivered on behalf of the Court). It would thus be an overinterpretation to conclude from this statement that the Court has ruled out as unconstitutional any and every consideration of the truth of religious beliefs.

It should also be kept in mind that *Abington v. Schempp* and the other major cases relevent to the role of religion in the public schools involved elementary and secondary schools, not (state-supported) universities. The distinction is important for at least two reasons. First, students are required to attend elementary and secondary schools, whereas attending a university is voluntary. Second, students in elementary and secondary schools are younger and, presumably, more impressionable. It may be, of course, that the Court, if asked to rule about religion courses in state universities, would hold them to the same standards established for the secondary schools. But the Court, even if it were to rule that the question of the truth of religious doctrines could not be discussed in secondary schools, might well hold one of these differences to be a *relevant* difference, so that what is impermissible in secondary schools would be permissible in colleges and universities.[21] In any case, the constitutionality of courses in the state university that would involve explicit consideration of the truth of religious beliefs has not been foreclosed. It can be argued, for example, that theologians should not in principle be enjoined from professing their belief in God and divine influence in the world any more than physicists are enjoined from professing their belief in quarks and in the efficacy of the four forces of physics.

The qualification "in principle" is important. I am interested in defending only a particular type of theologizing, not every type. To explain the type I have in mind will return us to the notion of "objectivity," raised earlier. It is being increasingly accepted that there is no such thing as absolute objectivity. Subjective bias inevitably colors the opinion of individuals (including scientists), and groups of individuals (including the scientific community), regardless of the safeguards taken to preclude it. Nevertheless, a significant degree of objectivity can be attained, and standards do exist for judging the relative objectivity of approaches. As I suggested in the first section, to be considered reasonably objective an approach must include submission to the criteria of self-consistency and adequacy to the relevant facts of experience. The canons of objectivity are violated if one rules out competing positions by reference to their inconsistencies, then excuses inconsistencies in one's own position. The canons of objectivity are also violated if one's theory is held in the face of strongly disconfirming evidence. (To be sure, it is permissible to put aside a certain amount of apparently disconfirming data as "anomalies" for a certain period of time: just how much such data, and for how long, are matters of judgment submitting to no mechanical rule. But reasonable, if not infallible, judgments can be made.) Objectivity also involves the capacity and willingness to understand the arguments of other individuals and groups who oppose one's theories, to discern which of these are well grounded, and to take these objections into account, thereby possibly modifying one's original theory. In short, to be objective is to allow one's opinions to be formed, finally, on the basis of reason and evidence, not prejudice, preference, emotion, or ungrounded faith. Theology that is objective in this sense should not be excluded from the university, anymore than should physics, biology, and psychology that are objective (only) in this sense.

It might be said, however, that the establishment clause puts religious belief in a special category. This clause erects a wall between religion and the state, while not erecting a similar wall between physics, biology, or psychology and the state. In reply, it can be pointed out that such a wall *does* exist. The state cannot mandate what theories are to be taught in physics, biology, and psychology. The state, for example, cannot get involved in the question as to which interpretation of quantum theory should be taught, or even whether quantum rather than Newtonian physics should be taught. Such questions are to be left to the "free market-place of ideas"; in other words, to the judgment of the professional organizations. As Justice Jackson said in a famous passage (in *West Virginia State Board of Education v. Barnette* [1943]): "If there is any fixed star in our constitutional constellation, it is that no official, high or petty, can prescribe what shall be orthodox in politics, nationalism, religion, *or other matters of opinion*" (italics mine).[22] The "wall of separation" between religion and the state is much more famous, and much more discussed, than the analogous walls of separation implicit, for example, in the right of free speech, but only because the issue of religion has been more volatile and its wall has been more often violated.

It has been argued that what the framers of the constitution meant to exclude by the Establishment Clause was only government support for any *sect*. For example, Sydney Mead, one of the leading authorities on American religious history, says that the secularization of the government means the "desectarianization of the government; that is, the civil authority must become neutral when the particularistic claims of the sects are concerned."[23] Such a position could presuppose the idea of a natural religion that is universal; the "particularistic claims of the sects" would then be divisive additions to the universal religion shared by all. Some scholars maintain that this view was held by some of the framers of the Constitution, and that they did not mean to separate the state from religion as such but only from sectarian religion.[24] Even if this is so, however, such a position would have to be rejected today. It is now generally agreed that there is no universal religion, no set of beliefs and practices shared equally by the various religions of humanity. The state, accordingly, cannot give support to religion vs. irreligion on the basis of the claim that the established religion is not a sect but the religion belonging to all humans *qua* human.

But there is another meaning of "sectarian," I suggest, that does provide a basis for distinguishing between the types of religious teaching that can and cannot be encouraged in the state university. Sectarian religious belief can be taken to mean religious belief that is advocated not on the basis of reason and experience, but on the basis of faith that these beliefs originated through special supernatural revelation. Sectarian beliefs are those that are said to be true because they were revealed, not because they provide the basis for an account of reality (or some portion thereof) that is more self-consistent and more adequate to the facts than competing accounts. The teaching of beliefs that are sectarian in this sense should not be encouraged by any university, state or otherwise.

But if a religious interpretation of the universe is not sectarian in this sense, if it is instead defended on the basis of its self-consistency, its adequacy to the facts of experience, and its illuminating power, then it should not be excluded from the state-supported university. I am, of course, taking "nonsectarian" to be synonymous with the approach I above called "objective." There is nothing in the establishment clause, or the Supreme Court's interpretation thereof, that implies that university professors could not profess their belief in a religious interpretation of the universe and of human experience if they did so in this nonsectarian or objective way.

The distinction between a "natural" or a "philosophical" theology, on the one hand, and a "dogmatic" theology, on the other, is also relevant to this discussion. For example, Robert Hutchins argued in *The Higher Learning in America* that the university needs the type of integrating, unifying perspective that theology provided in the medieval university, but that today this perspective would have to be supplied by metaphysics rather than theology.[25] When challenged by William Adams Brown in *The Case for Theology in the University*,[26] Hutchins replied that in saying that theology could not assist us he "was thinking only of dogmatic theology, which rests upon faith, or supernatural knowledge." He continued: "In metaphysics, which may assist us, I include natural theology, which is natural knowledge."[27] The term "natural theology" is often taken to mean a theological position that is universal, at least in principle, being based solely upon data that are equally accessible to people in all times and places, and not at all upon data that are unique to, or at least more heavily stressed in, some particular religious tradition. But this idea of a natural theology is today seen to be as problematic as that of a natural religion and therefore cannot be used to justify the legality of a type of theology in the state university.

The notion of a philosophical theology, however, can be understood differently from natural theology thus construed. A philosophical theology is philosophical (rather than dogmatic) because of how it advocates the truth of its doctrines, not because of where its doctrines originated. The question of where a particular idea first arose is irrelevant to the question of whether the *defense* of the idea is properly philosophical or not. That is, ideas that were first suggested by the Bible, Plato, the Bhagavad Gita, Charles Darwin, or Albert Einstein are fair game in principle for a philosophical theology. The theology is philosophical, as opposed to dogmatic, if it defends the idea in question in terms of its place in a worldview that is self-consistent, adequate, and illuminating, rather than in terms of its origin in an authoritative source. For a theology to be philosophical in this sense is the same as for it to be nonsectarian and objective. Such theology could be professed in a state university.

Making such a claim, it should be stressed, goes against a widespread opinion. For example, it is widely held that the reason so-called creation science cannot be taught in public schools is that its idea of the origin of the universe is derived from the book of Genesis and thus from the religious scriptures of a particular religious tradition. This was a central feature in the decision against Arkansas Act 590, which had legislated that creation science as well as evolution had to be taught.[28] The problem with Act 590, however, was not that creation science involves a notion of God and the creation of the universe that is derived from the Bible, but that the state was legislating that this position had to be taught (against the consensus of the scientific community that this position is indefensible on rational-empirical grounds). The basis for deciding what ideas are to be professed in the university should not be whether or not those ideas are "religious," in the sense of having their roots in some community of faith considered "religious," but whether or not there are good reasons, in terms of criteria generally accepted in the university, for considering those ideas to be probably true.

Having argued that the establishment clause does not preclude professors from professing their belief in theological ideas, I now make another and stronger claim: the establishment clause in fact implies that the advocacy of theological ideas (in the sense described above) *cannot* be excluded from the university by the state. The reason for this claim is (1) that irreligious, antitheological ideas (usually rooted in some "community of [anti]faith," such as the Darwinian community) are professed in the university and (2) that the state is enjoined by the Constitution from showing hostility to religion by giving more support to irreligious, antitheological ideas than it gives to religious, theological ideas.

I will take the second point first. In his opinion in *Abington v. Schempp*, Justice Clark said in reply to the first anticipated objection (which was that a "religion of secularism" would be established unless the proscribed religious exercises were allowed): "We agree, of course, that the State may not establish a 'religion of secularism' in the sense of affirmatively opposing or showing hostility to religion, thus 'preferring those who believe in no religion over those who do believe.' "[29] Justice Goldberg, in his concurring opinion, said that the Constitution prohibits any "hostility to the religious" on the part of the state.[30]

The first point, that antitheological views are indeed professed in the university, was sufficiently supported in the first section of this essay. Langdon Gilkey, an arch-opponent of creationism (and a witness against the creationist-supported Act 590 in the Arkansas trial), says that the creationists are right about one thing: their claim that science is often taught as religion, and that many scientists do teach a philosophical naturalism (in the sense of atheism) in teaching evolution.[31]

I am not saying that the state must legislate that theological ideas must be taught alongside the antitheological ideas. Such legislation would be parallel to the unconstitutional Arkansas Act 590; the state would be interfering in the professions' task to decide which ideas are worthy of advocacy. I am saying only that the establishment clause should prevent the state from prohibiting teachers from dealing openly with the question of the truth of religious beliefs, and even stating their own views.

The only way for the university to avoid this conclusion, it seems to me, would be for it to prohibit professors from professing any beliefs about the nature of reality, at least any such beliefs that could possibly conflict with any theological views (which would be virtually all such beliefs). All scientists and philosophers would have to take a strictly phenomenal, instrumentalist, or positivistic view of scientific theories. I have already argued that such a policy would be absurd, harmful, and impossible to implement. The only way for the state to avoid giving support to antitheological over theological positions is to allow theological as well as antitheological ideas to be professed. Indeed, I know of no reason to think that the state does not already allow this, and there is one ruling of the Supreme Court that provides some slight positive evidence that it does allow it.[32] What is lacking, it seems to me, is only a widespread realization of the fact that the teaching of theology in the state university, at least a nonsectarian, objective, philosophical theology, as described above, is not disallowed by the establishment clause. It might be argued, however, that the teaching of theology in state institutions would be prohibited by the free exercise clause. I turn now to this question.

B. Professing theology and the free exercise clause. The free exercise clause states that the government shall make no law prohibiting the free exercise of religion by citizens. One might argue that this clause would make it impossible for state-supported schools to allow theological beliefs to be professed by state-paid faculty members in the following way. It is clear that teachers cannot teach their own religious beliefs in the sense of seeking to indoctrinate students and demanding that students agree with them in papers and examinations. Everyone agrees that such teaching would violate the students' right to the free exercise of their own religion. But this right would be violated even if teachers professed their own beliefs without demanding assent. The reason is that teachers are authority figures with the prestige of their education, their profession, and the state behind them. For them to express their own beliefs about religious matters will inevitably exert a more-or-less subtle pressure upon students to agree with their opinions, and therefore quite possibly to disagree with the religious beliefs being taught at home and at church. For a Jewish or Christian teacher to express his or her belief in God will tend to inhibit the free exercise of religion on the part of Buddhists, secular humanists, and other nontheists. Likewise, for a Buddhist teacher to express his or her disbelief in a theistic divine reality in favor of Emptiness will tend to inhibit the free exercise of religion among Jews, Christians, Moslems, and other theists.

But this argument, applied consistently, would rule out the professing not only of theological beliefs but of much else besides. Not only neo-Darwinian evolution, but all evolutionary ideas about the origin of our present world, in astrophysics and geology as well as in biology, would have to be bracketed, because some religious groups still hold to a supernatural creation of the universe a few thousand years ago. In deference to those who believe in the Mosaic authorship of the Pentateuch, professors of history, religion, and literature (in "The Bible as Literature" courses) would be unable to teach a contrary theory as most probably true. Schools of medicine would be prevented from advocating the theory that germs contribute to some diseases because the Christian Science faith disagrees. Even more absurd consequences could be imagined—for example, if belief in a flat Earth were part of the religious creed of some students. One cannot reasonably maintain, therefore, that the right to the free exercise of religion would prohibit professors of theology from saying what theological ideas they find convincing. As with other rights enumerated in the Bill of Rights, it is not an absolute right, but only an objective, *prima facie* right, which in practice must be balanced against other rights with which it is in tension.

CONCLUSION

I conclude that there is no good reason to exclude the advocacy of theological perspectives in universities, including state-supported ones, and that there are good reasons to allow and even to encourage it. Part of my argument is that to institute this policy, or to encourage it more fully and openly, does not require any new legislation. It only requires a widespread recognition that it is already possible and desirable for theological perspectives to be professed. (Of course, it also requires the existence of professors with theological perspectives, and that is something that modernity has discouraged. This problem is beyond the scope of this essay. I will comment, however, that we seem to be entering a postmodern era, and that one feature of this transition may well be a recovery of, and willingness to express, explicitly theological perspectives on reality.)

The obvious implication of this recognition would be that professors with theological convictions in philosophy and religion departments would feel permitted, even encouraged, by their colleagues and the university administration to profess openly their convictions and their reasons for them in their teaching. For some, this might mean offering theistic interpretations of cosmic and biological evolution. For others, it might mean giving interpretations of the rise and evolution of religion that presuppose the reality of genuine religious experience, in the sense of a nonsensory experience of a holy reality. It might mean interpretations of human nature and destiny that are based heavily upon the teachings of a particular tradition, such as Christianity, Islam, or Buddhism. It might mean seeking a global theology, based upon the assumption that somewhat different truths are available from the various religious traditions, truths that could be integrated, perhaps along with modern insights, into a more adequate view of reality and human nature than is present in any of the historic traditions. Many other forms are possible as well.

But the profession of a theological perspective on human experience and reality as a whole need not be limited to teachers in philosophy and religion departments. A professor of theoretical biology, for example, who was convinced that the directionality and emergent novelty of the evolutionary process can best be explained in terms of a cosmic source of order and novelty could so argue in her or his presentation of evolutionary theory. A professor of astrophysics, convinced that the set of cosmological constants often summarized under the so-called anthropic principle (which would better be called the biogenic principle[33]) points to the reality of a creator, could argue this case. Professors of history convinced that human beings have genuine religious experiences of a divine reality, and that these experiences can best be understood as resulting from divine influence in the world, might include divine influence alongside other causal factors in their attempts to reconstruct historical events. Professors of psychology who believe that human motivation is in part explainable in terms of an awareness—perhaps largely unconscious—of a holy reality that draws them forward could advocate this view as a correction to reductionistic theories, or as a theoretical framework for humanistic and transpersonal psychologies. And so on.

This aspect of one's teaching should, of course, like any other aspect, be subject to evaluation by one's peers. But the criteria for evaluation would not include judgments about the origins of one's theological ideas. Pedigree would be ignored in favor of performance; that is, the judgment that the basic vision arose out of the Bible, the Bhagavad Gita, Plato, Marx, Darwin, Bohr, Einstein, Skinner, or Seth, and has been promulgated by a community of faith informed by that vision, would be irrelevant. The relevant question would be how the perspective is defended. The first question would be: Is it defended in terms of its self-consistency, adequacy to the facts, and illuminating power (rather than in terms of the claim, whether explicit or implicit, that its basic ideas are revealed truths)? The second question would be: How well is the perspective defended? Of course, peer review on this second question will involve problems of bias, as some professors will be so prejudiced against certain theological perspectives that it will be difficult for them to render fair judgments. But these problems will not be qualitatively different from currently existing problems (with, for example, capitalistic economists evaluating the work of Marxist colleagues, or vice versa, or behaviorist psychologists evaluating the work of Freudian colleagues, or vice versa).

The chief problem in moving in the direction I have proposed in less theoretical than practical. This problem is due to the long-standing convention that professors of astronomy, biology, history, psychology, and so on do not use theological categories, especially the category of divine influence, combined with the disciplinary structure of university education; hence professors in these fields often have little sophistication about the complex epistemic, metaphysical, and theological issues involved in speaking theologically. Because of these two features of modern university education, most professors, even those inclined to do so, would not be well equipped to bring a theological perspective to bear on their teaching. This dimension of their teaching would often be relatively amateurish. The uniqueness of this problem should not, of course, be overdrawn. The theoretical, causal analyses offered by professors of biology, history, psychology, and so on are often naive and amateurish, whether they be drawing upon Darwinian, Freudian, behaviorist, Marxist, capitalist, or other theories. The attempts to speak of divine influence upon the world in general and human experience in particular would probably not be qualitatively worse. In any case, the attempts to improve the situation could be similar to the attempts to overcome some of the worst features of the present disciplinary structure of the university with regard to other issues: team teaching, interdepartmental colloquia, sabbatical grants to work in other fields, transdisciplinary journals, and the like.

The university really should, I would argue in a longer piece in agreement with John Cobb, transcend its disciplinary structure.[34] Such a proposal would be in order in a book on "theology and the university," because reflection on this topic could lead to that more radical conclusion. But for now I limit myself to this more modest proposal. In it I have dealt less with theology as a distinct discipline than with the theological as a perspective that could be professed in relation to the subject matters of any of the disciplines. My argument has been that a theological perspective both could and should be expressed in a state university. In fact, for state universities to prevent such expression, whether overtly or covertly, would be to fall short of that neutrality between religious and antireligious viewpoints that is required, not only educationally but also constitutionally.[35]

NOTES

1. For a summary and discussion of the relevant rulings of the Supreme Court, see Robert S. Michaelsen, "Constitutions, Courts, and the Study of Religion," *Journal of the American Academy of Religion* XLV/3 (1977): 291–308.

2. See John B. Cobb, Jr., *A Christian Natural Theology: Based on the Thought of Alfred North Whitehead* (Philadelphia: Westminster, 1965), 252–70.

3. Robert Hutchins, *The Higher Learning in America* (New Haven: Yale University Press, 1936), 97.

4. Cobb worked out this understanding of theology in *A Christian Natural Theology* and in his earlier *Living Options in Protestant Theology* (Philadelphia: Westminster, 1962).

5. See James W. McClendon, Jr., and James M. Smith, *Understanding Religious Convictions* (Notre Dame: University of Notre Dame Press, 1975). John Cobb has commented, in response to Stephen Pepper's suggestion that worldviews are "world hypotheses," that the term *convictions* would be more accurate. See "Ecology, Science, and Religion: Toward a Postmodern Worldview," in David Ray Griffin, ed., *The Reenchantment of Science: Postmodern Proposals* (Albany: State University of New York Press, 1988), 99–113, esp. 101–02.

6. See Paul Tillich, *Systematic Theology,* vol. 1 (Chicago: University of Chicago Press, 1951); John Dewey, *A Common Faith* (New Haven: Yale University Press, 1934); Donald Cupitt, *Taking Leave of God* (New York: Crossroad, 1981); Henry Nelson Wieman, *The Source of Human Good* (Chicago: University of Chicago Press, 1946); Gerhard Ebeling, *God and Word* (Philadelphia: Fortress, 1967).

7. To think of God as a divine being distinct from the world is not necessarily to think of God as one more finite being among others. John Cobb and Charles Hartshorne (note 8) think of God as the all-inclusive, experiential unity of the world.

8. For examples of these arguments, see various writings by Charles Hartshorne, especially *Man's Vision of God and the Logic of Theism* (1941; Hamden, Conn.: Archon Books, 1964). I have explained the role these arguments have in Hartshorne's philosophical theology in "Charles Hartshorne's Postmodern Philosophy," in *Hartshorne, Process Philosophy and Theology,* ed. Robert Kane and Stephen Phillips (Albany: State University of New York Press, 1989), 1–33.

9. Neal C. Gillespie, *Charles Darwin and the Problem of Creation* (Chicago: University of Chicago Press, 1979), 127, 129–30.

10. See Garry Wills, *Inventing America: Jefferson's Declaration of Independence* (New York: Vintage Books, 1978), chap. 13, which is titled "Endowed by their Creator."

11. For a particularly forthright statement, see Richard Dawkins, *The Blind Watchmaker: Why the Evidence of Evolution Reveals a Universe Without Design* (New York: W. W. Norton, 1987).

12. See Langdon Gilkey, "Cosmology, Ontology, and the Travail of Biblical Language," *Journal of Religion* XLI (1961), and David R. Griffin, "Relativism, Divine Causation, and Biblical Theology," *Encounter* 36/4 (Autumn 1975): 342–62, rpt. in *God's Activity in the World: The Contemporary Problem*, ed. Owen C. Thomas (Chico, Calif.: Scholars Press, 1983), 117–36.

13. I have discussed this problem in *God, Power, and Evil: A Process Theodicy* (Philadelphia: Westminster, 1976), and in *Evil Revisited: Responses and Reconsiderations* (Albany: State University of New York Press, 1990).

14. To cite an example that was recently brought to my attention by Michael Corey, a student: In *The Symbiotic Universe* (New York: William Morrow, 1988), George Greenstein cites various facts about the nature of the universe that lead him to the conclusion that an omniscient being must have designed the universe, but then rejects this explanation, which he himself considers the "most sensible" one, on the grounds that "God is not an explanation" (28).

15. I have argued that to point to a "God-shaped hole" in one's cosmology is not necessarily to speak of a "God of the gaps" in "On Ian Barbour's *Issues in Science and Religion*: A Review Essay," *Zygon* 23/1 (March 1988): 57–81, especially the last section. John Cobb has shown how divine causation can be a fully natural part of the cosmic and historical causal processes in "Natural Causality and Divine Action," *Idealistic Studies* 3 (September 1973), 207–22.

16. Behaviorism and sociobiology are too well known to need documentation. For psychobiology, see William R. Uttal, *The Psychobiology of Mind* (Hillsdale, N.J.: Lawrence Erlbaum, 1978), esp. 9–10, 52–53.

17. Frederick Olafson, "Teaching *About* Religion: Some Reservations," in *Religion and Public Education*, ed. Theodore R. Sizer (Boston: Houghton Mifflin, 1967), 84–95, especially 84–86.

18. Cited in David E. Engel, "Abington v. Schempp; Murray v. Curlett," in *Religion in Public Education*, ed. David E. Engel (New York: Paulist Press, 1974), 12–19, especially 18.

19. Ibid., 12.

20. Cited in Sizer, *Religion and Public Education*, 39.

21. Robert Michaelsen in "Constitutions, Courts, and the Study of Religion" points out that, because the landmark decisions of the Supreme Court did not deal with religious studies in the public university, we must rely primarily on inference in determining the Supreme Court's position on this topic (295).

22. Cited in Sizer, *Religion and Public Education*, 23.

23. Sydney Mead, "Religion, Federalism, Rights, and the Court," in Engel, *Religion in Public Education,* 20–40, especially 26.

24. This view is discussed by Robert Michaelsen in "Is the Public School Religious or Secular?" in *The Religion of the Republic,* ed. Elwyn A. Smith (Philadelphia: Fortress, 1971), 22–44, and in "The Public School and 'America's Two Religions'," *Journal of Church and State* VIII/3 (Autumn 1966): 380–400.

25. Hutchins, *The Higher Learning in America,* vi.

26. William Adams Brown, *The Case for Theology in the University* (Chicago: University of Chicago Press, 1938).

27. Hutchins, vi.

28. See Langdon Gilkey, *Creationism on Trial: Evolution and God at Little Rock* (1985; San Francisco: Harper & Row, 1988).

29. Cited in Engel, *Religion in Public Education,* 18.

30. Cited in Sizer, *Religion and Public Education,* 39.

31. Gilkey, *Creationism on Trial,* 78, 96–97, 164.

32. In *Tilton v. Richardson* (1971), the Supreme Court upheld the use of federal funds for four Roman Catholic colleges in Connecticut, even though courses in theology as well as religion were offered, and even though the funds were provided under the Higher Education Facilities Act, which excludes funding for "any facility used for sectarian instruction." In justifying its ruling, the court noted the academic requirements and the professional standards of the courses in theology and the fact that the schools adhered to the principle of academic freedom. This case is discussed by Michaelsen in "Constitutions, Courts, and the Study of Religion," 298–99.

33. As suggested by Holmes Rolston III, *Science and Religion: A Critical Survey* (Philadelphia: Temple University Press, 1987), 67.

34. John Cobb has called for an end to this disciplinary organization of knowledge, and the related "disciplinolatry," in *For the Common Good: Redirecting the Economy Toward Community, the Environment, and a Sustainable Future,* co-authored with Herman E. Daly (Boston: Beacon, 1989), especially chap. 6.

35. I wish to thank John Cobb, Robert Michaelsen, and Jack Verheyden for helpful criticism of an earlier version of this essay.

2

Critical Theology as a University Discipline

A very popular error: having the courage of
one's convictions; rather it is a matter of having
the courage for an *attack* on one's convictions!
                                        —Nietzsche

The emergence of modern critical thinking—symbolized most vividly, perhaps, in the "radical doubt" of Descartes, and carried through most systematically in the "critical philosophy" of Kant—not surprisingly made precarious the place of Christian theology in the university. Theological reflection, for much of its history in the West, had been grounded on a principle of *authority* derived from the Christian belief that God had been decisively revealed to humanity in the history of Israel and especially in and through the ministry, death, and resurrection of Jesus Christ. Theological truth, therefore, was not thought of as something that humans discover (or create) in their work; it was, rather, something present and made available in the traditions of the church, especially in the Bible, which was commonly regarded as the very "word of God." Theology's task was to extract this truth from the traditional writings in which it was contained and to interpret it in such a way that its significance (for each new generation) was clearly expressed. What the truth is was already determined (who could call into question what God had revealed?): We humans were simply to believe and seek to understand. Christian theology, thus, understood itself to be working out of authoritative tradition, and its task was to interpret and pass on that tradition, certainly not to sit in critical judgment upon it.[1]

The rise of critical consciousness in modern intellectual life threatened this self-understanding of theology and, indeed, its very being. Because modern universities have increasingly come to see themselves as engaged essentially in critical thinking—about philosophical and scientific ideas; about religion and culture; about history, literature, and the arts; about legal, political, economic, and social institutions and ideologies; in short, about the whole range of human ideas and practices —the place of Christian theology in the university became, and has subsequently remained, quite precarious. Many, especially from F. D. E. Schleiermacher on, have sought to address this problem by rethinking the responsibilities of theology in the modern world. John Cobb has provided significant leadership in this task for the last thirty years. It is especially fitting, therefore, that appreciation for his work be expressed with a volume of essays on theology and the university, and I am happy to have been given the opportunity to contribute some of my own thoughts on this topic in honor of him.

I shall argue in this essay that, although it may quite properly be questioned whether authoritarian Christian theologies have any rightful claim on a significant role in modern university life, what I shall call "critical theology" does have important contributions to make to university studies; that critical theology should, therefore, be recognized as a legitimate discipline even in entirely secular institutions; and that it would be desirable for persons practicing this discipline to be appointed to full-time positions in departments of religious studies or even in independent departments of theology. It is important for Christian (and other) theologians to address themselves more self-consciously than has often been the case in the past to the cultivation and development of the critical potential of theological symbols and modes of reflection. This redirection will prepare them to take up more directly some of the major intellectual issues that modern universities need to address. To the extent that theologians fail or refuse to take up the critical opportunities and responsibilities that are peculiarly theirs, they can quite properly expect to continue to lack credibility in much contemporary university life.

I. DEFINITIONS: UNIVERSITY AND THEOLOGY

A large topic such as "theology and the university" involves many complex issues that cannot be elaborated upon in a brief essay of this sort; it is important, however, to set the stage for the central concerns of this essay in at least a few broad strokes.

What "theology" is, what its objectives are, and to whom or what it is responsible, are matters on which there is little agreement among theologians; there are, consequently, many different types and kinds of theology. The situation with regard to "the university" is no simpler: there is no agreement either within modern universities themselves or outside of them as to what the university is, what its purposes are or should be, and to whom or what it should be held accountable (or whether it is accountable to anything beyond itself). In fact, there are a good many different kinds of universities, that is, institutions that claim that title. In view of this complexity and ambiguity in the two central terms of our topic, how should we proceed? With respect to "the university," I shall make a stipulation; with respect to "theology," more preliminary discussion will be necessary.

I mean by "university" to refer to the higher learning in America at large; I shall, however, be confining myself to matters of especial concern to the humanities and the social sciences, those university disciplines that explore the nature of human existence and its meaning and purposes. Most institutions of higher learning in this country today would probably be considered "secular," but there are also many colleges and universities that are sponsored by churches and that describe themselves as "Christian." For the most part I will not be addressing myself to this latter segment of American higher education; in these institutions the presence of (some form of) theological reflection is already often regarded as appropriate for, or possibly even indispensable to, intellectual life. I wish to argue here the importance of theology to the modern secular university or college, institutions with no explicit religious commitments.

How now is "theology" to be understood for the purposes of this discussion? It should be clear that we cannot proceed with a completely open conception of theology, according to which whatever is claimed by someone or some group to be theology is admitted to the category. No institutions of higher learning define chemistry or economics or English literature or medicine or architecture in this utterly open way—such a completely normless approach would make it impossible to determine what is to count as *education* in a field—and there is no more reason to follow a totally open procedure of that sort with theology than with any other discipline. Our question thus becomes: What criterion can be formulated to help us identify and define the sort of theology that would be appropriate as a regular university discipline?

One might suppose that, because of the disagreements about what theology is and ought to be, it is not possible to specify such a criterion; but I do not think that is the case. Many claimants to the title of theology can be immediately ruled out of consideration for our purposes because of the importance given to "critical consciousness" in modern university life. For example, the theologies of religious groups that intentionally take an uncritical stance toward their own religious beliefs—by holding them, on dogmatic grounds, to be beyond questioning—can play only a very limited role in the life of a modern university. We need not, therefore, take these directly into account in formulating our criterion for determining the sort of theology appropriate for disciplinary status in the university. Some who think that all theology is intrinsically dogmatic and uncritical in character may suppose that by this move I have eliminated all possible candidates from further consideration. Such is not the case, although it is obvious that the field is now rapidly becoming much more restricted, and therefore more manageable.

In narrowing our field of candidates in this way I have already been implicitly invoking a criterion: I now want to propose this criterion as correct for defining the sort of theology appropriate to the modern university. Theology that is done with full attention to, and is thus an expression of, critical consciousness is what we are looking for: theology that opens itself willingly to severe criticism from outside perspectives (as well as from within). Theology that is formulated through the exercise of critical judgment with respect to all pertinent evidence and arguments (what we can quite properly call *critical theology*) has an important and distinctive role to play in university life today.

This characterization of critical theology is quite abstract and formal. How can we make it more concrete? It is helpful here to distinguish two different ways in which theological work may be of importance to the tasks and responsibilities of the university. The first is well known and widely acknowledged: Theological writings of all sorts are nearly always products of the intellectual activity of religious communities attempting to further their own self-understanding and the goals to which they are committed.

Such writings present careful articulations and interpretations of the symbols and meanings, the values and purposes, the activities, practices, and institutions of significance to their authors and the communities to which they have made themselves accountable. Texts of this sort from earlier periods of history have always been studied in the university by historians and others attempting to understand and interpret various features of human life in the past. Similarly, many different kinds of contemporary theological texts are of importance in the study of current religious life and culture, to sociologists and others concerning themselves with understanding modern worldviews, cultural values, and complexes of meaning; to philosophers examining value orientations and patterns of thinking about the meaning and problems of human life; to literary critics interested in exploring various types and styles of writing; to psychologists studying human motivation and self-interpretation; to scholars attempting to understand contemporary human religiousness and its various expressions; and so on. Virtually every kind of theology may find a significant place in university studies addressed to the examination, interpretation, and assessment of the many sides of human life and culture. This sort of study of theology can, however, be accomplished without appointing theologians to university faculty positions, although of course scholars with sufficient theological understanding to provide intelligent interpretation of these materials are required.

In my view, however, contemporary theological reflection has more to offer the university than mere documentation for various sorts of (nontheological) explorations and studies. In contemporary critical theological reflection, analytic tools, conceptual schemes, and ways of thinking are being developed that make possible grasping and interpreting features of human life and its meaning that nearly always escape the attention of other university disciplines. Such theological work can make available important resources for the university's proper tasks; it should, therefore, be given its own place within the intellectual life of the university. My reasons for making this claim should become clear as I sketch out more fully just what I mean by critical theology.[2]

II. CRITICAL THEOLOGY

Theology has often been characterized, following Anselm, as "faith seeking understanding." This has usually been taken to mean that the task of the theologian is to examine the content of (some particular) faith, with a view to understanding what it means and how it is to be interpreted to the community of faith and to others. There is another way in which Anselm's phrase can be interpreted, however. This way opens up a rather different conception of the theological task; or at least it leads to focusing attention on another dimension of theological inquiry that is of especial importance here. Theology, as "faith seeking understanding," may be seen as an inquiry into the role of faith-commitments in human existence, an inquiry into the significance of believing (or "faithing") in human life. In this reading, "faith" is taken in a generic sense (rather than the particular sense just mentioned), as pointing to fundamental features of human existence: that men and women live out of and on the basis of their trust in and loyalty to what they take to be most meaningful, precious, and important in life; that human lives are always oriented by some (perhaps implicit) "center [or centers] of value" (H. R. Niebuhr); and that it is out of underlying faith-commitments such as these that humans act and live in face of the unknown future into which they must inexorably move. The exploration of the role and significance of faith in human life (including such closely related dispositions as trust, loyalty, and commitment), and of the symbols that structure the various forms of faith, is by no means something of importance only to those with specifically religious interests; it is a matter central to the understanding of human being and well-being. Theology as "faith seeking understanding" in *this* sense, providing it is critical theology, quite properly belongs among university studies.[3]

From the time of the Enlightenment onwards, an increasingly self-critical strand of Christian theological reflection developed (nourished for many years by such writers as Kant, Schleiermacher, and Hegel). This critical moment in the theological tradition can provide the basis, I believe, for a new and distinctive conception of theology as essentially a critical discipline. It would be a discipline in which participating theologians carefully scrutinized their own faith-commitments in the context of similar examinations of a wide range of (competing) faith-orientations. A critical Christian theology of the sort I am envisioning here would, in contrast with more traditional "dogmatic" theologies, entertain, indeed pursue, the most radical sort of questioning of its own commitments. It would do so, however, as a contribution to a conversation in which similar radical exploration and questioning of other living faith-orientations—humanism, Buddhism, secularism, Judaism, Marxism, feminism, Americanism, hedonism, and so on—

was also being carried on. Attempting to examine and assess the major dimensions of one's own faith as openly and critically as possible does not mean that one does not consider such commitments to be a serious matter; on the contrary, precisely because of their serious import and consequence they deserve the most penetrating scrutiny we can bring to them. Critical theology, as an umbrella discipline within which the investigation of many (religious and secular) faiths was pursued, could provide the sort of context that would facilitate this sort of careful examination and assessment of diverse living faiths today. Such examination could in turn lead to the development of proposals for significant reconstruction of some (or all) of these orientations.

As envisioned here, critical theology would be a discipline that attempts (1) to uncover and explore the major faith-complexes that provide orientation within modern culture (and within the university itself), developing appropriate concepts and theoretical frameworks for articulating these studies sharply and clearly; (2) to develop criteria for comparing and assessing these faith-orientations, so that it would become possible to make critical judgments with respect to them; and (3) to make constructive proposals for transformations and improvements in these orientations that seemed appropriate and important. Theological reflection of this sort would address itself to some of the most important cultural problems faced by pluralistic societies such as our own: How should the diverse faith-orientations in such a society be understood? How is their fundamental human significance to be ascertained and assessed? Can these perspectives be helped to accommodate themselves to each other in ways that would be more beneficial to society as a whole? Moreover, it would be preparing intellectual tools and methods for helping to address humanity's major worldwide problem of finding ways to encourage the great diversity of human groups around the globe to live together more peacefully on our rapidly shrinking planet. It would be a "public theology"[4] working at a very important public task.

The university is the best location for carrying on theological investigations of this sort, for at least three reasons: (1) The research resources that the university can make available for such studies are unparalleled. (2) The traditions of academic freedom, which developed in the university and continue to be cherished there, provide an indispensable context and support for the sorts of sensitive (and possibly often unpopular) investigations that would be pursued and proposals that might be made. (3) The ongoing conversations in the university about questions of knowledge and value, morality and meaning, about the arts and the sciences and history in their complex interrelations with each other, and about the broad social and cultural issues of the day provide a setting indispensable for such critical theological reflection. Many of the issues to which such reflection must address itself are posed in their sharpest form in the university, and it is most likely from within the intellectual conversation in the university that critical theology can make its own most direct and significant contribution to culture at large.

The critical theology I am envisioning here is not a kind of generic theological reflection, unencumbered by any specific loyalties or faith-commitments. It is important to recognize that critical work of this sort can be carried on effectively only by persons who are well aware of what commitment to a specific way of life means, and what it may cost—that is, who know from within what a faith-commitment is and what it demands of individuals and communities. This does not mean, of course, that only avowedly religious persons can reflect upon faith-commitments. I emphasize again that we are concerned here with a broadly human quality or posture, one as evident in Marxists and secularists as in Methodists and Muslims. Commitment is an *act* or *attitude*, a posture of selves and communities, which is taken up in some sense deliberately (in decision) and is maintained deliberately (in loyalty and through reaffirmation). To the extent that this is the case, important dimensions of commitment can be known and understood only in and through the active participation of the knower and interpreter. If the objective of critical theological reflection is to gain some understanding of, and to assess the human significance of, this dimension of human being—our unavoidable involvement in (our faith in and commitment to) broad but specific patterns of living and doing, of thinking and being, of value and meaning—that reflection will have to be carried on by persons both self-conscious about such matters and trained to discern and to articulate them. The real faith-commitments and frames of orientation that order the lives of women and men today will have to be actively and effectively represented in the university theological conversation, if that conversation is to become truly critical.

Hence, in a fully staffed university program of critical theology, as I imagine it, there would ordinarily be persons with, for example, Roman Catholic, Afro-American, Protestant, Jewish, Buddhist, feminist, and positivist commitments, all actively engaged in critical examination of the faith-orientations of the communities with which they identify themselves, and in conversation with each other, and with others in the university, about the whole spectrum of positions they are collectively exploring. When we speak of a "discipline of critical theology" or a "department of theology," we are, or course, using the term *theology* in a generic sense, in which it refers to a range of studies exploring matters of "ultimate concern" (Tillich), foundational values, frames of orientation, ultimate points of reference, and the like. As envisioned here, however, these studies are to be conducted by persons with specific existential commitments to the positions that they are critically scrutinizing, evaluating, and reconstructing in relation to others engaged in similar activities from other points of view; the notion of totally uncommitted theologians is a contradiction in terms. Critical theology, then, is not to be understood as a discipline that attempts to transcend all particular commitments and perspectives through developing a universal or generic theological stance (an impossible, probably self-contradictory, project); it is to be seen, rather, as a pluralistic discipline that attempts to investigate and understand, and to find ways of assessing and reconstructing, the actual living faith-commitments to which men and women today give themselves.

This conception of critical theology stretches the term "theology" a good bit beyond its ordinary use. I am suggesting that we need secularist and Marxist theologians as much as Christian and Moslem ones, and that it is important that all of these together should explore the problematics of "faith." I recognize, of course, that "theology" is most frequently used to refer to specifically Christian thinking, and in addition that it is etymologically loaded in ways that may make it repugnant to thoughtful persons committed to other (religious or nonreligious) perspectives on life; "critical theology," therefore, may not be the most apt name for the new academic discipline I am suggesting. Nevertheless, because the kind of intellectual inquiry with which we are here concerned is clearly an extension and generalization of major themes of traditional theological reflection, and because no more appropriate title appears to be readily available, it seems to me justifiable to use this characterization at least for the present.

III. A PLURALISTIC, DIALOGICAL VIEW OF RELIGIOUS TRUTH

A significant transition or transformation in the self-understanding and faith-commitment of most theologians is required if they are to take part in the sort of critical theological reflection here being considered. Instead of undeviating attention to the claims of their own faith, and unequivocal commitment to the truth of those claims, theologians here would be required to take up a pluralistic stance from the outset, giving serious consideration to the claims of other perspectives and engaging in radical criticism and reconstruction of their own commitments, when this seemed appropriate and necessary. Such an attitude necessitates distancing oneself in certain respects from one's own tradition, taking a step back from simple unmediated commitment to it.

What is demanded here, however, may not be so far removed from what is required in more typical theological reflection as it initially seems. Certainly the critical theologian must step back from an utterly unequivocal (that is, a thoroughly uncritical) faith-commitment, but that is really nothing new to theologians (though they may not always admit this in their public pronouncements). All inquiries into faith necessitate the consideration of questions of many different sorts, some of them potentially quite damaging. A theologian will not be able to understand what is really at stake in such questions without looking carefully at the issues they pose for faith, that is, without seriously considering the alternatives they suggest. Theologians have always had to give some attention to ways of thinking that were significantly different from those endorsed by their own tradition; indeed, it was precisely through their taking into account such differing perspectives that they were often led to creative transformations of the tradition with which they were working. In critical theology, this concern with and interest in new ideas, questions, and criticisms would not be motivated primarily (as often in the past) by a desire to protect one's own tradition against enemies from without; it would, rather, be understood as constitutive of the theologian's proper task, a principal means of acquiring critical insights and perspectives to help in the assessment and reconstruction of major emphases in the faith-orientation with which one was working. Theologians have always, of course, appropriated insights and understandings from the likes of Plato and Aristotle, Kant and Hegel, Marx and Freud. In critical theological work, such appropriation would not be regarded as peripheral to the main theological task, as optional and possibly somewhat questionable. Rather, it would be central to what the theologian was attempting to do: contribute to the critical examination and constructive transformation of the faith-orientation to which he or she was committed.

In the past, most Christian theological reflection, as we noted above, took for granted a principle of authority. It was assumed that saving truth was present and available in the received tradition (especially the Bible) and that the theologian's task, therefore, was essentially a hermeneutical one, the task of interpreting the essentials of that tradition as faithfully, cogently, and clearly as possible. In an approach of this sort, religious truth seems to be understood in certain respects on the model of property: it is a *possession* of the tradition (and not available elsewhere), and it can be passed on from one generation to the next. With such a view it is especially important, of course, that the theologian interpreting the tradition be wary of distorting or diluting its truth with contaminants from without. Significant theological conversation, then, will be (for the most part) a matter internal to the faith-orientation itself, an essentially defensive activity concerned with protecting and preserving the truth that the tradition already possesses.

The critical theology outlined here as an appropriate university discipline stands in sharp contrast with this somewhat parochial conception of theological work. Here the theological conversation is not conceived as largely internal, confined to persons with closely similar faith-commitments; it is, rather, essentially open, with persons of other commitments welcomed as indispensable partners. It is, thus, a conversation that is premised upon and that encourages a notion of religious truth rather different from the traditional one based on the property model. I call it a "pluralistic" or "dialogical" conception of truth. In this view, religious truth is not so much a possession owned by a particular tradition as it is something expected to emerge in the conversation among persons of different faith-commitments, as they work together seriously in their collective attempt to understand and assess their diverse frames of orientation. Instead of taking truth to be a property of particular words, symbols, propositions, or texts, which can be learned and passed on (more or less unchanged) from one generation to the next, it is a living reality that emerges from within and is a function of ongoing living conversation among a number of different voices. In this model, religious truth is something that develops and is transformed in unpredictable ways as the conversation proceeds; it is not to be expected, then, that some final, complete, or unchanging truth will ever be reached.

Although the recent increase in interreligious dialogue seems to be moving many in the direction of a pluralistic and dialogical model of religious truth, I am not aware that a conception of this sort has been explicitly articulated elsewhere.[5] Even John Cobb, despite his emphasis on the necessity today (in our religiously pluralistic world) to move "beyond dialogue" to "mutual transformation" of our several religious traditions,[6] appears to think of some of the central Christian truth-claims as virtually certain, as providing foundations for human life that are absolutely secure and thus not really open to critical reconsideration: "When the Christian witnesses to Christ in the dialogue, the hope must be to do more than provide minor insights. Christ is understood only when Christ becomes the center around which life is lived." Although Cobb holds that "our present need is to learn through dialogue . . . to rethink our beliefs," and that the "Christian purpose in the dialogue with [for example] Jews must be to change Christianity,"[7] it seems clear throughout that he does not expect the reality made available through such fundamental symbols as "God" and "Christ" to be put into serious question. Moreover, Cobb apparently looks forward to a time when the present diversity of religious truth-claims can be grasped—to use the words with which he characterizes Whitehead's goal—in a single "conceptuality through which every type of human experience could be understood"; and he continues to think of Whitehead's work as a large step in that direction.[8] It seems unlikely, then, despite his remarkable openness to insights and image/concepts from religious and cultural traditions other than his own, that Cobb would be willing to regard truth itself as pluralistic through and through, and therefore to be conceived in principle as a dialogical reality.

My position here is that only such a radically pluralistic understanding of truth permits and encourages unrestricted openness in discussion of the most fundamental religious and human questions. Such a conception can be particularly helpful, therefore, in a situation in which persons of diverse religious and ideological commitments are attempting to understand and learn from each other's perspectives. Perhaps, as we increasingly move toward becoming a single interdependent humanity, this way of thinking about truth may in due course be seen as appropriate for human religious life generally. In any case, such a conception would greatly facilitate the sort of university theological conversation that I am sketching here. With a pluralistic and dialogical understanding of religious truth, all who participate in the conversation are accepted on equal terms. All are there to participate with the others in the search for truth; none are there claiming that they alone possess final religious insight or understanding. Each wishes to contribute whatever possible from the riches of the faith-orientation she or he represents, and will be listened to respect-fully and attentively; all expect to learn from the others, through appropriating with appreciation what they have to offer and through opening themselves willingly to probing questions and sharp criticism. With these sorts of attitudes and ground rules, it may be hoped, a thoroughly critical and yet significantly construc-tive exploration and assessment of a range of faith-commitments, and of the basic human need to take up such commitments and be loyal to them, could be carried on.

This suggestion, that the examination of human frames of orientation should be conducted with a pluralistic/dialogical con-ception of truth in mind, rather than a monolithic conception such as those usually found in the major religious traditions, is not in fact so innovative as it might at first seem. Modern historical studies have made it incontestably clear that every religious tradi-tion, and what is held to be Truth in that tradition, grew and de-veloped largely through internal dialogue and external exchange. Religious truth has thus always been pluralistic in the sense de-scribed here, emergent from conversations among many different voices over many generations. The efforts made, from time to time, to freeze it into authoritative, unchanging, monolithic forms have never been more than temporarily successful. In advocating the establishment of a dialogical setting within the university to explore, evaluate, and reconstruct various religious (and secular) insights into and understandings of human life and its meaning, I am simply proposing that we attempt to carry out more systemat-ically, deliberately, and constructively what has actually been go-ing on in the rivalries and interchanges among faith-orientations throughout history.

Historically, religious knowledge has all too often taken au-thoritarian forms, with truth believed to be accessible only to special elite groups who could interpret sacred texts and explain obscure ideas. This has fostered hierarchical social patterns easily subject to abuse: Religious knowledge and power were in the hands of the few, and the masses of ordinary people were expected simply to believe what they were told and to obey. The conversational model of truth I advocate here, in contrast, is neither esoteric nor hierarchical in character but is essentially democratic and open, a model that encourages cogent criticism of accepted positions and the consideration of insights and understandings from voices and points of view not previously taken seriously. This conception of religious truth avoids the nihilistic tendencies of an unqualified relativism, for it is truth—with its unique and undeniable claims upon us—that we are concerned with here; but simultaneously, in its acknowledgement that this truth is *pluralistic*—that no one voice or formulation can possess or adequately express it—this conception undercuts the tendencies, so prominent in traditional views, to become absolutistic, dogmatic, and imperialistic. Thinking of religious truth in this way would accordingly encourage just the kind of critical and constructive theological work that is appropriate to a nonsectarian university and much needed today in our pluralistic society.

IV. CRITICAL THEOLOGY AS PLURALISTIC

I hope this essay will not be understood as simply an advocacy piece for the kind of theology to which I am myself committed; in that case it would be taken as simply an example of one more kind of sectarian theology, this time a specifically academic sectarianism. The discipline of critical theology as conceived here would provide a context within which a *variety* of living religious and nonreligious faith-orientations can be openly and responsibly explored and assessed. It is neither an elitist academic "super-theology" that is seeking to swallow up all other positions, nor a "metatheology" that stands above or beyond the others. Rather, it is constituted from the outset as an ongoing dialogue about fundamental issues of life and death, a dialogue conducted by persons representing diverse living faith-commitments and having different methodological concerns. Only in this way can its thoroughly critical character be insured.

A critical conversation of this sort, devoted to exploration of the deep-lying questions about human ultimate loyalties and frames of orientation, would gradually, one can hope, move the entire university to address the religious dimensions of the massive social and cultural problems with which humanity today must come to terms.

NOTES

1. For a thorough historical analysis and deconstruction of this traditional authoritarian approach to Christian theology, see Edward Farley, *Ecclesial Reflection* (Philadelphia: Fortress, 1982). A somewhat earlier but very influential analysis of many of the issues raised by the authoritarian dimension in theological work is to be found in Van A. Harvey, *The Historian and the Believer* (New York: Macmillan, 1966). For my own brief

analysis of, and reasons for rejecting, an authoritarian approach in Christian theology, see *Theology for a Nuclear Age* (Manchester: Manchester University Press and Philadelphia: Westminster, 1985), chap. 2, and *An Essay on Theological Method* (Atlanta: Scholars Press, 1975, rev. ed. 1979).

2. I will not in this essay illustrate my argument by taking up specific theological symbols and modes of analysis and showing how they can contribute directly to the critical reflective work of the university; such examples can be found scattered through my writings over the years. See, for example, "Metaphysical Assumptions and the Task of Theology," chap. 10 of *Relativism, Knowledge and Faith* (Chicago: University of Chicago Press, 1960); "The Secular Utility of 'God-Talk'," chap. 11 of *God the Problem* (Cambridge: Harvard University Press, 1972); "The Idea of Relativity and the Idea of God" and "Metaphysics and Theology," chaps. 3 and 9 of *The Theological Imagination* (Philadelphia: Westminster, 1981).

3. In recent years Wilfred Cantwell Smith in particular has emphasized the usefulness (for religious and anthropological studies) of thinking of faith as a generic human quality (see especially *Faith and Belief* [Princeton: Princeton University Press, 1979], *Belief and History* [Charlottesville: University of Virginia Press, 1977], and *Towards a World Theology* [Philadelphia: Westminster, 1981]); but he is by no means alone in this emphasis. Contemporary theologians such as H. Richard Niebuhr (from *The Meaning of Revelation* [New York: Macmillan, 1946] to *Radical Monotheism and Western Culture* [New York: Harper and Bros., 1960] and the just published *Faith on Earth* [New Haven: Yale University Press, 1989]), Paul Tillich (*Dynamics of Faith* [New York: Harper and Bros., 1957]), Bernard Meland (*Faith and Culture* [London: G. Allen and Unwin, 1955]), and Schubert Ogden (*The Reality of God* [New York: Harper & Row, 1966]) have all presented interpretations of faith as a generic human quality. They have been dependent on earlier writers such as William James (see especially *The Will to Believe and Other Essays* [New York: Longmans, Green and Co., 1897]), Josiah Royce (*The Philosophy of Loyalty* [New York: Macmillan, 1908] and *The Problem of Christianity* [New York: Macmillan, 1914]), and George Santayana (*Skepticism and Animal Faith* [New York: Dover, 1955]). Recently James W. Fowler (along with some others) has utilized the generic notion of faith as a basic concept in the psychological study of human development (see, for example, *Stages of Faith: The Psychology of Human Development and the Quest for Meaning* [San Francisco: Harper and Row, 1981]).

4. For a recent discussion of the idea of "public theology," see Linell E. Cady, "A Model for a Public Theology," *Harvard Theological Review* 80 (1987): 193–212.

5. In recent years there has been increasing interest among philosophers and theologians in conversation or dialogue, as a proper goal for intellectual activity, instead of the more traditional pursuit of truth (see, for

example, Richard Rorty, *Philosophy and the Mirror of Nature* [Princeton: Princeton University Press, 1979] and *Consequences of Pragmatism* [Minneapolis: University of Minnesota Press, 1982]; Jürgen Habermas, *Theory of Communicative Action*, 2 vols. [Boston: Beacon Press, 1984, 1987]; Richard S. Bernstein, *Beyond Objectivism and Relativism* [Philadelphia: University of Pennsylvania Press, 1985]; Helmut Peukert, *Science, Action and Fundamental Theology: Toward a Theology of Communicative Action* [Cambridge: M. I. T. Press, 1984]; Francis Fiorenza, *Foundational Theology* [New York: Crossroad, 1984]; David Tracy, *Plurality and Ambiguity* [San Francisco: Harper & Row, 1987]; Peter Hodgson, *God in History: Shapes of Freedom* [Nashville: Abingdon, 1989]). My suggestion that (religious) truth should be understood to be specifically pluralistic and dialogical in character is in harmony with this growing interest in conversation and "communicative action." I have elaborated this notion more fully in "Religious Pluralism and Religious Truth" (forthcoming).

6. Dialogue "that does not intend to go beyond itself stagnates," he argues. "In a successful dialogue both partners are engaged in fresh thinking. . . . *Beyond* dialogue, I suggest, lies the aim of mutual transformation" (John B. Cobb, Jr., *Beyond Dialogue: Toward a Mutual Transformation of Christianity and Buddhism* [Philadelphia: Fortress Press, 1982], viii, xi, 48).

7. Ibid., viii, 51, 49.

8. Ibid., 147.

3

God: The Last Taboo?
Science, God, and the University*

Not only in European countries, but also in America, atheism—a theoretical, but especially a practical atheism—today demands an account of our belief in God as it never did in the past. In the course of modern times this belief has been increasingly on the defensive and today has often been silenced, at first by a few people and then by more and more. Atheism as a mass phenomenon, however, is a phenomenon of the most recent times. The question is forced upon us: How did it get so far? What are the causes? Where did the crisis break out?

I. WHY HAS GOD BEEN REJECTED IN MODERN TIMES?

God been rejected in modern times mainly for two reasons: First, God was invoked and science opposed. Catholic apologists even today are inclined to make light of the condemnation of Galileo by the Roman authorities on faith, approved by Pope Urban VIII himself and carried out, in the Catholic universities, with all the resources of power at the disposal of inquisitors and nuncios. But this declaration was regarded in practice in Catholic theology as an infallible and irreformable decision; it nipped in the bud the modest attempts of open-minded theologians to think out afresh the biblical message in the light of a new scientific worldview. God was invoked, not only by the Church, but also by the state, not only by Rome, but also by Lutheranism and Calvinism, when proceeding against scientists. There was suppression of dissident opinions on both sides.

All the pressures of the teaching authorities poisoned relations between the churches and theology on the one hand and the new philosophy and natural science on the other, right up to the present time (I think even "Humanae vitae" is a consequence of this development and of this attitude). It was claimed that it was a question of defending the biblical faith in God, but in fact what was defended was the Greco-medieval worldview. Over and above this it was a question also of defending the legally assured supremacy of theology in the hierarchy of the sciences, the authority of the Church in all questions of life, and in the last resort quite simply blind, obedient submission to the ecclesiastical doctrinal system. It is not surprising that since then the Catholic Church especially (but also other churches) has been widely regarded as the enemy of science. Not even the Second Vatican Council in the present century ventured expressly to rehabilitate unjustly condemned scientists, from Galileo to Teilhard de Chardin.

In the complex development toward modern secularization, this kind of belief in authority—in the Bible, in the Church—hostile to reason, philosophy, and science has very seriously discredited in modern times not only the Church, but also the Christian idea of God. The rejection of religion as a whole was always linked with the rejection of institutionalized religion, rejection of God with rejection of the Church. This is true of the early rationalist critique of religion in the eighteenth century, of the classical critique of religion in the nineteenth and at the beginning of the twentieth century, and of the present-day critique of religion on the part of Neo-Marxism or critical rationalism. The history of the neo-positivist Vienna circle around Moritz Schlick and Rudolf Carnap (many of them of Jewish descent) and also the origins of Sigmund Freud's work show how much the hostility of Church and theology to reason and science contributed to both the radically antimetaphysical attitude of the then rising analytical philosophy and the radically antireligious attitude of psychoanalysis at the same time.

How many opportunities were missed at the beginning of modern times! What a fine new synthesis would have been possible! How Christian faith, as in the High Middle Ages, might have taken up opportunely the influences and conclusions of the new sciences comprehensively interpreted and where necessary even credibly criticized and relativized! All for the sake of a more profound and comprehensive understanding of both natural science and religious faith. Did not the leading representatives of the new mathematical-mechanical natural sciences believe in such an agreement? Pascal, Copernicus, Kepler, Galileo, Leibniz, Newton, Boyle: all were not only believers in God, but also professing Christians. Even Voltaire and the men of the French Enlightenment propagated a mechanistic worldview and ideological tolerance not as atheists, but as deists: for them God always remained, admittedly at a distance, the creator and steerer of the world-machine.

It is not an exaggeration to describe the history of the relation between theology and science as the history of a continual defensive action, of a continual retreat, on the part of theology. This may be illustrated schematically by the example of cosmology. There was a time when God was regarded as directly responsible for whatever could not be otherwise explained: Weather and victory in battle, sickness and healing, happiness and unhappiness were explained as the result of God's direct intervention. When everyday things came to be increasingly explicable by science there had to be a retreat. God remained necessary, however, to direct the orbits of the planets. When these orbits were explained by gravitation, there was a further retreat, although God's intervention continued to be required to explain the deviations in the planetary orbits (even the great Isaac Newton accepted this). When the "Newton of France," Pierre Simon Laplace, produced a scientific explanation of the deviations and God appeared to be a superfluous hypothesis for the explanation of the existing universe, theologians concentrated on the question of the beginning of the world and—against Charles Darwin's theory of evolution— vehemently defended a literal interpretation of the biblical accounts of creation. After that, from the theory of the direct creation of the whole world by God there was a withdrawal to the position that God directly created life and human beings, then to the position that God directly created the human soul. Finally, as it seems today, the idea of any direct supernatural intervention of God in the evolution of the world and humanity has been abandoned.

It is obvious that a theology of this kind leaves God without any function. God no longer seems necessary either for the explanation of the world or for the conduct of life. In natural science, at any rate, God could not play a part if scientific method was to remain neat and exact. For many it was thus clear, once and for all, that religion was not a scientific, but merely a private, affair. Consequently for many, science replaced religion even in the private sphere.

We must come to the second aspect of this struggle: God was invoked and democracy opposed. The history of Europe up to the beginning of this century makes it abundantly clear that secular and spiritual rulers, throne and altar, state constitution and church constitution provided mutual support. Political and denominational tutelage corresponded to one another; hence, emancipation from the absolutist state meant also emancipation from the absolutist church and vice versa. The heretic was an enemy of the state, and a political opponent was a heretic. Even in the field of politics a continual strategy of defense and withdrawal was practiced. Was there anything that was not forbidden or condemned by the churches in the nineteenth and twentieth centuries: democracy, liberalism, socialism, freedom of opinion, freedom of the press, freedom of conscience, freedom of religion? The failure especially (but not only) of the Catholic Church to meet sociopolitical problems with more than pious intentions, almsgiving, and individual works of charity seriously discredited belief in God at an early stage. How greatly the socioethical potential and sociological relevance of the message of Jesus Christ has been neglected through the centuries! How much did the association of an individualized belief in God with princely absolutism and its unscrupulous power politics make this belief increasingly incredible to the rising bourgeoisie? Belief in God was opposed, because it was used by princes ruling by God's grace as a means of preventing the diffusion of the "light of reason" and of liberty, equality, and fraternity, thereby keeping the people in tutelage and servitude.

After churches and clergy had come to be the main support of the unsocial, corrupt, and bankrupt *Ancien Regime*, the cry of the Jacobins ("priests to the lampposts") and the public deposition of God in Notre Dame in Paris were scarcely surprising. For the first time in world history, atheism had become a political program. This was a bourgeois-liberal atheism, soon to be followed, after the October revolution in Russia, by a proletarian-socialist atheism that developed into a power in world politics through the Communist movement.

All this has to be our Confiteor, the confession we have to make honestly and sincerely. Of course, there are also questions to be put to both political and scientific atheism.

With regard to political atheism, belief in God, to be sure, has to be proved in both individual and social practice; believers in God who do not live in a truly human, truly moral, truly social way are certainly a strong argument against belief in God. In this sense political atheism is decidedly right, but at the same time it should be remembered that believers in God who do not live in a truly human, moral, social way cannot make belief in God untrue in itself. A theory that is not often put into practice can still be true. Even a program that people continually ignore can still be right. Even a message that is disregarded can still be good. It may also be admitted that the churches, which exist to proclaim God, can by their theory and practice discredit belief in God and have often done so. But at the same time it should be remembered that, when the churches are credible, they can keep the question of God open, and this too they have done.

With regard to scientific atheism, modern science (including, obviously, the social sciences by analogy with the natural sciences), by proceeding in a way that is methodologically irreproachable, must necessarily leave out God, who in fact cannot be empirically observed and analyzed like other objects. In this sense scientific atheism is decidedly right. But we may ask again if an open-mindedness in principle toward reality as a whole must not be required of both natural and social scientists.

There is no science which has for its object all aspects of the world, including human life and action. Today physicists, biologists, medical doctors, psychologists, and sociologists are concerned with the analysis of data, facts, phenomena, operations, processes, energies, structures, developments. But the theologian (perhaps also the philosopher) now as formerly may rightly be concerned with other questions, of ultimate or primary interpretations, objectives, values, ideals, norms, decisions, and attitudes.

We have expressly stated that the failure of theology and church with regard to the natural and human sciences had a great deal to do with the fact that both scientific and political atheism were able to gain acceptance in the eighteenth century with individual precursors, in the nineteenth century with numerous educated people, and in the twentieth century finally with the great masses in East and West. Yet again we may ask if this failure can justify the modern natural and human sciences' increasingly regarding their methods and conclusions as absolute; in becoming often a quasi-religious *Weltanschauung*; in negating the question of God without discussion; in largely replacing belief in God with belief in science and progress. Here also should apply the principle that many philosophers and specialists in the natural and human sciences have meanwhile come to recognize: critical rationality, yes; ideological rationalism, no. Rationality should not be irrationally made absolute. There must be no intellectual pride. Nor of course may rationality be piously or impiously passed over or sacrificed. There must be no intellectual sacrifice, no *sacrificium intellectus*. Rationality must in fact be taken seriously as an element, but only as an element, within the whole of reality.

II. CAN A RATIONAL, SCIENTIFIC PERSON STILL BELIEVE IN GOD?

Yet, precisely in the light of critical rationality, the question immediately and rightly arises: Can a modern, rationally thinking, scientifically trained person still believe in God? Ever since Immanuel Kant's critique of the proofs of God, most scientists have taken it as proved that pure reason is bound to the horizon of our visible, calculable experience in time and space and cannot effect the transition from the "visible" to the "invisible," cannot reach the transcendent beyond time and space, beyond experience. Even someone who does not subscribe to Kant's critique of the proofs must admit that there is no purely rational demonstration of God's existence that is universally convincing. Proofs of God turn out in practice to be less than cogent. It is not without reason that there is no single proof that is generally accepted even by believers.

I cannot treat the whole problematic of the proofs of God. I would only like to say that we must not judge them too hastily. Insofar as proofs of God seek to prove something, I agree with their critics that they mean nothing; insofar as they bring God into the discussion, they mean a great deal. As firm answers they are inadequate and unconvincing; as open questions they cannot be rejected. Their probative character is eliminated today, but not their content, and what matters today is precisely this unprovable content of the proofs of God. But how are we to find a rational approach to God? How can we convince the modern scientific mind today if we cannot produce proofs?

Must we from the outset abandon any hope of finding a rational approach to God? Must we throw ourselves blindly into God's arms and perhaps just in this way fall into nothingness? At this point must we simply believe? Has belief then nothing to do with thought? Is not belief without thought unthoughtful, unconsidered, irresponsible faith? Is belief in God perhaps merely something for devout visionaries? These objections are justified. Belief in God certainly is not to be proved, but neither is it merely to be asserted and invoked. It is to be verified and justified, verified by reality and justified in the light of reason. Here the thinking person cannot allow himself to be obstructed by any dogmatic prohibition of questioning: neither in the name of an unjustified faith nor in the name of an arrogant reason.

At the same time, however, what must be admitted from the outset is the conclusion that can easily be drawn from discussion with Feuerbach, Marx, Nietzsche, and Freud: that a negative answer, a no to God, is possible. Atheism cannot be rationally eliminated. All the suffering and misery of the world, of humanity and society, provides a simple excuse at all times for saying that there is no God.

The other conclusion, however, can also be drawn from discussion with the great atheists, namely, that a positive answer, a yes to God, is possible. If atheism cannot be rationally eliminated, neither can it be rationally established. Atheism is, as Kant himself likewise observed, also unprovable. There is in fact no conclusive argument for the necessity of atheism. Reality, profoundly questionable as it is, and also the experiences of trust, security, love, truth, and meaning, give us reason to say that there is a God. All this means that a yes or no to God involves a question, a challenge, a decision: a decision that must be justified in the light of reason.

It is regrettable that so many false battles have been fought in modern times between science and belief in God, between theology and atheism. No thinking person today can dispute the fact that the critique of religion by Feuerbach, Marx, and Freud was largely justified. Feuerbach was absolutely right in thinking that religion contains an element of projection. But this is not to say that Feuerbach proved that religion is *merely* a projection. It can also be a relationship to a wholly other reality. Marx, too, was absolutely right in suggesting that religion can be opium, a means of social appeasement and temporary consolation, of repression. But it can also be the means of comprehensive enlightenment and social liberation. Freud, too, was absolutely right in maintaining that religion can be an illusion, an expression of psychological immaturity or even neurosis, of regression. But again it does not have to be such; it can also be the expression of personal identity and psychological maturity.

Thus both the strength and the weakness of the psychological argument for atheism are clearly seen. God is said to be a pure projection. It must certainly be admitted that belief in God can be psychologically explained. But there is no question of a simple choice between a psychological and a nonpsychological viewpoint. From the psychological viewpoint, belief in God always displays the structure and substance of a projection and is always open to the suspicion of being merely a projection. But the fact that it is a projection by no means decides whether the object to which it is related exists or does not exist. A real God can correspond to the wish for God. Why should I not be allowed to wish that death is not the end of everything, that my life has a meaning, that there is meaning in the history of humanity, in a word, that God exists?

Both the strength and the weakness of the often repeated argument, based on the philosophy of history, that religion has come to an end, are also clearly seen. The strength of the argument lies in the indisputable, all-embracing secularization process of modern times. But does this in itself mean the end of religion? Can science replace faith? Does secularization as such mean religionless secularism? As seriously as the problem in particular of both theoretical and practical nihilism must be taken even today, Nietzsche's prognosis of the death of God has turned out to be wrong. Instead of the "abolition" of religion by atheistic humanism, as announced in Feuerbach's projection theory, there is now (despite all secularization) in many places a new humanism, both theoretical and practical, fostered by believers in God. The atheistic-humanistic belief in the goodness of human nature and in human progress, by contrast, is itself now suspected of being a projection.

Instead of religion's "withering away" with the advent of atheistic socialism, as proclaimed by Marx's opium theory, there is now (despite all violent suppression) a new religious awakening in many places, even in socialist countries. The atheistic-materialist belief in the rise of a socialist society, by contrast, seems to countless people today to be itself a form of consolation serving vested interests, and the revolution becomes the opium of the people. Instead of atheistic science leading to a "breakdown" of religion, as prophesied in Freud's illusion theory, there is now (despite all hostility to religion in certain sectors of science) a new understanding for ethics and religion. The atheistic-scientist belief in the solution of all problems by rational science, by contrast, itself now seems to many to amount to an illusion.

But you will ask: Even if there is no conclusive argument for a no to God, how can I say yes to God? An appeal to the Bible is always possible. But this appeal is convincing for the most part only to someone who already believes in God. In any case, one consideration is fundamental: the fact that God is can be accepted, not on the basis of a proof, but only in a reasonable trust (rooted, of course, in reality itself). That is to say, I can reasonably commit myself to and rely on the fact that the reality which we can experience—which we see, hear, measure, weigh, calculate, manipulate—does not explain itself, is not the ultimate and primal reality. This reality of world and humanity is substantiated, sustained, and embraced by a primal ground, primal support, and primal purpose. Belief in God, then, is a matter of trust. The ambivalence of the whole reality of world and humanity forces a decision on us: We are expected to decide, without intellectual constraint, but also without rational proof. Belief in God is a venture that cannot be proved rationally from the outset and from outside, but whose reasonableness and meaningfulness dawn on the person from within in the very process of deciding (inner reasonableness) against an ultimate meaninglessness, insignificance, nothingness of human life and history. Faith has reasons that reason itself does not know: It is a reasonable trust!

What is the difference, then, if God does exist? I would like to formulate here a series of propositions. If God exists (and I am confident that God does exist), then the basic question of Leibniz, "Why is there something and not nothing?" (restated by Heidegger as the "miracle of miracles": "Why is there anything existing at all and not nothing?"), would find an answer. A liberating, surpassing, transcending of "one-dimensional man" into another dimension—as Herbert Marcuse demands, but in a way fundamentally different from that proposed by Marcuse—would become a real alternative even now. The infinite yearning of human beings—who, according to Ernst Bloch, are restless, unfinished, never fulfilled, and always setting out again on their way, making further demands, gaining more knowledge, seeking further, continually reaching out for what is different and new—would have meaning and would not finally be left unfulfilled. Even all the undeniable suffering, unhappiness, pain, age, death, and also the menacing final stage of boredom in a totally managed world: all these things would in fact not be final, but could refer to what is wholly other. The yearning of Max Horkheimer and countless other people for perfect justice, for absolute meaning and eternal truth, for a life without suffering, would not be unrealistic, but in the end open to fulfillment, to infinite fulfillment.

Yes, if God exists, then the signs and symbols of transcendence, then the demands for a new consciousness and a new definition of values, then the question of the great whence and whither, the why and wherefore of human life and the world's history, would refer not to nothing, but to the most real reality.

All this can make clear that what is needed most today is not a scientifically or theologically substantiated dissociation, diastasis, of science and belief in God, but a new fruitful synthesis arising from mutual critical respect. Science always raises critical questions with regard to any kind of belief in God. But belief in God also always raises critical questions with regard to any kind of science.

III. HOW CAN GOD BE CONCEIVED IN A SCIENTIFIC AGE?

If God exists, how would God have to be conceived against the background of modern science? First of all we must make some negative demarcations: God must not be thought of as a Supreme Being dwelling in a literal or spatial sense above the world. God is not an (almighty) absolutist ruler exercising unlimited power arbitrarily over the world and humankind. It is this naive, anthropomorphic idea of God as a supramundane being above the clouds in a physical heaven that has especially prevented scientists from reflecting seriously on the question of God.

Neither may God be conceived as an objectified, hypostasized "opposite" existing in a metaphysical sense outside the world in an extramundane beyond, in a world behind our world. God is also not a kind of constitutionally ruling monarch, bound on his side by a constitution based on natural and moral law and largely withdrawn from the concrete life of the world and humanity. This rationalistic-deistic idea of a God as an extramundane being beyond the stars, in the metaphysical heaven, should no longer be an impediment to raising the question of God for serious discussion, even among scientists.

In modern times, many from Spinoza, Hegel, and Schelling to Teilhard de Chardin, Whitehead, and Martin Buber have contributed substantially to the preparation of a new understanding of God and the world. And consequently—aware of our debt to them—we may now quite positively say: God certainly is not the world, and the world is not God: but God is *in* this world and this world is *in* God. To think of God in this way presupposes not a dualistic but a uniform understanding of reality. God is not to be thought of merely as a part of reality, a (supreme) finite being alongside finite things. Instead God must be thought of —to paraphrase some of the great classical formulas—as the infinite in the finite, the unconditioned in the conditioned, the absolute in the relative, the transcendent in the immanent. God then as the here and hereafter, all-embracing and all-pervasive, most real reality, in the heart of things, in human beings, in the history of humanity, in the cosmos. Hence God is to be understood as the simultaneously close and distant, worldly and unworldly, God. A God who does not make human freedom impossible, does not restrict it, does not play it down, but makes it possible, sustains, and perfects it. We may trust that, as the one who sustains, supports, guides, God is always ahead of us in all life and action, but also in breakdown and failure.

All this means certainly that the question of the God of the ancient worldview is obsolete: God as a miracle-working helper in need, as a stopgap, who is always invoked when we cannot go further with our human science and technology or cannot cope with our personal life. But the question of the God of the *new* worldview is not obsolete: the God who—even for scientists—can be the answer to those fundamental questions which—even for them—cannot be brushed aside and which again point to the intrinsic reasonableness of belief in God, and to its very practical relevance.

Who are we? The answer is: Defective beings who are not what they might be and expectant, hoping, yearning beings who are continually excelling themselves. But why are we like this? What is the explanation of this strange pressure constantly to transcend ourselves? What explains it, not only practically, provisionally, but finally, definitively? Is there no answer to this? Or is the question even permissible? *If* God exists, then it can be understood at the deepest level why we are very finite, defective beings and yet infinitely expectant, hoping, yearning beings.

Where do we come from? We can go back over the chain of causes, finding one cause after another. But the series breaks down when we try to explain the whole. What then is the cause of all causes? Do we not at this point come up against nothingness? But what does nothingness explain, except precisely nothing? Should we be content with matter or energy, ascribing to them divine attributes, eternity and omnipotence; or even with hydrogen, which really raises the question of the source? What is before the Big

Bang? Is there no answer to this? Is the question even permissible? If God exists, then there is an absolutely fundamental answer to the question of the origins of hydrogen energy and matter, to the question of where the world and humanity come from. Where are we going ? We can aim at one goal after another. But one goal after another is attained and we are still no nearer to giving a meaning to the whole, to the totality of human life, to the totality of human history. What then is the goal of all goals? Is nothingness perhaps both beginning and end? But nothingness no more explains the end than it does the beginning. Is the end to be a totally technicized or radically revolutionized society? Are not both these possibilities today more questionable than ever? Is there no answer to this? Is the question even permissible? If God exists, then an answer may be attempted on a higher plane to the great question, Where are human beings going, to what is human life and human history directed?

IV. CONSEQUENCES FOR THE UNIVERSITY

I turn now to some consequences of these reflections for our universities. Are these most basic questions merely the individual's private concern and not a matter supremely relevant to the public at large? Are we not to be allowed to speak publicly about all this also in our universities (and also outside the department of theology or religious studies)? At a time of unparalleled elimination of taboos, is God to be the last taboo? No, the question of God is too important and too explosive to be left solely to theologians.

It was once thought at the university that only the jurist could speak of law, only the psychologist of the psychical, only the sociologist of society. Meanwhile, criticism of "one-track-specialization" and the requirement of interdisciplinarity have borne fruit. Today we have become largely aware of the sociopolitical implications and interests, assumptions and consequences of each department, even linguistics, history of art, applied mathematics, and logic. Unless we are completely mistaken, the time is coming when people will begin to be aware not only of the sociopolitical but also of the closely connected ethical-religious dimension of each department.

This is not to say anyone is to be permitted at any time to speak incompetently on any subject. But certainly, in the department concerned, basic ethical-religious questions are not to be ignored or suppressed, but taken seriously and discussed, if necessary between different departments: for instance, in astrophysics the question of the origin of the universe, in quantum mechanics or molecular biology questions of chance and necessity, in jurisprudence questions of legality and morality, in economics the question of ethical motivations and objectives, in medicine the question of living and dying. Should we not then have the courage to admit when science has reached the end of its knowledge and planning, or when it has come up against questions of trusting faith?

We have heard it already: fortunately today relations between science and religion, and especially between natural science and religion, have perceptibly relaxed: militant atheism has largely become obsolete. It is true that agnosticism is still widespread among scientists: someone who is not against religion is not necessarily for it. But, at a time when we are able to do more than we can be permitted to do, there is a growing awareness that the serious problems of human beings, of society, of science and technology, and of ambivalent progress and growth raise questions that relate as never before to reality as a whole. What standards and norms are we to observe in state and society, in medicine and genetics, in atomic physics and space research? What priorities are to govern our decisions? Where should we spend public money? From what standpoint should we organize our basic life? To what should we commit ourselves in practice? All these are questions of ethics; they are also all questions of religion.

The faith of an entire epoch is coming to an end today. Not indeed the old faith in God as the great atheists predicted. What is waning is that modern faith which dates from the Enlightenment and the Industrial Revolution and which for many people has replaced belief in God: faith in an everlasting, unstoppable, eternal, immutable progress, a progress with divine attributes. Faith in the quasi-automatic progress of scientific knowledge, of technical realization and of industrial production, a faith that had been turned by the philosophers of history—Comte, Hegel, Marx—into a universal worldview. This optimistic faith in the power of science, technology, and industry—advancing in a straight line, in an evolutionary way, or dialectically by revolution—this faith is now coming to an end. I say nothing against scientific, technological, economic progress as such. What I oppose is a faith in progress: a faith that relies on eternal, automatic progress, as people formerly relied on divine providence, a faith that does not orient progress to basic human values and thus does not control, correct, or humanize it.

Yet we should not draw hasty conclusions. Belief in God is by no means the only alternative to belief in progress. In the all-embracing crisis of meaning, of orientation, of norms (rendered more acute by an unsatisfying, now often pointless division of labour, and by ruined leisure), a variety of escape routes is possible: flight to the total utopia of a social order, supposedly free from conflict, from domination, from pressure to produce results; or activist rebellion and even terrorism; or flight into privacy and inwardness, into a political resignation, to nostalgia; even the "Great Refusal" or simply flight into easy characteristic adaptation without inner loyalty.

The modern democratic state cannot provide any final answer to the question of meaning if it is not to become itself totalitarian. A political party, including people of different trends of thought and belief, neither can nor will answer ultimate questions or preach ultimate truths; it cannot and will not demand or provide a uniform "ultimate substantiation." Ultimate and primordial questions, answers, truths, substantiations, and interpretations were and are the concern precisely of religion, unless the latter is to be replaced by a quasi-religion or some other substitutes for religion. Even a person who cannot answer these questions would not deny that people in one way or another, sooner or later, are going to be faced with them.

It is good that politicians and scientists in particular are becoming increasingly aware of the absence of meaning in our society and that the question of meaning, raised by so many people and left unanswered, is now recognized as a political issue of the highest importance. Obviously there are no ideal religious solutions for present-day difficulties. The answer to the question of God is in no way an answer to all the urgent questions of the day. But the question of God has a deep, indirect influence by bringing basic convictions, basic attitudes, basic values, to bear on them. Ought we not, then, particularly at our universities, to respond to the present crisis by attempting to get to the bottom of political-ethical-religious questions affecting both the individual and society, to which students often respond with the greatest seriousness? Ought we not all together in all sections of science and in all departments to be continually wrestling anew with the basic question, the cui bono, the why and wherefore also of the different sciences?

In recent times we have gone through so many forms of atheism, experienced so many types of agnosticism, tried so many variations of nihilism, come across so many kinds of blind faith in allegedly supreme values such as nation, people, race, class, science, progress. People have always believed in some kind of God—if not in the true God, then in some kind of idol. Belief in God has been seen to reach the heights and the depths. But after so many crises, surprisingly much has been clarified and many difficulties against belief in God have been cleared up. It is not necessary to be against belief in God just because we are for heliocentrism and evolution, for democracy and science, for liberalism or socialism. On the contrary, let us state this very clearly: we can be for true liberty, equality and fraternity, for humanity, liberality and social justice, for humane democracy and controlled scientific progress, *because* we believe in God. A short time ago an English Nobel Prize winner, when asked if he believed in God, is said to have replied: "Of course not, I am a scientist." I hope that a new age is dawning when the answer will be: "Of course I do, I am a scientist."

I have tried as succinctly as possible to provide answers—incomplete, but unequivocal. They are meant to provoke a free, reasonably justified decision, or perhaps the revision of a decision. One thing is certain: Today, against the background of modern science, the question of God calls afresh for a decision from unbelievers and believers. There is no question of going back, only of going forward. As we look ahead to the third millennium we must think again about what we could not discuss but only suggest here: namely, that the God of philosophers and scientists and the God of the Bible need not be mutually exclusive, but could even be mutually inclusive. This, of course, would mean the appearance of the more godlike God: that God before whom the modern individual, without having to give up his or her reason and science, could again—as a philosopher of our time has said—"pray and offer sacrifice, again fall on his or her knees in awe, and sing and dance."[11] A vision? A projection? An illusion? A suggestion? A hope—not more than this, but also not less.

NOTE

*This essay is a slightly revised version of a lecture that I gave at the School of Theology at Claremont on 17 December 1981. It is here published for the first time in English. This essay comes out of the experiences of a teacher of theology at a secular university (Tübingen), where theology is one academic discipline among others at a big state university. I am happy that I can dedicate this lecture to my colleague and friend John Cobb, who has followed my work with great sympathy and respect. I admire him both as a human being and as a theologian who is open to questions of today's society ranging from philosophy to natural sciences, from questions of culture to the dialogue with world religions. But John Cobb has always affirmed at the same time his strong Christian convictions. He combines in an convincing way the ability to dialogue with the ability to affirm his Christian standpoint. I am especially grateful for his pioneering work in interreligious dialogue which he serves not only by his publications but also by his various dialogue activities, above all his engagement in the Society for Buddhist-Christian Studies, to which I also belong and which is of utmost importance for the future of the relationship between Christianity and Buddhism. I am convinced that his retirement from his position at the School of Theology will not mean retirement from theology. On the contrary, if I know John Cobb, he will use his new freedom to serve theology in his very special way.

4

Theology in the University:
The Question of Integrity

It is not too much to say that the fate of professional theology in the modern world is very much tied up with theology's being typically located in the university. Whereas in the ancient world a theologian was generally a bishop, and in the medieval world, usually a monk, in the modern world, since the Reformation and the Counter-Reformation of the sixteenth century, a theologian has typically been a university professor.

Of course, even much academic theology has continued to be done outside the university in free-standing schools and seminaries all through the modern period right up to the present. But somewhat as even rural areas in an urban society such as ours are, in their way, urban in culture, even such nonuniversity schools of theology have been importantly determined in their culture by university theology. One indication of this in recent American theological education is that the faculty of nonuniversity schools of theology are commonly appointed from persons whose graduate study in theology has been done in universities.

In the course of the modern period, however, universities themselves have undergone fundamental change—from the pattern established by the great medieval universities, in which theology not only had an integral place but was also, as the phrase went, "queen of the sciences," to the so-called secular universities of today, where theology is either completely excluded or else enjoys only residual status. Theology's place, relative to other fields and disciplines, is at best ambiguous, doubtful, and insecure. Of a piece of this change is that modern universities have become increasingly self-conscious about their autonomy as academic institutions and about the freedom that properly belongs to their members, especially the relatively permanent members that make up their faculties. In this connection, individual faculty and the professoriate collectively have also become more and more professionalized, particularly with the establishment of organizations like the American Association of University Professors (to which I shall refer hereafter as the AAUP).

The upshot of all this is that, in America, at least, it is now universally held within the academic community that institutional autonomy and academic freedom define the university. Indeed, already well before the founding of the AAUP in 1915, William Rainey Harper, president of the newly formed University of Chicago, argued that

> When for any reason, in a university on private foundation or in a university supported by public money, the administration of the institution or the instruction in any one of its departments is changed by an influence from without, when an effort is made to dislodge an officer or a professor because the political sentiment or the religious sentiment of the majority has undergone a change, at that moment the institution has ceased to be a university, and it cannot again take its place in the rank of universities so long as there continues to exist to any appreciable extent the factor of coercion. . . . Individuals or the state or the church may found schools for propagating certain special kinds of instruction, but such schools are not universities, and may not be so denominated.[1]

Considering that this understanding of the nature of the university has become ever more widely accepted in American higher education, we should not be surprised that even church-related universities now commonly understand themselves accordingly. This had become clear already a generation ago from the well-known typology employed in a report of the Danforth Commission on Church Colleges and Universities.[2] According to this typology, church-related institutions of higher learning tend to fall along a spectrum defined on one end by the "defender of the faith" type of institution and on the other end by the "non-affirming" type. Institutions of the first type seek to entrench their students in a particular religious position and therefore limit their autonomy and academic freedom accordingly. Institutions of the second type, by contrast, are so lacking in any explicit religious commitment as not only to enjoy unlimited academic freedom and autonomy, but also to be barely distinguishable from secular colleges and universities. Distinct from both of these extreme types, however, is the "free Christian (or Jewish)" type of institution, which, while it is explicitly confessional in its commitment, understands its autonomy as an institution and the academic freedom of its members to be indispensable to its proper service of the faith it confesses. Its distinctive mission or vocation precisely as a church- (or synagogue-) related institution is to be a fully free and autonomous university or college. If many Protestant institutions have long since conformed to this third, intermediate type, it is significant that even Roman Catholic universities and colleges have increasingly come to understand themselves in the same way ever since the 1960s and the changes in Roman Catholic praxis and theory sanctioned by the Second Vatican Council.

In the course of these changes in the self-understanding of the university, however, the place of theology has become increasingly uncertain. Given the usual way of understanding and practicing it, as thinking and speaking performed in direct service of the church and its witness, theology has been typically viewed as not being really of the university even if it happens to be in the university. Here, at least, the institutional autonomy and academic freedom that are now understood to define the university can no longer apply and must, in the nature of the case, be suspended. Such is the case even if it be recognized only tacitly rather than openly under the guise of a tendentious redefinition of what such autonomy and freedom are supposed to allow.

Significantly, even the AAUP has developed principles and policies that have at least appeared to allow for certain exceptions to its otherwise strict insistence on academic freedom and institutional autonomy as definitive of the university. Thus in its 1940 *Statement of Principles on Academic Freedom and Tenure*, which is still binding, there occurs what has come to be referred to as "the limitations clause." According to this clause, "Limitations of academic freedom because of religious or other aims of the institution should be clearly stated in writing at the time of the appointment." Developments during the 1970s and 1980s, however, have finally forced the AAUP to reexamine this clause so as to determine exactly how it should be understood and applied. The developments to which I refer are the growing number of cases involving church-related institutions in which issues of academic freedom have once again arisen and which have, therefore, come before Committee A, which is the AAUP's instrument for investigating and disposing of such cases. Often enough, as it happens, these cases have directly or indirectly raised the question of theology in the university.

Recognizing this, the members of Committee A, meeting in June 1987, authorized appointment of a four-member subcommittee, including theologians, to review the whole matter of the limitations clause and its recent application to particular cases and then to report back to the committee. As it turned out, I was the Protestant theologian who was asked to serve on this subcommittee, the Roman Catholic theologian being my friend and former colleague at the University of Chicago, David Tracy. Our final report was approved for publication by Committee A at its meeting in June 1988 and then published in the September-October 1988 issue of *Academe*, together with some critical reactions and an invitation to readers generally to submit additional comments. There is no need here to say anything about the procedure we followed in conducting our review or about the course of our deliberations in arriving at the substance of our report. It will be sufficient to summarize its two main conclusions, which are directly relevant to the theme of this essay.

We concluded, first of all, that, when the limitations clause is interpreted, as it should be, in the context out of which it was formulated and in relation to the long history of discussion of which it was a part, its purpose is not what it has often been supposed to be both by institutions invoking it and by Committee A in applying it to particular cases. Thus, for example, in the early 1960s a Roman Catholic institution, Gonzaga University in Spokane, Washington, had permitted the termination of appointments of faculty members upon the commission of a "grave offense against Catholic doctrine or morality." The AAUP committee investigating this case observed in its 1965 report that the 1940 *Statement* recognized "the propriety of limitations, suitably indicated, on academic freedom because of the religious aims of the institution," although the committee was critical of the lack of specific guidance that had been provided by the institution's statement of this particular limitation. Whereupon Gonzaga University, exercising, as it claimed, "its right under the 1940 *Statement*" to specify the limitation more exactly, revised its faculty handbook to include the following statement:

> Intelligent analysis and discussion of Catholic dogma and official pronouncements of the Holy See on issues of faith and morals is encouraged. However, open espousal of viewpoints which contradict explicit principles of Catholic faith and morals is opposed to the specified aims of this University.

With this, the investigating committee declined any further critical comment, although it did go on to criticize other portions of the handbook in some detail.[3]

The same understanding of the purpose of the limitations clause was emphasized in the 1967 AAUP report of a Special Committee on Academic Freedom in Church-Related Colleges and Universities. Although this report rightly recognized that the clause has to be understood in its context and against its historical background, it went on to allow that "At some point in the scale of self-imposed restrictions a college or university that comes under them may, of course, cease to be an institution of higher education according to the prevailing conception." Having thus introduced the notion of a scale of restrictions, some of which are, but others of which are not, inconsistent with the idea of an academic institution, the report went on to observe that some of its later statements further defined the "area of acceptable restriction." It then supplied guidelines for demarcating this area of acceptability, saying that any limitation or restriction must be "essential" to the religious aims of the institution.[4]

As a result of our close review of the context and history of the limitations clause, we became convinced, and argued in our report, that, contrary to this understanding, it in no way intends to legitimate or render acceptable restrictions on academic freedom, provided only that they are essential to "the religious or other aims" of the institution. Crucial for our alternative understanding was a gloss on the history of the discussion given by Committee A in its report for 1939, at a time when negotiations for the 1940 *Statement* were all but concluded:

> There are a few institutions of the proprietary or sectarian type which carefully specify in advance that which is to be

affirmed and taught concerning certain subjects and which pledge in writing members of their faculties to uphold by precept and example the points thus made clear. The present officers of this Association have felt that such institutions were free thus to restrict members of their faculties and have wasted little time or sympathy on complainants who, having thus definitely pledge [sic] themselves by formal contract, have later wished both to retain their appointments and to recover the freedom we seek to defend for other teachers and scholars. The difficulty is not with the few institutions which are thus frank and precise in their agreements, but with those which covet for themselves classification with the freer colleges and universities and yet would impose upon members of their faculties an obligation to conform to certain of the beliefs and practices of the administrative officials of the institution or of the supporting organization. To repeat, this Association would not deny to a group which desires to do so the right to support an institution for propagating its views. It merely insists that such an institution ought not to be represented to the public as a college or university for the promotion of the liberal arts and sciences, in which scholars and teachers are free to seek and impart truth in all of its aspects. Furthermore, such an institution ought to be careful to stipulate in advance of employment the particulars in which it insists that members of its staff adhere to prescribed doctrines and practices. Otherwise, it must be assumed that a member of its staff is free to engage in the normal activities of a teacher and scholar.[5]

In the light of this and other clear indications to the same effect, we concluded that the AAUP's position at the time of the 1940 *Statement* and its limitations clause rested on the same presuppositions contained in its founding *Declaration of Principles:* (1) that any institution has the uncontested right to impose or accept limitations upon its own autonomy and the academic freedom of its members; but (2) that any institution exercising this right thereby forfeits any moral right to proclaim itself an authentic seat of higher learning and assumes the moral responsibility of publicly declaring itself the proprietary institution it in fact is, including stipulating in advance the limitations it places on academic freedom.[6]

The second of our two conclusions had to do with "professional education," and, specifically, theological education, in the university. Contrary to the prevailing view that theology, at least, can only be an exception to the principles of academic freedom and institutional autonomy, we concluded that theology's right to be in the university depends on its being in fact of the university, and therefore bound by essentially the same principles binding on any other field or discipline, department or school.

> [T]here is no principled basis to distinguish professional cler-
> ical education from professional education generally. . . . A
> school of law endowed by its creators to train students as
> *laissez-faire* or Marxist lawyers, and measuring its faculty
> against a requirement of faithfulness to the doctrines thus set
> down, has every right to exist; but it has no right to class
> itself as a seat of legal learning on a par with free institu-
> tions. Neither would a school of law with commitments to
> religious orthodoxy. To the same effect, if theology is an aca-
> demic discipline, it must be treated as any other discipline.
> Higher education is not catechesis, and this is no less true for
> professional clerical education than for any other professional
> calling.[7]

But is any wrong done by allowing an unfree school of theology a place in an otherwise free university? Such is the last question raised in the second section of our report, and we answered
it thus:

> [I]t is difficult to maintain that an entire university forfeits its
> status simply by housing a component that requires creedal
> orthodoxy as a consequence of its singular religious mission.
> But a wrong it is. It is a wrong to the individual scholars so
> constrained, who are denied the liberty of inquiry and expres-
> sion ostensibly afforded their colleagues in other disciplines,
> and who, if their later inquiries lead them to fall afoul of con-
> secrated authority, must forfeit their posts. It is a wrong done
> to colleagues in other disciplines, who may never be secure
> that their academic freedom will indeed be insulated, for the
> power to muzzle, once permitted within a university, may
> prove difficult to constrain—especially given shifts in denom-
> inational doctrine and leadership. Consequently, it is a wrong
> done to the institution, for it must labor under a cloud of
> suspicion that the teachings and writings of its faculty may
> not be truly free. In sum, the housing of an unfree school
> within a free university is a contradiction: it may be *in* the

university but, being unfree, it is not *of* the university, and it has no business being there.[8]

Now I realize that this second conclusion, like the first, reflects nothing more than the thinking of a four-member subcommittee, and that, while our report has since been approved for publication by Committee A, it still has to be critically received and perhaps amended by the professoriate generally, including, presumably, the theologians belonging thereto. But whether, or with whatever refinements and amendments, it may finally become AAUP policy, I do not have the least doubt that the understanding it expresses of theology's right to a place in the university is the understanding that is bound to prevail—if, indeed, it does not already prevail—throughout the academic community. Sooner or later, it will be clear to all that at stake in theology's presence in the university is the integrity of the university. Either theology is an academic field or discipline essentially like every other and, therefore, bound by the same principles of academic freedom and institutional autonomy; or else, being an exception to these principles, theology has no moral right to be reckoned on a par with the other academic fields and disciplines and, therefore, is not an integral part of the university.

In point of fact, however, theology continues to be generally understood and practiced in such a way, in the churches and even by many, if not most, academic theologians, that its right to a place in the university is anything but secure. That this is so is made particularly clear by the recent and well-publicized case arising from Professor Charles E. Curran's being denied the right to continue to teach Catholic theology at the Catholic University of America. Because this was one of several such cases that our subcommittee had to consider, I had already studied it in some detail before being appointed to the AAUP committee responsible for investigating the case. By the time this further responsibility was discharged, however, I had had occasion to read statements by Professor Curran and his counsel that sought to explain and justify his position against that taken by Catholic University and its chancellor. The crux of his defense is that the only Church teaching that he ever questioned or dissented from in his own teaching and scholarship as a theologian falls into the category of noninfallible teaching. In other words, at no point had he ever questioned or dissented from the infallible teaching of scripture and dogma as interpreted by the teaching office of the Church. What is striking about this defense, however, is its clear implication that, if Professor Curran had ever dissented from, or even questioned, such infallible teaching, his right to teach at Catholic University would have been forfeited and could have been legitimately denied him, provided, at least, that such would have been the finding of his scholarly peers proceeding in accordance with academic due process. In short, at this crucial point of principle, Professor Curran's understanding and practice of theology was no different from that of the Cardinal Archbishop of Washington, who, acting *ex officio* as chancellor of the university, had initiated the proceedings to withdraw his canonical mission as a Catholic theologian. But it is just this understanding and practice, accepted by theologian and chancellor alike, that our subcommittee found to be incompatible with the academic freedom and institutional autonomy definitive of the university.

The same point becomes clear in another recent case involving Southeastern Baptist Theological Seminary in Wake Forest, North Carolina. Like any number of other institutions related to the Southern Baptist Convention, Southeastern Baptist recently came under the control of a new board of trustees, most of whose members belong to the extreme fundamentalist majority currently dominating the convention. As a result of this development, the faculty at Southeastern Baptist organized themselves into a chapter of the AAUP and entered the complaint that, because their trustees had now denied their proper role in the appointment and promotion of faculty and had subjected them to new doctrinal restrictions, their academic freedom as well as the autonomy of their institution had been violated. But without questioning that there were, indeed, serious violations of academic freedom and due process in this case and that the trustees of the seminary clearly changed the rules on persons already appointed to the faculty, I am most struck by the fact that, even before the fundamentalist takeover, the so-called academic freedom of the faculty and the autonomy of the institution had been severely compromised by restrictions in the form of required subscription to stated articles of faith. In other words, from the standpoint of the second conclusion in our subcommittee report, Southeastern Baptist Theological Seminary and its faculty had never enjoyed real institutional autonomy and academic freedom to begin with. Of course, being a free-standing seminary, it is not located in a university. On the other hand, the action of its faculty and their appeal to the principles of academic freedom and institutional autonomy provide a good example of the point I made earlier, that even nonuniversity schools of theology have come to be increasingly determined by the culture of the university and of the academic theology done within it.

Obviously, there are complexities even in such relatively clear-cut cases as these that call for a much more nuanced treatment than I am able to give here. But I am satisfied that, even if all the relevant complexities were taken into account, the bottom line would not be significantly different. It is simply a fact that, as theology is still widely understood and practiced, not only in the churches but by academic theologians themselves, it remains an undertaking that cannot be an academic field or discipline on a par with every other in the strict and proper sense of the words. Far from being subject to the same academic freedom and institutional autonomy by which the university is now defined, theology is, in fact, a restriction on, or an exception to, such freedom and autonomy.

Of course, apologists for the usual understanding and practice of theology frequently argue that academic freedom and institutional autonomy are, in effect, analogical concepts that have somewhat different meanings in different contexts, or as applied to different academic fields or disciplines. Indeed, these apologists reason, such freedom and autonomy are never absolute, because they are always subject to certain limitations. No scholar-teacher is free to ignore the overriding obligation to tell the truth, and the autonomy of any institution is circumscribed by the well-being of such other communities as it exists to serve. But, then, if we reject, as we must, unlimited freedom and autonomy, we must also realize that our concepts of them have a range of meanings depending upon particular context and application. We are then in a position to recognize that what these concepts mean as applied to the church-related institution and to the theological scholar-teacher need not be simply the same as in any of their other applications. On the contrary, the institution's autonomy in such a case allows for its freely acknowledging church authority, and the academic freedom of the theologian may very well include fidelity to, and respect for, the teaching office of the church.

The objection to this argument, however, is that it is a futile attempt to have it both ways. Even if one grants that institutional autonomy and academic freedom are never absolute and that they may, indeed, have a range of meanings, what they are supposed to allow cannot be redefined beyond certain definite limits. If an institution yields to church authority in any properly academic decision or proceeding, it thereby forfeits its autonomy as an academic institution. If a theologian's fidelity to, or respect for, the teaching office of the church in any way limits what he or she can teach or publish as a proper conclusion of theological inquiry, then his or her academic freedom consists in nothing but the words. The prevalence of such argument, however, is clear evidence of the situation in which we find ourselves, thanks to the way in which theology for the most part continues to be understood and practiced in both the church and the academy.

My conviction is that this situation is particularly unfortunate because there is good reason to believe that the conventional understanding and practice of theology that create it are as unnecessary as they are problematic. Through the efforts of a number of theologians working out of different ecclesial traditions and cultural contexts, there has already emerged a clear alternative, from which it follows that theology need not be in any way a restriction on, or an exception to, academic freedom and institutional autonomy but may be every bit as subject to them as any other field or discipline rightly claiming a place in the university.[9]

The key to this alternative understanding and practice is to distinguish clearly and sharply, although without in any way allowing a separation, between Christian faith and witness, on the one hand, and Christian theology, on the other. The basis for this distinction is that, in general, it is one thing to make or imply claims to validity by means of our various acts, thoughts, and statements, while it is another, very different (though also closely related) thing to reflect critically on our claims to see whether or not they are really valid. Thus Christians can believe and bear witness to their faith only by making or implying several such claims to validity, to the effect that their witness is not only fitting to its situation but also adequate to its content and, therefore, both appropriate to Jesus Christ and credible to human existence. But in the circumstances in which they typically make or imply such claims the question naturally arises as to whether their claims are valid. Some or all of the same claims to validity are made or implied by others, Christians or non-Christians, for contrary forms of faith and witness. Thus the very act of bearing Christian witness establishes both the possibility and the necessity of a certain form of critical reflection whose task is to validate (or invalidate) the several claims to validity that that witness either makes or implies. If one holds, then, as those arguing for the alternative understanding and practice of theology typically do, that it is just this form of critical reflection to which the phrase "Christian theology" properly refers, one is free to understand and practice Christian theology consistently and without qualification as simply another form of the same critical reflection that is embodied in some way or other in any academic field or discipline.

This is so, at any rate, if one assumes, as I do, that the whole point of any such field or discipline, whether in the humanities and sciences or in the various professional areas (engineering, law, business, medicine, and so forth), is somehow to advance essentially the same process of critical reflection in a deliberate, methodical, and reasoned way; that is, by so reflecting on the claims to validity made or implied in some area of life and praxis as to validate (or invalidate) them. My contention is that when Christian theology is understood and practiced as it should be, it is not just another form of bearing Christian witness, which is rightly subject to the teaching office of the church, but, rather, a distinctive form of essentially the same process of critical reflection embodied in one way or another in all the other academic fields and disciplines.

This means, of course, that theology's service to the church and its witness, while both real and important, can never be direct but must always be indirect, in essentially the same way in which all of the other forms of critical reflection can be of only indirect service to the other areas of life and praxis that they exist to serve. One might say that this is the price that must be paid for theology's being a genuine form of critical reflection. No form of reflection can be really critical unless it is free not only to validate the claims to validity on which it reflects but also to invalidate them. This qualification implies that its service to the particular area of life and praxis that it exists to serve can only be indirect. Therefore, theological reflection, also, can be genuinely critical only if its service to Christian witness is always indirect and it remains free to invalidate all claims of witness, even when they are made or implied by the teaching office of the church. This point explains in turn why the principles of academic freedom and institutional autonomy must apply as fully to theology as to every other field or discipline in the university. If the whole point of theology is critical reflection on the validity claims made or implied by Christian witness, it must be fully subject to these principles and so in no way a restriction on, or an exception to, them.

It is not my purpose in this essay, however, further to develop and defend this alternative understanding and practice of theology for which I have argued elsewhere.[10] My purpose here, as indicated by my subtitle, is simply to clarify the question of integrity that is raised by theology's continuing to be present in the university.

I could not accomplish even this, however, without making one final point. Clearly, theology's being in the university raises the question of the university's integrity as an academic institution that is fully free and autonomous. But no less clearly, in my view, it also raises the question of the integrity of theology itself. Whatever else is to be learned from the long history of Christian theology, one thing seems certain: it is always wrong for theology simply to adjust its claims (including, not least, such claims as it may make about itself) to the understanding and practice of the world around it. This means in the present case that how theology is to be understood and practiced can never be responsibly determined simply by theology's looking to the modern university and the principles by which it is defined. On the contrary, theology must also look to its own essential nature as Christian theology, fully realizing that it is at least possible that those who continue to defend the conventional understanding and practice of theology are right: it cannot be understood and practiced in accordance with its nature unless it is recognized openly or tacitly to be a restriction on, or an exception to, the defining principles of academic freedom and institutional autonomy. I do not hesitate to say that if they prove to be right, I, for one, would feel obliged to give up my alternative understanding and practice, even though in my case this would be to give up theology altogether as no longer a defensible undertaking.

Obviously, this is not what I and a number of other theologians expect finally to come of our efforts. But I trust that the point I am making is clear: if the only theology that could be of the university as well as in it would be Christian theology in name only, then the question of integrity—of theology's integrity as well as the university's—would not really have been answered after all.

NOTES

1. Quoted in the report of the subcommittee of Committee A on Academic Freedom and Tenure of the American Association of University Professors, "The 'Limitations' Clause in the 1940 Statement of Principles," *Academe* 74/5 (September–October 1988): 54 (hereafter referred to as *Report* [1988]). For reasons that are made clear below, I am indebted to this report throughout the essay and owe a special debt to the work of Matthew W. Finkin, who not only drafted the report but also did the historical research lying behind it.

2. Manning M. Pattillo, Jr., and Donald M. Mackenzie, *Eight Hundred Colleges Face the Future* (St. Louis: Danforth Foundation, 1965), 66–69. Cf. *Report* (1988), 53–54.

3. *Report* (1988): 53.

4. *Report* (1988): 52–53.

5. Quoted in *Report* (1988): 54.

6. Cf. *Report* (1988): 54–55.

7. *Report* (1988): 55.

8. *Report* (1988): 55–56.

9. See, for example, Hans Küng and David Tracy, eds., *Paradigm Change in Theology: A Symposium for the Future*, trans. Margaret Kohl (New York: Crossroad, 1989); also Charles M. Wood, *Vision and Discernment: An Orientation in Theological Study* (Atlanta: Scholars Press, 1985).

10. See especially my *On Theology* (San Francisco: Harper & Row, 1986).

WOLFHART PANNENBERG

5

The Task of Systematic Theology
in the Contemporary University

In the history of Christianity, there was always a fundamental question to be faced and to be answered: the question of why an individual person should commit herself or himself to be a member of the Christian church. In the case of a Jew, one is born as a Jew. But one is not born as a Christian; one has to be reborn. Certainly, since the fourth century, baptism, in most cases, has become a matter of early childhood. The difference from the assumption of being a Christian by birth does not seem tremendous. Nevertheless the sign of baptism has to be appropriated in the course of one's life. Otherwise, it becomes an empty sign. It is not that the life of a Christian first begins with personal conversion. It does start with baptism, but one's baptism has to be remembered and reappropriated again and again until death. Thus, being a Christian remains a very personal affair.

There are all sorts of particular reasons and factors in each individual story for becoming a Christian. But in any event one has to become a believer. Christian belief has always been belief in God and in Jesus Christ. This is what makes a Christian: to confess to Jesus Christ that in him God has acted to restore and reconcile the human race and through the human race all of creation. Again, there is a significant difference from being a Jew or, say, a Hindu. One is a member of the Jewish or Hindu people by birth. It may be important to confess to the faith of the fathers and to obey the traditional rules of life, but personal confession is not constitutive of being a Jew or a Hindu. In the case of the Christian, his or her personal confession to Christ is constitutive of being a Christian. It is bound up with one's baptism. It is not the only issue in baptism, of course. In our baptism God called our life once and for all, beyond our capacity of answering God's call at any particular moment. But still, our confession of faith belongs to the integrity of our baptism. It is only in our personal faith as individuals that our baptism is alive.

The problem involved in this situation becomes sharpened when we consider that it is precisely the Jewish God, the God of the Hebrew Bible, whom the Christian believes and confesses to be truly God. What should motivate a person to embrace the God of another nation? We may say it is Jesus and his teaching. But Jesus was a Jew himself, and most Christians are not. To a Jew, it may be natural to honor the God of his or her forebears, although even that is not a condition for being a Jew. In the case of the Christian, however, whose background is Gentile and who only becomes a member of the Christian community by confessing to the God of Israel, we must ask: Why should such a person do so?

Here we are at the core of our subject, the need for systematic theology. It all depends on the question of truth: If we suppose that the God of Israel and of Jesus is the one and only true God, then and only then is there sufficient reason for believing in that God, even if one is not a Jew.

In each personal story of becoming a Christian or of personally appropriating the call that claimed our lives in the event of our baptism, there will be many factors and motives contributing to our involvement in the Christian faith. Many of those factors and motives may be more or less accidental, but all of them, even our most personal experiences, would turn out to be superficial or deceptive, if the God whom Jesus proclaimed, the God of Israel, were not the one true God. In being a Christian, everything depends on the reality of God. This explains the fundamental importance, not only of belief and dogma, but also of theology in the history of the Christian churches. We cannot honestly identify ourselves as Christians if the story of Jesus Christ and of his God is merely a story, in the sense of a fairy tale; if it is fiction, not history. The Christian faith cannot live by relating the history of Jesus as if it were just a myth of Christian ancestors. The problem with the term "story" is that it obfuscates the truth-question. I suspect that the term "story" is so popular precisely because it allows one to slide over this question. The story of Jesus Christ has to be history, not in all its details, to be sure, but in its core, if the Christian faith is to continue. The same applies to the term "myth": There must be a real God, not just a mythical one, if we are to entrust ourselves to God.

The question of truth in religion is not only a theological question. It is not even primarily theological. Prior to theology, there is a feeling of reliability, or an awareness, only vaguely perceived, of the mysterious reality that encompasses and pervades our lives. To most people, beauty speaks of truth in more powerful ways than any intellectual argument does. Nevertheless, whatever we take as true in experiential immediacy may be challenged. All momentary certainty stands in need of further confirmation and interpretation, and it is only by reference to the unity of all our experience and of all our knowledge that we can determine what is true. Coherence provides the final criterion of truth. It can serve as such a criterion because it also belongs to the nature of truth: Whatever is true must finally be consistent with all other truth, so that truth is not only one, but also all-embracing. It is thereby closely related to the concept of the one God.

Considerations such as this belong to the level of reflection, not to the realm of experiential immediacy. Nevertheless, the Christian experience and the Christian community of faith need the work of theology, because it is on the level of reflection that all claims of truth are to be judged. The missionary proclamation of the Christian church, asserting that the God of Jesus is the one and only true God and that this God truly raised Jesus from the dead, entails a need for theological reflection, a need for an examination and confirmation of its truth-claims on the level of reflection. If theology properly faces that task, it can be of invaluable help in encouraging the preacher and in strengthening the good conscience of every individual Christian that the teaching of the church is true. If theology does not properly face its particular task regarding the truth-claims of the Christian tradition, then it easily happens that clergy are the first to become insecure and evasive about the message they are supposed to preach. When they become doubtful about the truth of the gospel, they will tend to replace it by other "causes" and the believers will be disturbed, because they no longer hear in church what they rightfully expect to be taught there.

The task of theology is not only to investigate the origin and the original content of the Christian faith and of the doctrines of the church, and the changes they underwent in the course of history, but also to determine the truth contained in that tradition. All theological disciplines share in this task, but undoubtedly it is the special task of systematic theology. To the degree that the question of the truth-content in the documents of the Christian tradition is dealt with in biblical exegesis and in church history, those disciplines share in the special task of systematic theology.

The content of truth inherent in the documents of the tradition has to be determined again and again; in each historical situation a new effort is needed to distinguish the truth of the gospel and of the dogma of the church from the evanescent forms of language and thought that at one time served to express such abiding truth. To make that distinction is possible only in terms of one's own thought and language, rooted in a contemporary setting. Therefore, the task of distinguishing in a particular traditional assertion the core of truth from the passing forms of language and thought arises again and again. In each historical epoch, systematic theology has to be done all over again. Yet the task is always the same, and the truth that systematic theology tries to reformulate should recognizably be the same truth that had been intended under different forms of language and thought in the great theological systems of the past and in the teaching of the church throughout the ages.

The task of the theologian in relation to the traditional language of Christian teaching is a critical as well as a systematic task. It has to be critical, because the distinction has to be made between what is historically relative in the traditional teaching and what is its abiding core. This task arises even in biblical exegesis, because the biblical writings are also historical documents. Therefore, time and again the substantial content of the biblical witness has to be reformulated. But the truth-content of traditional teaching cannot be determined in dealing with details only. It needs systematic presentation. Systematic presentation is itself a test of the truth-claims of each of the specific assertions that enters into a comprehensive account. The reason is that truth itself is systematic, because coherence belongs to the nature of truth. Therefore, the attempt at systematic presentation is intimately related to the concern for the truth that is searched for in the investigation of traditional teaching.

The most illuminating example of the task of systematic theology is provided by the doctrine of God. It is also the most comprehensive subject of systematic theology. If we take the title of systematic theology literally, it promises a systematic treatment of the doctrine of God.

In the context of Western culture, even today the word "God" is almost exclusively used in the singular. One may or may not believe in God (or in "a" God), and one may refer to God as a human projection or myth, but it is always (or almost always) the one God who is talked about. Such a way of using the word God implies as its semantic minimum the idea of a power on which all finite reality depends. In another way, the same idea is expressed in the minimal description that the word God refers to a power that determines everything. Such a minimal description does not provide a full concept of God. It does not say what kind of power or determination it is that is referred to, whether it is a power of natural force or of vengeance or of arbitrary decree or of justice or of love. To answer this question yields different concepts of God. In any event, the word God refers to a power. A God without power is no God at all, although that power need not be violent; it may work by way of persuasion. God may be personal or, like Spinoza's God, impersonal. Although the God of the Bible is certainly personal, this is not necessarily a requirement of the idea of God in general, although the word "God," because of its religious origin, carries personal connotations. In any case, there has to be some kind of power. Even the gods of polytheism are conceived as powers. In the case of the one God, there is only one such power, and accordingly all finite reality must be understood as depending on it. One may raise the question, then, whether or not the idea of God as only one implies that God's power must unlimited (except for the requirement of consistency with the divine nature). If the oneness of God implies the absence of any but self-imposed forms of limitation, the consistency of the word God in philosophies such as that of Alfred North Whitehead is in doubt, because the one God is thought by Whitehead to be limited by the existence of a world that is not his creation and by its creativity.

So much about the notion of God as only one. Now the idea of God as determining all finite reality implies that no finite reality can be understood in its depth without reference to God. For practical purposes, there may be descriptions of the world of finite things and even of human beings that abstract from their dependence on God, although the Christian faith affirms this relation to God as constitutive of their existence. However, if talk about God has any claim to truth, it must be possible to show that secular descriptions of reality are indeed abstracting from the fullness of its nature. It may be the case that the fullness of reality, even that of finite things, escapes our human capacity for insight, so that we cannot obtain exact and precise knowledge except for the abstract models we construct. But even then it must be possible to uncover in the nature of things what it is that our abstract models leave behind by the act of abstraction. It must be possible to point to traces of dependence upon God, if that is indeed constitutive of the nature and existence of an entity. If, to the contrary, the nature of things were thoroughly explained without any reference to God, it would follow by implication that there is no God. The very idea of the one God implies that all finite reality depends on him. Hence, such dependence has to be made plausible if someone insists on the reality of God. And it can be made plausible only by entering into the arena of competing interpretations of finite reality.

The plausibility of assuming the reality of God cannot be established by simply calling on some particular experiences. One has to establish the plausibility of the idea that all finite reality depends on God, not only human beings and the course of their history, but also the world of nature. But how can that ever be achieved? The only way it can be done is to present a coherent model of the world as God's creation. This is precisely what theology has always tried to do. Such a doctrine of creation cannot demonstrate in every detail the dependence on God of all the forms of finite reality. At its very best, the doctrine of creation could design a model of how the world looks if considered as God's creation, and of how we have to think of God if we are serious about speaking of the creator of the world. Actually, it is in rather general terms that theology in the doctrine of creation explicates the claim that all finite things, their differences and particularities notwithstanding, depend on God for their nature and existence. What theology can possibly achieve in this respect is always far from adequate. But even so, the theological doctrine of creation should be able to nourish and substantiate the confidence that the world of finite reality is indeed susceptible to a coherent interpretation as being created by God. In such a way the doctrine of creation in its turn substantiates the truth-claim involved in the use of the word God.

But it is not only a systematic description of the world as creation that is required in order to substantiate an affirmation of the one God. If the term creation is restricted to the bringing into existence of finite entities, then it takes more than the act of creation to substantiate belief in a God who determines everything. If the God who created finite entitites could not also sustain them, he could not be trusted as the one God in whose hand everything is placed. Because the creatures have their existence in a temporal process, they would have to rely on powers other than God for the achievement of what they desire in their developing existence if God had only given them the beginning of their existence. In view of the experience that finite existence is continuously in danger and seems to fall prey to the powers of destruction, the question is inevitable: Will the God who granted such existence also assist his creatures to overcome the evils that surround them? Or will the creatures in this respect be left to some other power? If the latter, the creator God would not be the all-determining reality, and the discussion would be about polytheism. Or could one imagine that God, existing as the all-determining reality, had created his creatures simply in order to watch them pass away? Such a God, certainly, would not be love. His creative activity would be capricious. Could that be consistent with other characteristics implied by the notion of the one God? In any event, Christian theology at this point goes beyond the minimal description of God in terms of an all-determining reality. It is the character of that reality and of his power that needs clarification here. According to Christian theology, the nature and power of God is love. This is first expressed not in his sustaining and redeeming activity but in the very act of creation. To grant existence to creatures is an act of love, if it does not serve another purpose but is itself the purpose of the creative act. But God cannot be at the same time love and omnipotent (as the all-determining reality must be supposed to be), if he leaves his creatures to the powers of evil and destruction.

It is the old problem of theodicy that arises at this point. It expresses the challenge that a loving and all-powerful Creator has to meet in the face of the forces of evil and destruction that pervade the actual world. Therefore, beyond creation in the more restricted sense of the word, something more is needed to prove the plausibility of the assumption of God's existence: The redemption and final salvation of the creatures is part and parcel of the demonstration of the reality of God. Not only the doctrine of creation is related to the task of substantiating the truth-claim of the Christian language about God, but so are christology, soteriology, and eschatology (the doctrine of final salvation). It is only in the event of final salvation that the reality of God will be definitively established. The entire process of divine economy leading to that final consummation amounts to a self-demonstration of God's existence.

One could include all of this in the notion of creation, because it is only in the eschaton that God's work of creation will be completed. If such a broad notion of creation were adopted, one could simply say that the interpretation of the world and of its history as God's creation substantiates the truth-claim of Christian language about God. In any event these claims can be supported only in the form of a systematic and integrative interpretation of the world of experience, corresponding to the oneness of God as well as to the unity of truth expressed by the requirement of coherence as a criterion to judge any particular claim to truth.

So far, I have argued that systematic theology is necessary to substantiate the truth-claims of Christian language about God. This task is met by attempting a comprehensive and coherent account of the world as God's creation, including the economy of God's action in history. To provide such a comprehensive interpretation on the basis of a Christian doctrine of God is more or less what has been done in systematic theology since the days of the early church when, in a context of Hellenistic culture, Christians, and especially Gentile Christians, had to justify their faith in the Jewish God and in Jesus as his final word. Explicitly, such a defence of the Christian faith in God by way of a systematic exposition of Christian doctrine as well as of the world of creation and history has been attempted since Origen's work on principles. This approach to theology produced classical systematic work like that of Thomas Aquinas, who was the first to state clearly that everything in theology is concerned with God. This statement unites the doctrine of God in the more rigid sense of the word and the doctrines relating to the economy of God's action in the world. The two belong together like the immanent life of the trinity and the economic trinity. Therefore, everything in theology is concerned with God, so that God is the one and only subject of theology.

In modern times, the systematic treatment of Christian doctrine has not only continued, but has even acquired additional importance. Since the beginning of the modern period, the Christian faith has had to face new challenges, the combined impact of which gives even more weight to the task of systematic reconstruction.

One of these challenges (and I shall restrict my argument to only two of them) resulted from the rise of modern science and the development, on its basis, of a program of a complete, purely secular interpretation of reality in general and of human life and history in particular. This program is embodied in the modern university. This development, which has been of preeminent consequence in shaping modern culture in general, tended to render a Christian interpretation of the world superfluous, at least in public discourse. A second major challenge, also embodied in the modern university, has been the criticism of all forms of arguing by recourse to authority. It is this second modern challenge that requires a more detailed discussion at this point, because it helps to clarify the specific function of systematic theology in the modern situation. It will finally bring us back to the other and even more awe-inspiring issue.

From classical antiquity to the seventeenth century, an argumentation by or from authority had been considered perfectly rational. In many areas of thought, authority was considered indispensable as an educational means for the individual to obtain autonomous insight. In some areas, and especially in the realm of history, all our information was understood to depend permanently on authority. The only problem, then, could be whether or not a particular authority was reliable. All this changed in early modern times. After the period of religious wars in early modern history, all argument by authority fell into disrepute. Authorities were understood as divided and as purely conventional. Above all, authorities were seen to be merely human. To follow the lead of authorities would involve the risk of falling prey to prejudice. Authority and reason were no longer seen in harmony, but in opposition; it became the battlecry of modern culture to follow the light of reason, not the prejudices of authority. The modern university is the institutionalization of that battlecry.

In a special way, this applies to history, the former domain of authority. The modern science of history is based on a method of critical examination of all the relevant documents from the past. Modern history aims at an autonomous reconstruction of historical processes on the basis of such critical examination of the documents of the past. Historical knowledge is no longer considered to be dependent on the acceptance of some authoritative tradition. Even in the field of history, then, reason has been opposed to authority.

What is the impact of all this on systematic theology? Until modern times, the systematic reconstruction of Christian doctrine was understood to be based on some prior acceptance of authority, the authoritative teaching of the church and the authority of the

biblical writings. In the course of medieval theology, the correlation between these two authoritative sources of Christian doctrine
was increasingly determined in such a way that the basic authority
was attributed to the scriptures. In the Reformation the authority
of scripture was opposed to the authority of church teaching. The
latter was not completely denied, but it was considered derivative
and subordinate. In early modern times, all such authority, the
scriptures as well as the teaching of the church, came to be considered merely human. Scriptural criticism began by producing evidence of the human, not divine, character of the biblical writings:
diversities and contradictions in biblical reports, indebtedness to
now obsolete beliefs about nature, and so on. Thus in modern biblical exegesis the Bible came to be regarded as a collection of historical documents. Perhaps this approach does not necessarily
exclude the interpretation of the Bible as inspired by God, but certainly it would be a very different account of the inspiration of
scripture than that of premodern Christian thought.

The rise and victory of modern historical-critical exegesis
meant that systematic theology could no longer take the divine
truth as a guaranteed presupposition of theology. Traditional Protestant dogmatics had not been much different from medieval scholastic theology in assuming that the divine truth of the Christian
doctrine was secure before the work of theology even began. Systematic argument was not understood as the arena where the
truth-claims of traditional teaching are judged, but only as explication of the truth presented authoritatively in the inspired scriptures. To be sure, medieval and even Protestant dogmatics did in
fact determine what was to be regarded as the true content of traditional teaching and of the scriptural witness. But the tension
between this implication of its own praxis and the assumption of
a presupposed guarantee was not perceived before the rise of historical criticism and the modern suspicion against any appeal to
authority.

Even in the modern situation, however, theology did not dare
to rely on its own systematic reasoning in facing the question of
truth. Instead, the principle of authority in its function of an *a
priori* guarantee of truth was replaced by that of personal experience and belief. Theology now was conceived as explication of
the content of personal or communal faith, the truth of which
had to be presupposed as a matter of personal decision. William W.
Bartley III pointedly characterized and attacked this attitude as
"the retreat to commitment" (in his book by that title). It actually
represents a retreat from the arena of public critical discourse of

truth-claims of all sorts, a retreat into some sheltered corner of personal preference. The impact of this attitude on Christian thought did a great deal of damage to the righteous claim of Christian teaching to be taken seriously as a candidate of rational discourse.

But theology does not really need to retreat to subjectivism. The discipline of systematic thought in coherently restating the content of Christian doctrine can stand on its own without a prior guarantee of truth. Of course, most persons who engage in such an enterprise will be confident from the outset that some sort of Christian teaching will prove to be true. But such confidence is a psychological incentive, not part of the argument. In a similar way, the theologian may be persuaded by the authority of the church or by the authority of the Bible. There is indeed a spell of authority emanating from the Bible and the Christian church, although not everybody might be sensitive to its fascination. But, again, such spiritual authority must not be mistaken for a basis of argument. It should rather motivate an effort at examining its truth-claims. In the course of such investigation and examination, the authority cannot function as an argument. In fact, it would ruin the argument, if it were used that way. (Anselm of Canterbury was more sensitive to that problem than most theologians of later periods have been.)

In the discussions of systematic theology, then, in the sequence of its argumentation, in its construction of coherent models of the world as determined by God's action, the question of truth should be regarded as open. Of course, if it turns out to be true that there is a God, that Jesus is risen and that everything is in his hands, then this has been true all along. It does not depend on the effort of the theologian. Presumably, this was the most profound reason to attribute to some authority prior to theological reasoning the power to guarantee the divine truth. But the scriptures themselves tell us that the universal recognition of God's glory will not occur before the eschaton. Until then, the truth of his revelation will continue to be in dispute. Therefore, our knowledge is imperfect, as Paul says (1 Cor. 13:9), and this applies most of all to theological knowledge. We are called to accept this situation and not to demand a final guarantee of truth before we even start to think. The modern criticism of authoritarian argument, on the one hand, and of the retreat to subjective commitment, on the other, has caused many theologians to surrender Christian apologetics and dogmatics, to surrender even the Christian truth-claims themselves, and to turn to what are considered "relevant issues" of the time. But there is no reason to lose heart and to sell out just because there is no *a priori* guarantee of truth.

The effort at systematic reconstruction of Christian doctrine is even more needed than in earlier periods of the church, because it is now clear that the truth-claims of the tradition have to be dealt with in this framework. The results will remain provisional, but that is in keeping not only with the spirit of modern science, but also with Paul's understanding of the provisional form of our knowledge, due to the incompleteness of salvation history itself. To engage in systematic theology in this way is quite compatible with personal confidence in the ultimate truth of the Christian doctrine, even more so than on the basis of a prior commitment to authority. A Christian should be ready to leave it to God himself definitively to prove his reality; he or she should be content only to perceive vaguely and to adumbrate the infinite wealth of the truth of God. Certainly we need to be reassured of that truth; precisely that reassurance is the duty of systematic theology.

Systematic theology done in this way is not confined to the task of restating the traditional doctrine in view of contemporary insights in the fields of biblical exegesis and doctrinal history as well as in the secular disciplines. It should be an effort in constructive thought in order to exemplify how the God of the Bible can be understood as Creator and Lord of all reality. Theological systematics must therefore integrate the wealth of insight gained by all the secular disciplines of the university into the mysteries of nature, human life, and history. In a strict sense, it is only by way of such an integration of secular insight into theological systematics that the truth-claims of the traditional doctrine can be restated. Such an integration of achievements of the secular disciplines into theology, however, cannot consistently be the selective transfer of some isolated results. It requires a critical reflection upon the methodical framework of the research done in those disciplines. The transposition of details into the framework of theology will consequently take the form of a critical transformation that nevertheless must remain accountable to the standards of those secular disciplines. It will not be possible to do this without creating new dispute and controversy. But the systematic theologian must not shy away from interdisciplinary controversy within the university. This controversy can open our eyes to see new possibilities. Controversy is far better than unrelated coexistence, because in controversy we are still concerned for the truth which is only one. The prospect of general agreement may be somewhat dim, although the bold outlines of some agreed synthesis may occasionally become visible. The dangers of dilettantism are always close at hand. But then, even in theology the excitement of systematically exploring the truth of God must not be mistaken for having that truth itself at our disposal.

This is how I understand the need for and the task of systematic theology in the contemporary university.

II. THEOLOGY, THE UNIVERSITY, AND THE COMMON GOOD

6

The University and the Common Good

In 1858, President Henry Tappan of the University of Michigan wrote:

> Of all mere human institutions there are none so important and mighty in their influence as Universities; because when rightly constituted, they are made up of the most enlightened, and the choicest spirits of our race; they embrace the means of all human culture, and they act directly upon the fresh and upspringing manhood of a nation. To them must be traced science, literature and art; the furniture of religious faith; the lights of industry; the moving forces of civilization; and the brotherly unity of humanity.[1]

Tappan was in the grand tradition. The purpose of the university has never been understood simply in terms of ideals for the internal life of the scholarly and teaching community. Supporters of the university have always tried to legitimate their claims for the importance of their particular university ideal by arguing that

97

the embodiment of that ideal not only best serves the internal life of the university community as such but also makes a significant and necessary contribution to the well-being of the society as a whole. In other words, the purpose of the university is finally defined in relation to a vision of the good for society.

The debate about the purpose of the university is therefore a moral debate in which the contesting parties make the claim that the university ought or ought not to do and be this or that. This is true even of so-called descriptive accounts of the function of the university such as that of Parsons and Platt.[2] Their descriptive work presupposes that the good society is one in which there is a relatively stable social equilibrium within which change occurs in an orderly fashion and in continuity with the present shape of institutions. This presuppostion is value-laden and could itself bear moral examination, but that is not my purpose here. I propose to argue that the purpose of the university can best be understood in relation to the concept of the common good. I am aware of the ambiguities surrounding this concept, but I believe that some such notion of the good of the whole is necessary as a proper context for understanding the purpose of the university, and the idea of the common good has fewer disabilities than its chief competitor, the idea of the public interest.[3]

I propose no grand solution to the problem of the university, nor do I have my list of great books which on reading would prove to be salvific for all places and all times. My aim is much more modest. I hope to show that, as we become more clear about the idea of the common good, we may be able to initiate a form of public discourse about the purpose of the university that might at least point to the moral limits of university practice in the context of a broader understanding of our community of support and our community of responsibility.

I begin with the "hermeneutics of retrieval," the recovery of past traditions and the appropriation of those traditions for current practice. In the process, the tradition is significantly modified by its being related to a new context for practice; at the same time, current practice is called into account by the power of the tradition. With this in mind, I begin with an analysis of the notion of the common good and then show how that notion has been related to the discussions of the purpose of the university at important moments in its history. I next provide a brief analysis of the dominant understanding of the American university today and highlight some of the key questions that should be considered within the university about its relationship to a contemporary understanding of the common good. I then make my proposal for bringing discourse about the common good back into the university, discourse that is essentially theological.

I. THE COMMON GOOD AND THE PURPOSE OF THE UNIVERSITY IN MEDIEVAL THEOLOGY

At the time of the founding of the great medieval universities, the proper end of the entire social order was believed to be the promotion of the common good. It was Thomas Aquinas who resurrected this Aristotelian idea and gave to it a distinctly Christian shape. With respect to the moral teleology of the *natural* order, there is no significant difference to be noted between Thomas and Aristotle on the idea of the common good. For Thomas, however, the highest good was not a natural good but a *supernatural* good. Because of this, the common good was finally the good of the whole cosmos, properly related to God. In the light of this fact, the highest common good of the human community was the salvation of souls. Whatever else Thomas may have said about the common good, this for him was the essential matter. However, he also fully explored the natural common good, a conception that he draws almost entirely from the writings of Aristotle. This concept became the dominant social-ethical ideal of medieval times.

What was the common good?[4] First it is important to remember that for Aristotle and for Thomas, the highest natural good is happiness, or living well. It is beyond my interests here to develop fully the content of living well, but, in general, the good life in Aristotle is the virtuous life, and the highest virtues are the intellectual virtues. The good life, therefore, is the life lived according to reason, and the moral life consists in living according to the moral virtues, which are achieved by the ordering of the will according to reason.

Furthermore, Aristotle's notion of living well rests on the anthropological assumption that human beings are social in two senses. First, a single human being cannot survive physically in isolation. We require community for sustenance and protection from the time of our birth, simply as a condition for living. But the most important dimension of our sociality is the second: In order for rational beings to live the good life, they require discourse with other rational beings for the perfection of their virtues. The heart of the sociality of human beings is communication at all levels from early life on. It is this process of opening oneself up to the

other and receiving from the other such openness that causes community to be. In other words, it is mutual acts of speech or, in
Thomas's terms, "sounds charged with intentionality" that make
community possible and necessary. The sociality of human beings
is grounded, therefore, not only in their survival needs, but also in
their highest possibilities for living well.

In the light of this understanding of community, we can say
that the common good, for Thomas and Aristotle, is relational. It
is an order of relationships that at once promotes the good of the
individual and unites her with others in pursuit of a common end.
The good of the whole is indeed the good of the parts, but it is
always more than that. The common good consists not only of
the sum of virtue deriving from virtuous persons in a given city.
It also consists of those conditions, such as peace, unity, and justice, that make possible relations among individuals that will
promote mutual communication for the purpose of living well.
The common good of any city, then, rests on the friendship of persons and the conditions that make it possible for those friendships
to endure.

The common good was primarily a political ideal, but it was
not simply defined in terms of the interests of the city as such. To
be sure, the common good included the maintenance of the government of the city, but under a wise ruler the city was to sustain
a durable order with justice that embraced diversity and yet maintained peace. No other human community could provide these
conditions adequately for the whole. Smaller groupings, such as
the family, have their own common goods as well, and much of
what is said about the common good of the city applies to these
smaller groupings too. Yet, like that of the individual, the good of
smaller groupings must be seen as subordinate to the common
good of the city. Even as the individual is morally required to promote the good of the whole family, so the family is required to
promote the common good of the city. The same is true for other
groups. It was assumed that, in the best of times, the good of the
individuals, of smaller groupings, and of the city coincided, but
should a situation arise in which the good of the individual or
smaller groups conflicted with that of the city, the good of the city
would certainly take precedence.

It is important to note that this conception did not mean that
individuals and families were viewed simply as instrumental to
the good of the city. Although the discussion is subtle, the conception of the common good, for Aquinas, was stated in such a way as
to make clear that the authority of the ruler to impose sacrifices

on the individuals of the city for the sake of the whole had to meet the test of morality. The sacrifices had to be in the service of the greater moral health of the society, which in the long run would support even more adequately the good of the individual. Criminals could be punished and soldiers conscripted, for example, not to promote just any interest of the city, but only to maintain the city's commitment to the common good, defined as peace, justice, and prosperity. Above all else, nothing could be done by the ruler that could endanger the "separated" or supernatural good of any single individual. In this sense, the natural common good could finally never be defined apart from the supernatural common good of the cosmic order.

In this account of the common good, there are three closely related elements. First, there is the common good of the individual and subsidiary groups. Secondly, there is the common good of the city. Finally, there is the "separated" or supernatural common good.

At no point, to my knowledge, does Thomas write specifically about the university and the common good. In the light of his own use of Aristotle, however, it is safe to presume that, if he had done so, he would have argued that the theological and moral end of the university is, like that of any other human community, to promote the common good in its own life and in the life of the realm. For Thomas, this view would clearly have required that, whatever else the university did, it should serve the growth of piety for the sake of human salvation. The most important subject to be taught would be theology, and it would be important that theology avoid errors that might endanger the highest common good, the salvation of souls. This separated common good was of crucial importance for the moral health of the society. Moreover, in the light of his deep interest in and dependence on Aristotle, it is very likely that Thomas would also have placed great emphasis on the role of the university in transmitting the tradition of classical learning and promoting rational discourse among the students and faculty, the very activity that constituted the possibility of the common good as he understood it. This role would constitute the internal common good of the university community.

Thomas was, however, very much part of the medieval Paris circle of theologians who believed that the university was one of an entire range of social organizations seen to be the work of God regulating the political, educational, and religious life of the people.[5] In the thirteenth century, Alexander of Roes argued that the conception of a Christian society required "preservation of centers of relative autonomy in order to secure Christian society against aberrations in name of piety or patriotism." The proper functioning of Christian society as a whole, therefore, required coordination in three institutions, "the *sacerdotum*, the *imperium*, and the *studium*." In his view, the university was to be the prophetic arm of the comprehensive work of God. In other words, it was to the university that Alexander looked to remind both the rulers and the church of their proper bounds, so that the proper conditions for the well-being of the whole could be maintained.[6]

Like Thomas's thinking about the common good, medieval thinking about the university viewed the internal function of the university to be preserving the learned tradition of antiquity in such a way as to support true piety among the people. The roots of this idea of learning appeared at least as early as the fifth century in Jerome's call for a "learned celibacy."[7] To be sure, the study of the ancients was always carried on under the authority of the scriptures, and classical teaching was always to be brought into conformity with Christian revelation, but the result of this kind of pedagogy was to unite the love of God and the love of learning in what Jean Leclerq has called an "integral Christian humanism," a concept that functions even in the present time as a significant element in the Catholic understanding of university education.[8]

By way of summary, then, in medieval theology the university had two important relations to the common good. With respect to its own internal good, the university was to promote true piety by engaging in rational discourse uniting the love of God and the love of learning. This role was in itself important for the whole society. But the university was related more directly to the common good of the realm in the critical role of assisting the ecclesiastical and political authorities to avoid excesses in a coordinated attempt to promote the common good of the whole social order.

II. THE TRANSITION TO THE MODERN UNIVERSITY

By the end of the fourteenth century, the uneasy balance involved in medieval Christian humanism began to break apart, and the new, antitheological humanism of the Renaissance captured most of the major German universities during the latter part of the fifteenth and the first half of the sixteenth century. For a brief period in the sixteenth century, an alliance between the leaders of the Protestant Reformation and the neohumanists seemed possible, but that possibility soon faded. The subsequent conflict between the Protestants and Catholics led to a growing dogmatism in both groups, and the impact on the universities was disastrous. In the seventeenth century, the relative autonomy of the great medieval universities collapsed. Protestants, and to some degree Catholics as well, insisted on confessional universities. The neohumanists, for the most part, were expelled from the universities in Germany. The university was to serve only the common good of the church, and the transmission of the tradition was reduced to the transmission of religious orthodoxy.[9]

It was against this state of affairs that Thomasius Wolff of the University of Halle protested. He denied the authority of theology and Aristotelian philosophy and insisted that laws and morals were to be based on rational knowledge about human life and society. Wolff based his own thought on mathematics and physics and insisted that philosophy was to pursue the truth with complete freedom.

It is here that we can mark the transition to the modern university, a transition of monumental proportions. In the older versions of the university, all instruction had been based on the assumption that the truth was a given, and that the responsibility of the university was to transmit that unchanging truth to each generation. In the late seventeenth century, beginning at Halle, all of this was turned on its head. From that time until the present, the basic assumption of the modern university has been that truth is to be discovered by scientific (*wissenschaftliche*) investigation. Research is the fundamental purpose of the university, and the task of instruction is to lead students to develop their own research capacities and to communicate the results of that research broadly in the scholarly community.

If at Halle the new science reigned, at Göttingen it was the new humanism that dominated the understanding of the university. The new humanism shared with the integral humanism of medieval times its fascination with the classics of antiquity. What was decidedly different was the relation to theology. The new humanist had little or no interest in theology. The philosophy faculty assumed leadership at Göttingen, and the focus was upon a reasoned cultivation of the sense of the good and the true, not in the service of true piety, but as the fruit of reason and for the sake of the development of high culture.[10] If one combines conceptually the reforms at Halle and at Göttingen, all of the ingredients are present to anticipate the new idea of the university that was launched with great fanfare and national support at Berlin at the end of the first decade of the nineteenth century.[11]

One of the leading voices in the discussion of the new university was a theologian, Friedrich Schleiermacher. Following somewhat the pattern suggested by Wolff at Halle, Schleiermacher argued that research was the primary function of the university. The overarching goal of all research was the discovery of a comprehensive and unified principle of knowledge by which the whole of knowledge and its parts could be interpreted and integrated. The key to this search was not only freedom to teach and to learn, but also free communication of ideas between the various special fields of knowledge. "It is," said Schleiermacher, "the duty of all scholars to re-unite in comparative studies that which by virtue of language appears in separation." The essential purpose of the university, he concluded, was "to generate and to train the scholarly spirit," the final outcome of which would be "a totally new form of the intellectual life."[12]

The university was to provide an important service to the state as well. It was to develop an intellectual elite that was broadly "cultured," one whose personalities were formed in accordance with a cultural ideal or a system of the highest and most universal ethical and aesthetic norms. This particular legacy of German neohumanism and Protestant pietism was not explicit in Schleiermacher's essay, but it appears clearly in Hegel and other writings on the new university published at the same time. Here one finds the final contours of the modern university in Germany. University instruction had two purposes. The first was to promote in its internal life free communication of ideas generated by research in the various specialized sciences. The second was to educate persons who would form a leadership class to a clear worldview composed of the highest values of liberal culture. As Karl Jaspers was later to write of this university ideal, the university was to be "the intellectual conscience of an era . . . aiming to stand for man's humanity *par excellence.*"[13]

The architects of the new university were not interested in the old language about the common good. They were mostly Protestants, and they had little other than historical interest in Catholic theology. In addition, the whole medieval structure of thought, of which the notion of the common good was an integral part, had collapsed under the onslaught of the Enlightenment. In fact, the idea of the common good had been so much identified with rulers and the monarchy that, in seventeenth-century

England, a new term, *the public interest,* had emerged as another way of articulating concern for the good of the whole.[14]

Although the language is missing, it is obvious that the formal criteria for the natural common good are met by the idea of the modern university. Its chief internal good was the promotion of rational scholarly communication, that social activity which Thomas and Aristotle deemed central for the perfection of virtue. Moreover, its own self-understanding of its purpose included the commitment to contribute to the cultural and moral health of the state by educating the sort of leadership required for general excellence in human living.

But there is a significant difference in the idea of the modern university: the primacy of research in the purpose of the university. As Jaspers was to underscore a century later, even though both teaching and research were important in the university as conceived by German idealism, it was research that was most important. One must have competent researchers in the university, he argued, even if the researchers were bad teachers.[15]

Although the German idealists clearly understood the university to be related to the common good, a significant shift had occurred in the way in which that relationship was understood. The focus was primarily on the internal good of the university as a subsidiary unit of the society and its service to the national state. There is no formal counterpart to the transcendent dimension represented by the Thomistic separated good. Quite the contrary: By the end of the nineteenth century, a significant number of professors in the German universities thought that, because High German culture was clearly superior to any other human cultural achievement, it was the mission of the German state to disseminate that culture as widely as possible for the good of the world. This narrow focus on the German state as the objectification of universal values led to an intellectual imperialism and made the German universities easy prey for the ideology of political imperialism that took them by storm in the early twentieth century.[16]

III. AMERICA AND THE RESEARCH UNIVERSITY

From colonial times, American colleges were seen to be servants of the commonwealth. In a fashion similar to the patterns established in England, especially at Cambridge, that service was provided by educating leaders who were schooled in the classics.

The virtues of intellectual discourse were to be honed in such a way that the students would develop an appreciation for rational thought; it was assumed that these habits of mind would be transferred to the tasks they undertook in the service of the nation. The colleges in America sought to develop in the students Christian intellectual habits associated with Christian character. It was a learned ministry that the founders of Harvard hoped to provide for the commonwealth, and that ministry was by no means confined to the ordained clergy. What they had in mind was a broadly understood Christian leadership class.[17]

Later, there were others in America, including Jefferson and Franklin, who thought that the common good might be served better by schooling that was more practical and egalitarian. The need of the newly forming nation was for an educated citizenry who could understand and implement democratic institutions. These citizens also needed to have the sort of technological skills that would give rise to innovation in commerce, so that the economy of the new nation could prosper.[18]

The great struggle for the soul of the American university occurred during the last decade of the nineteenth century and the first decade of the twentieth. Two of the competitors were the older liberal ideal and the Franklin-Jefferson vision. This latter vision cohered nicely with the nineteenth-century American preoccupation with national development and prevailing egalitarian sentiments. Not only was university education to be made available to all persons who had the capacity for advanced learning, the fields open for specialization were viewed as equally important as long as they were useful for the preparation of persons to find jobs and to make a contribution to the nation's welfare.

A third competing vision was, in part, borrowed from the modern university ideal developed in Germany. Even though those who conceived the modern German university gave primacy to research, what they had in mind was not primarily highly specialized advanced research, but research closely related to teaching. They certainly meant to require of all faculty competence to do advanced specialized research, but that research was to take place in the academies outside the university proper. Within the German university proper, the organizing goal was the conceptualization of the unity of knowledge, which necessitated not only careful research in the various disciplines of the university but also cross-disciplinary communication. In the late nineteenth-century American version at Johns Hopkins, however, this primary focus was eliminated, and the specialized institutes or academies became the model for the university itself. The university would serve the common good of the nation by becoming an advanced research center focused on the pursuit of knowledge for its own sake. This was the proper way for the university to serve the whole: simply fulfilling its unique role by striving for the highest standards of excellence in the research function.

Partisans of these ideals generated a heated debate over the future of the university, but none achieved complete dominance. Most of the leading universities incorporated aspects of each of the competing visions into their curricula by the end of the first decade of the twentieth century. During the first quarter of the century, most of the universities continued to experiment. It was a time of proliferating professional, vocational, and extension programs, a developing research emphasis, and general expansion. Increasingly, the elective system was adopted as a device for managing the conflicts surrounding the curriculum, and university administration expanded to offer all sorts of services to the students and to supportive constituencies. Development offices emerged to organize massive public relations efforts and to orchestrate fundraising campaigns made necessary by expansion.[19]

The moral fervor of partisans of the competing visions waned, and the institutions came to terms with the necessity of offering something to each of the interests impinging on their lives. Most of this development occurred without organized faculty resistance, for obvious reasons. What the new institutions offered was a safe setting for the practice of the emerging academic professionals, and it reflected a pluralistic understanding of the needs of higher education. Those needs were to be met in an institution that could command broad community support; the institution was to be legitimated in the eyes of the public by the services it provided to the society as a whole. The common good was still in view, but it had become diffuse. It was assumed that the common good was pluralistic and that everything the university did somehow enriched the life of the nation and served it well. By the end of the 1920s, this view was quite widespread.

About that time, two reformers called for major changes. One of these, Abraham Flexner, was preparing his series of lectures at Oxford University which were later to be published under the title *Universities: American, English, German.* He was a strong advocate of return to the German research ideal, which he thought was best exemplified by the model developed by Daniel Colt Gilman at Johns Hopkins. Flexner was highly critical of the emerging pattern of the American universities, charging that they had become nothing more than "academic service stations" for any and all constituent groups that sought institutional legitimation for training of any sort. He argued that a continuation of that pattern of development would prove to be disastrous for the American university as such. By trying to serve every conceivable interest, the university would effectively serve none. Above all else, the university was to be a graduate research center, and it could best serve society precisely by doing what it alone could do: research of the highest academic quality.[20]

A few years later, Robert Maynard Hutchins, in his Storrs Lectures at Yale, presented a very different vision, even though he was of much the same mind as Flexner about the intolerable situation in the universities of America. Hutchins's idea of the university was in some respects, like Flexner's, a revival of Schleiermacher's vision. It also bore some resemblance to the vision of John Henry Newman for the new Irish university at the middle of the nineteenth century. According to Hutchins, there would be no place in the university for attention to the practical application of knowledge at all. Ideas were of the essence. But neither was advanced specialized research to be a significant feature of the life of the university. Such research that was to be done in the university was to be related to teaching. Advanced specialized research would be carried on in separate graduate schools that would be related to, but not part of, the university. Learning in the university was to be rooted in the classics; the central goal of the university was to be general intellectual conversation that would challenge the mind with great ideas. The philosophers were to provide leadership in the conversation about the unifying principles of knowledge, and teaching would regularly be interdisciplinary.[21]

It was Flexner's ideal, however, that prevailed. Hutchins's vision really did not survive him at Chicago. Most of his disciples retreated to specialized colleges or to the undergraduate programs in the universities. One might attribute to his influence some of the impetus for the general education movement as well. Yet even though Hutchins continued to make similar proposals for university reform through the early 1960s, there is little evidence that his ideas have had a major impact on the shaping of the university. With Flexner it is somewhat different. Although he had profound influence on medical education, he was not a major influence on the development of the American university as such. Still, the ideal he championed reigns supreme today. It is research that dominates the definition of status and function in the most prestigious American universities.

But the research university today is a far cry from the Johns Hopkins of Flexner's time. It has been profoundly shaped by other influences. In fact, the interest and support of the federal government has had the greatest impact on the design of the contemporary American research university. Beginning with agricultural research after the Morrill Act in 1862, and expanding to meet industrial and military needs during World Wars I and II, government funding defined the direction of the university's contribution to the common good. That contribution was to be research that had possibilities for direct application to the development of industrial and military technology, both of which were seen to be vital to the strength of the nation. As a result, the ideal of pure and disinterested research merged with the American ideal of practicality, so that the modern American university evolved into an institution for science-based technological innovation. This is not the same as the old German research academy from which Gilman of Johns Hopkins and later Flexner drew their inspiration. Rather, it combines the functions of the nineteenth-century German academy with the French ecole polytechnique and the German technologische Hochschule (a combination that Hutchins and Flexner opposed for different reasons).

Not all of the impetus giving rise to the dominance of the research function was external. Internally, the faculty was rapidly evolving into one of the most professional of the professions. Very early, the focus on research encouraged the movement toward academic specialization. So, too, did the development of graduate departments organized along the line of fields of specialization. Increasingly these departments controlled access to the academic profession. Linked to other departments in academic guilds, they developed the power to validate paradigms of knowledge and to rate individual contributions to knowledge in relation to the dominant guild paradigms. As a result, graduate research faculties began to exercise powerful influence in almost all of the institutions of higher learning in America. In this sense, although it is true that residual reminders of the old liberal college persisted, they were not significant in the shaping of the life of the university. University presidents and faculty members regularly gave rhetorical expression to their commitment to older liberal ideals and at times struggled mightily, if unsuccessfully, for the establishment of general education. Yet, those who applauded the dominance of research and those who deplored it increasingly agreed that, at least in practice, the research function was the core function of the modern American university. More and more it was on the basis of published research acceptable to the major guilds that both university and individual personal prestige were established and maintained.[22]

Increasingly, however, even this reward system was modified as research of certain kinds proved to be commercially profitable. After World War II, there emerged a new professional type, the "academic entreprenuer." It was no longer the master who had something to profess or the pursuit of truth for its own sake that fired the imagination of the academy. It was not even intrauniversity politics and international guild recognition that excited the primary interest of the emerging princes of the academy. Rather, visions of grants, consulting contracts, and, above all else, personally controlled research institutes invaded the dreams of the academic entrepreneur. The professionalization of the academy had taken a decisive turn. The research function conceived as the pursuit of truth for its own sake was distracted from its pursuit by the vision of a pot of gold. Public service as an ideal of the profession was often confused with private gain from research that could meet the demands for technological and social development as conceived by governmental and private funding sources.[23]

IV. THE DECADES OF TURBULENCE

Life in the university seemed rather settled in 1963 when Clark Kerr, in his Godkin Lectures at Harvard, confidently announced that the days of major university reform were over. What he saw ahead for the university was a future much the same as the present. The university would develop in response to the needs of its constituents and the pressures they exerted. In this situation, Kerr argued, the task of the university president was not to present any grand unifying vision but rather to mediate the competing claims so that the life of the university could proceed with a commitment to progress and peace.[24]

Ironically, Kerr hardly had time to return from Harvard to California before he was confronted by the "free speech" movement, which marked the beginning of massive student and faculty unrest in all of the major universities in America. The ensuing upheaval sparked the revival of the debate about the meaning and purpose of the university with an intensity heretofore unseen. Critics produced a new flood of jeremiads, but the complaints fell into patterns not too different from the presidential proposals and faculty tirades a half century or more earlier.

On the one hand, the university was seen to be a medieval institution in the midst of modernity, a community of intellectual monks who had little interest in the world outside its campus. It was argued that under the banner of "knowledge for knowledge's sake" and "value-free inquiry," together with a host of other slogans with similar meanings, the university had abdicated its position as servant to society. The result was a growing gap between what was taught in the university and what was required for living in the world. Moreover, some of the critics berated the university faculty for both their active and passive moral failures. They charged that while some of the faculty blithely ignored the urgent needs of the society in the name of dispassionate inquiry, others sold their souls to corporate America and to various governmental agencies to secure funding for research that was, in many cases, inappropriate to the university.[25]

On the other hand, the university was seen by critics of a different mind to be an institution that had tried to serve so many interests that it had lost any sense of direction. These critics argued that the institution's character was determined by the marketplace rather than by any clear understanding about its distinctive purpose. Equally problematic for many of the same critics was the call to the university by some of the more radical professors to engage in all sorts of inappropriate activities in the name of moral responsibility to the society. They argued that the distinctive service that the university could render to society was to be itself: an institution devoted to the pursuit and transmission of knowledge for its own sake.[26]

Then, of course, there was the debate about the relative weight given to research and teaching. There is little argument among the parties to the debate about the fact that research is in fact both conceptually and operationally the central function of the modern American university. The dispute was about the appropriateness of this emphasis on research and its impact on the quality of teaching and learning in the university.

Barely beneath the surface of these disputes was the growing uneasiness of some segments of the university faculty with the controlling paradigm of knowing. Drawn primarily from the natural sciences, and reenforced by the influence of positivism in philosophy and the social sciences, that which Parker Palmer has called the *objectivist* understanding of knowledge dominated university epistemological discussions.[27] Critics such as H. D. Aiken decried the stranglehold of empiricism and the capitulation of the social sciences and the humanities to models of knowing inappropriate to their subject matter. Aiken urged a return to more broadly conceived epistemological paradigms, or at least recognition of the existence of a plurality of paradigms of knowing.[28]

In all of this turmoil there were dire predictions about the future of the university. Irving Kristol announced the loss of the university's soul.[29] Robert Nisbet denounced the university's hubris and doubted the viablility of the institution as such.[30] Charles Frankel commented despairingly that there was no such thing as a university in America.[31] Never before have we witnessed such passionate apocalypticism among the dispassionate! But strategy did not match passion, and the decades of turbulence passed without much change. As Kerr observed in a short codicil to the 1982 edition of his lectures, what was remarkable after the previous two decades was how little had changed.[32] Leaders like Derek Bok of Harvard observed that the American university still was an institution with high standards of excellence, and he was of the opinion that no serious observer would want to change very much about them. In his view, the university served the comon good or the public interest by offering quality education and by advancing knowledge through research.[33] Bok never argued that the university was perfect, but he was sure that whatever problems there were in the university could be managed with adjustments here and there.

V. PROBLEMS CREATED BY THE DOMINANCE OF THE RESEARCH IDEAL

No one can deny that the American research universities do some things quite well. On close analysis, however, Bok's optimism seems to me to be misplaced. He overlooks some serious problems related to abiding institutional distortions created by the dominance of the research ideal in the university. First, rational discourse among the faculty in the university is now largely confined to discourse within specialized departments. Through the guilds, that conversation is broadened, but only geographically, in relation to other similarly specialized departments in research universities. Thus, the sort of discourse that might yield a sense of the good of the whole simply does not take place in the university. Not even discourse about the internal common good of the university takes place unless an issue of academic freedom or faculty governance is at stake. Then the specialists might begin to act in the interests of the common good of the whole, but only in terms of the academic profession itself. Other cross-specialty conversations are usually confined to discussions of promotion and tenure, student prizes, or visiting lecturers. Even here, the number of faculty involved in the community of discourse is very limited.

The fact that an increasing number of the faculty are located in semiautonomous research institutes affiliated with the universities adds to the problem.[34] They teach very few students, and they are only peripherally involved in other common faculty responsibilities. The combined effect of these developments makes the prospects for a community of discourse about anything resembling the common good—even the university's good—quite discouraging.

Second, it is not only the prospects for faculty discourse that are discouraging. Discourse between faculty and students is limited because the emphasis on research has devalued the teaching function for the most highly respected and widely recognized faculty members. To be sure, there is always an official affirmation of the value of good teachers, but the modern university has never departed from Jasper's preference for a good researcher, even if she or he is a bad teacher. The summary of the most recent Carnegie Foundation study by Ernest Boyer clearly indicates that teachers in general are not valued very highly in America, and the university setting is no exception.[35] Teaching is a very low priority for most of the leading research faculty. Moreover, that low priority is in part a function of the system of rewards inside the university itself where status, power, and money flow to those whose research is most widely recognized and most readily marketable. Even research directly related to teaching is not valued nearly so highly as that which is more marketable.

Third, because certain kinds of research are so much more marketable than others, the importance of some kinds of research and knowledge has diminished considerably in the university. If the government is prepared to fund a five-million-dollar program of biological research that might have significant military applications, there is little hope that research on art in the fifteenth century, which must be funded by the university's own meager research budget, will command as much administrative attention as its scientific counterpart, which is likely to contribute significantly to university revenue. The faculties in the humanities simply do not wield as much power and influence in the university as do the natural science and social science faculties. The message is not lost on the students either. As the most recent study by the

National Endowment for the Humanities has indicated, they have deserted the study of the humanities in droves during the last decade.[36] The effect of all this is the gradual demise of the faculties that have traditionally been the primary focus of discussions about values and virtues pertaining to the common good.

I am not suggesting that the research university should be something else. I am too much of a realist for that and, in any case, I strongly believe that research is one of the most important functions of the university. What I am suggesting is that the complete dominance of the research function has created distortions in the life of the university that render any conversation about the common good generally problematic and, in many instances, impossible. If the university is to be a servant of the common good, these distortions must be addressed.

VI. TWO RESPONSES TO RECENT CONTROVERSIES: SHILS AND BOK

One response to the recent decades of turbulence has been to turn inward. Members of the International Council on the Future of the University, alarmed by what they believed to be irresponsible action on the part of faculty during the upheavals of the 1960s and 1970s, appointed a special study group on the ethics of the academic profession. Their report, *Academic Ethics*, prepared by Edward Shils, explicitly limited its attention to concerns about the professional obligations as distinct from those obligations and responsibilities that might arise for faculty members from their roles as citizens, family members, and so on.[37] As a professional, the faculty member in the university has two sets of responsibilities. One of those is to the students, the colleagues, and the institution where he or she serves. The other is to the truth. These two obligations come together in the commitment of the faculty to create and sustain in the university a community of discoverers. This internal good of the university is the highest good for the academic profession, and it serves the larger society best by attending strictly to those matters in the life of the university that are crucial to its internal integrity. As Shils puts it: "The fundamental obligations of university teachers for teaching, research and academic citizenship are the same for all academics. All these activities are necessary for the university to perform its indispensable tasks for modern societies and modern intellectual culture.[38]

This report is a very thoughtful addition to the literature on professional ethics, but it does not give sufficient attention to the obligation of the university to the common good of the whole. The assumption of the report is that the university best serves the common good of the society by strict attention to the integrity and balance of its own inner life of teaching and research. That assumption is precisely what was at stake in the controversies over the purpose of the university during the decade or so of turbulence that preceded the formation of the study group. In light of this, the report almost appears to be a rearguard action on the part of the more conservative faction in the university. It simply will not do to allow the internal questions of professional ethics to preempt questions about the public responsibilities of the professions for the common good. These larger questions point beyond the requirements of personal integrity to the morality of structures of reward and their impact on the university as well as the society.

By the mid-1980s, Derek Bok's complacency had been shaken, and he was manifesting a growing concern about all aspects of life at Harvard. In his book *Higher Learning,* Bok indicated that he was deeply troubled by the growing dissatisfaction about the teaching and learning process inside the university and recommended urgent attention to the question of *how* students learn in addition to the ongoing attention to *what* they should learn. Furthermore, citing a study by Howard Bowen, Bok called attention to the fact that higher education does not seem to be a significant factor in shaping student attitudes toward certain ethical ideals and practices. That concern has become more and more urgent for him. Like most sensitive leaders in the nation, he is aware of a serious decline of the sense of responsibility for the common good of the whole among professionals and nonprofessionals alike. He recognizes that what counts in the prevailing professional ethos is neither public virtue, public service, nor the common good. On the contrary, the prevailing ethos supports an individualistic pursuit of private gain. Bok sees this to be a serious corrupting influence on the professions themselves as well as a destructive force on the quality of public life. In his President's Report of 1986–87, he issues a strong call to the university to respond to this situation. He urges more teaching of ethics, not only in the professional schools but also in the undergraduate curriculum.

Specifically, Bok calls for more courses on applied ethics and greater attention to the processes of moral reasoning. He does not believe that the university itself or any of its professional schools provides adequate training of this sort. Consequently, he urges concrete steps to prepare persons to teach such courses and steps to initiate curricular reforms that will not only make room for the election of such courses but also make them an integral part of existing degree programs.[39]

With Bok's proposals, the emphasis shifts from concern about the practice of academic professionals to the formation of students. He assumes, as did von Humboldt in Germany and Newman in Oxford, that by affecting student perspectives the university fulfills its role as servant to the common good. It could be that his proposals will force the general discourse of the community more in the direction of ethics in the practice of the professions, but even he is not very sanguine about the possibilities. He concedes that thousands of such courses are already being offered in universities and colleges with, as yet, little recognizable effect. He still believes, nonetheless, that better ethical instruction eventually could lead to a heightened consciousness in professionals of their responsibility for the wider common good.

I support the call for applied ethics and better teaching of ethics. The necessary discussion about the design of such courses and the focus on professional responsibility implied in Bok's proposals would surely raise the level of discourse in the university and expand its horizons beyond the narrow limitations of the Shils report. But alone they are not sufficient. The institutional distortions inhibiting discourse about the university's responsibility for the common good would still be a serious problem until those distortions arising from the dominance of the research function itself are addressed.

VII. HOPEFUL SIGNS

In the foregoing discussion, I have assumed that two conditions are essential if the university is to make its contribution to the common good. The formal condition is renewed university-wide discourse. The material condition is that the subject matter of that discourse must be the common good of the whole. To those conditions, I want to add one explanatory note. In the contemporary context we must return to Thomas and not to Aristotle. For Aristotle the horizon of the common good was the boundary of the city. Thomas's theological commitment to the "separated common good" enlarged his horizon so that the common good was finally conceived to be the proper relation of the whole cosmos to God. While I am not suggesting an identical formulation of the common good, I do think that some cosmic vision is required today. The larger issues of the common good are transnational; they involve the proper relation of all of the parts of the natural world to the whole. Pollution of the oceans and air, the "greenhouse effect," the threat of nuclear war: all of these are issues drawing us to some global notion of our common good, which transcends individualism, nationalism, and anthropocentrism. It is discourse about the university's proper contribution to the discussion and resolution of issues of such magnitude for which I am calling.

I am aware of the usual faculty reaction to calls for interdisciplinary discourse. But I am an optimist, and I believe that there are signs that the time is right for the universities to take certain steps to renew the conversation about the common good. In the first place, most of the university community is already convinced that the major issues and problems facing the world do not yield easily to the specialized organization of university disciplines and departments. Second, the natural sciences, which stand atop the university epistemological and power pyramids, are experiencing changes in perspective that are facilitating some scientific cross-disciplinary interest. At the 1988 meeting of the British Association for the Advancement of Science, for example, a full day was devoted to discussion of the importance of biological investigation for physics. This is but an illustration of what seems to be a larger epistemological shift. As the late Heinz Pagels wrote in *The Dreams of Reason,* a radical change is occurring in the organization of natural sciences from narrow specialization toward a more comprehensive or ecological science.[40] This new perspective may make it increasingly difficult to conceive of human good in less than global terms. Even now it is no longer possible from a natural scientific perspective to conceive the human good apart from the good of the whole natural order. Because the paradigms of knowing in the natural sciences are so influential in the university, a shift in the focus of research in the natural sciences will likely have a great impact on the other areas of university study.

It is to natural science, moreover, that the world's political and economics leadership looks for guidance and promise in matters directly and indirectly affecting human survival. The natural scientists will make the discoveries that are matters of life and death for the world, and their own understanding of the interrelationship and interdependence of all sectors of the natural order will inevitably introduce into those decisions considerations of global consequences. In other words, considerations of the common good of the world will figure prominently in the selection and implementation of scientific research.

This is not altogether a recent development. From the beginning of the development of the atomic bomb, sensitive nuclear physicists had serious misgivings about the potential destructiveness of their research. According to Lord Zuckerman, they thought it must be possible to impose reason upon reality. He proposed that research and development be subjected to the control of public discourse about its potential destructiveness.[41] Recently this sort of proposal has been given a new impetus by the work of the Committee for Responsible Genetics, an interdisciplinary group of scholars who secured the signature of more than five hundred scientists on a pledge refusing engagement in research intended for use in the development of biological weapons. What is becoming apparent is that more and more of the best minds in scientific research are insisting on the necessity of discussing the appropriateness of pursuing any research in which the result might be harmful to the common good of the whole. This insistence means that the old distinction between fact and value, so revered in earlier epistemological debates, is of diminishing interest. If the natural scientists continue to take the lead, the conditions of interdisciplinary discourse will change.

Equally encouraging is the internationalization of scientific discourse. As Sir Eric Ashby has said, the language of natural science is the new Latin of human conversation. This is the one mode of discourse based on internationally recognized modes of validating, testing, and sharing knowledge. Given the dominance of the natural sciences in the university, the possibility is raised that university discourse will increasingly become internationalized. That augers well for the development of conversations about the common good in a global context.

VIII. A MODEST PROPOSAL TO PROMOTE DISCOURSE ABOUT THE COMMON GOOD

In the light of these positive signs, I now come to my modest proposal. I propose first that all institutes affiliated with the university be subject to the usual procedures for making decisions about appointments, remuneration, and continuance in the university. This means that the directors and personnel of any affiliated institutes would be full members of the university faculty and administration and subject to the patterns of governance applicable to all other parts of the university. Second, I propose that all members of the faculty be required to engage in a regular pattern of teaching in the university graduate and undergraduate programs. Third, I propose that any research that is sponsored by the university or its affiliated institutes be funded by a Center for Research and Teaching. I also propose that awards be offered by the center for creative and excellent teaching as well as for innovative contributions to curriculum development.

The center would be partially funded by income derived from marketing university-based research. Fifty percent of all the proceeds from university-sponsored faculty research should return to the center fund and not to departments or individuals (as is the case with some present licensing arrangements). This suggestion is a variation on the proposal at Harvard for the Medical Science Partners plan to establish a subsidiary corporation to invest in research and reap some of the profits to support further research.[42] In my proposal the purposes would be generalized and the funds held by the university. I propose that the center be subject to faculty direction, and that the decisions about what research to fund be public faculty decisions. Finally, I propose that the evaluation of research proposals include, in addition to discussion of the merits of the proposals, some debate about what is and what is not appropriate research for the university in light of its responsibility for the global common good.

I anticipate four objections to the proposal. First, it might be objected that the type of discourse I am advocating would be very frustrating to researchers who would have to wait interminably for decisions from a new layer of bureaucracy for permission before pursuing new forms of research. But it is already the case that any research requiring significant funding must be subjected to review either by faculty committees and university administrators or by granting agencies outside the university whose criteria may or may not include those appropriate to the university's proper concern for the common good. The difference my proposal would make is that the university would itself provide a review, utilizing criteria for judgment appropriate to the university's concern for the common good.

Second, critics could argue that the resolution of debates over the ethical criterion I have introduced would be impossible, and that would make decision-making about research proposals unacceptably cumbersome. I do not deny that this might present a problem, but there is already precedent for the introduction of ethical criteria into the research review process. For example, I served for several years on a medical school ethics board that subjected all internal research proposals to scrutiny utilizing ethical criteria.

Early in the formative stage of the review committee there were intense discussions of appropriate criteria, but a working consensus did emerge over time. Moreover, by the second year, 75 percent or more of the proposals submitted were approved with no need for extensive discussion. Researchers soon understood the criteria and, as the committee continued its work, most of the proposals submitted for review were designed with ethical criteria in mind.

Some critics of the proposal might suggest that the introduction of ethical and peer review into the entrepreneurial arena of competition for research grants would result in a massive exodus of research-oriented faculty from the universities. I doubt this sort of apocalypticism, primarily because I do not believe that most university faculty would be opposed to some discussion of the issues I have raised. In any case, research that is done without serious reflection on the consequences of that research for the common good of the world is, in my view, not compatible with the nature of the university; those who are not willing to subject their research to rational discourse about the ethical limitations of scientific research do not belong in a university committed to the common good.

Perhaps a more serious criticism might arise from the perception that such a process of review would be in conflict with academic freedom. One would certainly want to proceed with extreme caution here. The review process must be seen to be fair, and the constitution of the review committee would have to be fully representative of the research interests in the university. Under the proposal no one would be prohibited from doing research. Only university funding and university sponsorship would be at stake. The intent of the proposal is not to prohibit research but to encourage the university as a community of scholars to take some ethical responsibility for the research that their institution sponsors and funds. One might even argue that the open discourse that would be generated by the proposal would actually increase academic freedom. Here it is important to note the historical roots of academic freedom. This privilege is grounded not in the general notion of free speech but in the concept of the university.[43] As I indicated earlier, it was freedom to teach and freedom to learn that were sought by the founders of the modern university, and these freedoms were for the purpose of advancing communication in the university. If academic freedom is understood as the privilege of free communication in the university, open discourse about research proposals and the purposes and limitations of university-based research would certainly serve to advance that freedom. It could provide a new initiative for vigorous discourse and open debate on a wide variety of issues. That debate and discourse might even provide something of a counter to the power by which certain faculty or schools of thought limit the entry of new paradigms for research into the life of particular universities by their control over the process of the validation of knowledge. Such a development would significantly enlarge academic freedom within the university. But now I have become utopian!

Realistically, I must admit that I do not think that these proposals would be adopted easily (if at all), but even if they were to be seriously considered, the discussion of the university and the common good would quickly move from the abstract to the concrete. I think that the self-interests of the leading academic professionals would ensure broad faculty participation. That in itself would raise the ethical intensity of the discussion and expand the scope of interdisciplinary discourse—not a negligible contribution to the internal good of university life. Properly supported, continuing discourse of this sort might even create an ethos in the university characterized by a consistent concern for the common good as one of the criteria for educational excellence. From that ethos we might reasonably expect a new generation of leaders with a vision reaching beyond narrow professionalism and nationalism toward a cosmic vision of the good of all parts of the created order properly related to each other.

It should be plain by now that my proposal involves nothing less than the return of theological discourse to the university. Even if the terms *God* and *theology* are not used, discourse about the common good of the whole creation is theological through and through.

NOTES

1. Henry P. Tappan, "Idea of the True University," in *American Higher Education: A Documentary History*, vol. 2, ed. Richard Hofstadter and Wilson Smith (Chicago: University of Chicago Press, 1961), 517.

2. Talcott Parsons and Gerald M. Platt, *The American University* (Cambridge: Harvard University Press, 1973).

3. Carl J. Friedrich, ed., *Nomos V: The Public Interest* (New York: Atherton, 1962); especially the articles by Brian Barry and Frank Sorauf. See also Virginia Held, *The Public Interest and Individual Interests* (New York: Basic Books, 1970).

4. In the following discussion I have relied on a number of sources, especially the following: Richard A. Crofts, "The Common Good in the Political Theory of Thomas Aquinas," *The Thomist* 37 (1973): 155–73; Bruce Douglass, "The Common Good and the Public Interest," *Political Theory* 8 (February 1980): 103–17; Jacques Maritain, *The Person and the Common Good*, trans. M. R. Adamson (London: Geoffrey Bles, 1938); Heinrich A. Rommen, "The Nature of the Common Good," in *The State in Catholic Thought* (New York: Greenwood, 1945), 306–08; Aldo Tassi, "Anarchism, Autonomy, and the Concept of the Common Good," *International Philosophical Quarterly* 17/3 (September 1977): 273–83; *Aristotle's Politics*, trans. Benjamin Jowett (New York: Modern Library, 1943); Aristotle, *Nicomachean Ethics*, trans. Terence Irwin (Indianapolis, Ind.: Hackett, 1985); Jaime S. Velez, "The Doctrine of the Common Good in the Works of St. Thomas Aquinas," Ph.D. diss. (South Bend: University of Norte Dame Press, 1950).

5. Kevin M. Cahill, "University and Revolution," in *America* 157/4 (22 August 1987): 77–78.

6. George H. Williams. *Wilderness and Paradise in Christian Thought: The Biblical Experience of the Desert in the History of Christianity and the Paradise Theme in the Theological Idea of the University* (New York: Harper & Bros., 1962), 172.

7. Ibid., 156.

8. Jean LeClerq, *The Love of Learning and the Desire for God: A Study of Monastic Culture*, trans. Catharine Misrahi (London: SPCK, 1978), 139–41.

9. Friedrich Paulsen, *The German Universities and University Study* (London: Longmans, 1906), especially 14–16.

10. Ibid.

11. For a complete discussion of the emergence and decline of the modern German universities, see Fritz Ringer, *The Decline of the German Mandarins: The German Academic Community 1890–1933* (Cambridge: Harvard University Press, 1969). On Berlin, see especially chap. 1.

12. Friedrich Schleiermacher, "Reflections Concerning the Nature and Function of Universities," trans. and ed. Gerhard E. Spiegler, *The Christian Scholar* 48/2 (Summer 1965): 141–43.

13. Karl Jaspers, *The Idea of the University*, ed. Karl W. Deutsch, trans. H. A. T. Reich and H. F. Vanderschmidt (London: P. Owen, 1960), 134, 145.

14. J. A. W. Gunn, *Politics and the Public Interest in the Seventeenth Century* (Toronto: University of Toronto, 1969), especially Introduction and chap. 1.

15. Jaspers, *The Idea of the University*, 58.

16. See Alice Gallin, *Midwives to Nazism: University Professors in Weimar Germany* (Macon, Georgia: Mercer University Press, 1986), and Robert P. Erickson, *Theologians Under Hitler* (New Haven: Yale University Press, 1985).

17. Charles F. Thwing, *A History of Higher Education in America* (New York: D. Appleton, 1906), 34. See also John S. Brubacher and J. Willis Rudy, *Higher Education in Transition: A History of American Colleges and Universities, 1636–1976*, 4th ed. (New York: Harper & Row, 1977), 14–16, 42–43.

18. Thwing, *A History of Higher Education in America*, 112–16, 192, 202, and Laurence Veysey, *The Emergence of the American University* (Chicago: University of Chicago Press, 1965), chap. 1.

19 Most of the material for the preceding discussion was drawn from Veysey, *The Emergence of the American University*, chap. 1.

20. Abraham Flexner, *Universities: American, English, German* (New York: Oxford University Press, 1930).

21. Robert M. Hutchins, *The Higher Learning in America* (New Haven: Yale University Press, 1936).

22. See Parsons and Platt, *The American University*, 103. See also Burton J. Bledstein, *The Culture of Professionalism: The Middle Class and the Development of Higher Education in America* (New York: W. W. Norton, 1976); Magali S. Larson, *The Rise of Professionalism: A Sociological Analysis* (Berkeley: University of California Press, 1977); and Christopher Jencks and David Riesmann, *The Academic Revolution* (Chicago: University of Chicago Press, 1977).

23. Clark Kerr, *The Uses of the University*, 3rd ed. (Cambridge: Harvard University Press, 1982), 90.

24. Ibid., 36–38.

25. See, for example, Theodore Roszak, ed., *The Dissenting Academy* (New York: Pantheon Books, 1968).

26. See the articles in Sydney Hook, Paul Kurtz, and Miro Todorovich, ed., *The Idea of a Modern University* (Buffalo, N.Y.: Prometheus Books, 1974).

27. Parker J. Palmer, *To Know as We are Known: A Spirituality of Education* (San Francisco: Harper & Row, 1983).

28. H. D. Aiken, *Predicament of the University* (Bloomington: Indiana University, 1971).

29. Hook et al., *The Idea of a Modern University*, 90.

30. Ibid., 78.

31. Ibid., 98.

32. Kerr, *The Uses of the University*, 151.

33. Derek Bok, *Beyond the Ivory Tower: Social Responsibilities of the Modern University* (Cambridge: Harvard University Press, 1982), 75.

34. See Robert Nisbet's discussion in *The Degradation of American Dogma: The University in America, 1945–1970* (New York, Basic Books, 1987), chap. 6.

35. Ernest L. Boyer, *College: The Undergraduate Experience in America* (New York: Harper & Row, 1987).

36. Lynne V. Cheney, *NEH, Humanities in America: A Report to the President, the Congress and the American People* (Washington, D.C.: National Endowment for the Humanities, 1988).

37. Edward Shils et al., *The Academic Ethic: The Report of a Study Group of the International Council on the Future of the University* (Chicago: University of Chicago Press, 1983).

38. Ibid., 104.

39. Derek Bok, *Higher Learning* (Cambridge: Harvard University Press, 1986).

40. Heinz R. Pagels, *The Dreams of Reason: The Computer and the Rise of the Sciences of Complexity* (New York: Simon and Schuster, 1988).

41. Solly Zuckerman, *Nuclear Illusion and Reality* (New York: Viking, 1982), 106.

42. From a report in the *Los Angeles Times*, 15 September 1988.

43. See the excellent discussion in John R. Searle, *The Campus War: A Sympathetic Look at the University in Agony* (New York: World Publishing, 1971), 184–86.

CATHERINE KELLER

7

Toward an Emancipatory Wisdom

Wisdom is radiant, and does not grow dim.
By those who love her she is readily seen,
and found by those who look for her. . . .
Watch for her early and you will have no
 trouble;
you will find her sitting at your gates.
Even to think about her is understanding
 fully grown;
Be on the alert for her and anxiety will quickly
 leave you.

Wisdom 6:12–17

I. MILLENNIAL SUSPICIONS

This essay is written not so much about John Cobb's theology as from and for it. Yet it involves me not only in a Cobbsian critique of university irresponsibility, but in questioning my own dependencies as a feminist on academic liberalism, process liberalism, and, indeed, on a male mentor.

The urgency of the topic of theology and the university takes on transacademic significance now, at the end of the millennium of the university. While secular modernity (presumably now in a state of rapid detumescence) rose after the middle of this millennium, the first universities were founded close to its beginnings. But I do not intend to announce, with millennialist fervor, the end of the university. That would unduly trivialize the apocalyptic moment. Rather, I am concerned with how theologians ensconced in university structures understand our role at this point in history: a point supersaturated with ecological, economic and (despite superpower depolarization) nuclear threat.

Surely the university ought to be devoting itself—ourselves—to the cultivation of wisdom that can find a way toward a just and sustainable earth-future. I can state such an ethical imperative from within the boundaries of university theological discourse and structure. Therefore such devotion must not be impossible. But it is not forthcoming, although world crisis is. Why not? Where is our freedom? Where is our wisdom?

The university offers an indispensable space in which self-understanding, social criticism, and utopian imagination can and do sometimes take shape. Theology, despite or because of its tensions with the modern university, has a significant but not queenly role to play in this opening. Paradoxically, however, and at great cost, the transformative potentiality of this space is undermined by the very structures that hold the space open. Something in the dynamics of the freedom of academia seems to maintain the self-enclosure of this very opening. That is to say, the possibilities for critical and innovative thought that do occasionally sprout up in patches within various institutions of "higher learning" are cultivated within walls that often seem to prevent substantial social disseminations. These boundaries mark the divisions between and even within the disciplines, as well as the separation of the disciplines as a whole from accountability to the world. Perhaps most important, they reconstruct themselves within the subjectivities of the university-educated, who then bear them along as the shape of their own reason. Even when we may be seeking the wisdoms of freedom, justice and sustainability, we may in fact, because of the structures in which we work, be inoculating ourselves and our students against them.

I do not believe that such is necessarily true. These walls are formidable by force of habit, history, and social location, but there is no reason to assume that they are impenetrable or insurmountable. In my experience, both process theology and feminist theology offer important, at points convergent, insights into the dilemmas posed by "academic freedom." As a recipient of university graduate education, I was empowered by John Cobb to bring the insights of feminism and Whitehead into "creative contrast" with each other and with the *status quo* of academic theology. Yet the longer-term dynamism of this process of contrasting convergence has also motivated me, as educator, to question and criticize the ease of the convergence. But when I gaze back toward Claremont I find that Cobb's own incessant development has brought about certain transformations of process theology which themselves tend to converge with my divergence. (Another case of back to the future?)

In the present context I wish to consider the obstacles and the openings to emancipative theological work in the university. But I do this with no *a priori* certainty that such criteria would be anything other than the sort of self-deceptions that beset university consciousness in the first place. I say this not to invalidate my own remarks in advance. Rather, as I hope will become clearer along the way, a certain self-suspicion seems appropriate inasmuch as I, from the relatively privileged vantage point of a white North American academic (whatever else I am), undertake to criticize the academy. One hopes by such institutional autocritique somehow to alter or subvert the institution. But an essential dimension of my argument concerning the self-deceiving character of academic freedom is that such self-critique can be a way of having the cake of our freedom to criticize while eating the benefits of the institutional structures criticized. In other words, what is perhaps too loosely called "cooptation" must figure in any authentic consideration of the role of the university at the end of its millennium. But I am not interested in staring too long into the many-mirrored hall of academic self-distortions. Let us see rather if in the spirit of John Cobb's work we may move toward something I will call *emancipative wisdom,* which brings us into confrontation with the conception of freedom presumed by the academy.

II. FRAGMENTATION AND FREEDOM

John Cobb's December 1988 address to the American Academy of Religion was a jeremiad. He called all of us in the academy to accountability for the failure of the university to provide adequate intellectual leadership with which to face "the fate of the earth." He analyzed how the wretched situation of our planet's present ecology, economy, and militarization constitutes an emergency that the university seems organized to ignore. This gross irresponsibility is evidently no accident. The kind of disciplinary fragmentation that prevents meaningful confrontations between the sciences and the humanities, or between economics and political science, and between either of the latter and ethics, reflects a globally pervasive fragmentation. The intra-university divisions express and perpetuate the mentality sustaining the division of all life according to competing interests. The academic addiction to specialization not only breeds triviality, it directly or indirectly subserves the special interest governing much of our political and economic life. Cobb's speech was a political act of great seriousness. It chanelled the academic prestige now vested in Cobb, as a leading, perhaps the leading, North American Protestant theologian, into the dramatic power of an exposé, delivered at a peak moment of the great self-congratulatory religious festival of our discipline. Because of Cobb's successful dedication of much of his life to the creation of interdisciplinary forums aimed at transforming the fragmenting dualisms of the modern worldview, he has the credentials in praxis that legitimate such a critique. I know of no institutionalized interdisciplinary effort, within or without the field of theology, comparable in scope and quality to that which the Center for Process Studies has undertaken for so many years on such sparse resources. Especially in recent years, as Cobb has worked to transform process theology into political theology, he has become a model for a kind of self-transformation that one only hopes scholars will increasingly emulate. This is no running jump onto the liberation bandwagon. He has been reaching deeply into resources that his highly articulate metaphysics and faith provide for their own transformation.

Yet as his own speech suggested, the structural forces of the modern university make such metanoia unlikely. The demands of the academic guilds seem to exhaust and redirect most of the vision and energy of developing scholars. Why is it that one so rarely can describe even the best equipped of doctoral students, let alone junior faculty, as flourishing? Is the anxious malaise emitted by upwardly mobile academics expressive of some ultimately transformative creativity? Or is it not rather symptomatic of the internalization of the fundamental fragmentation? If wisdom is being sought, rather than professional achievement, would not this "anxiety quickly leave you" (as promised in the passage quoted at the outset)?

The constraints binding creativity and the anxiety therefore pervading consciousness work so systematically now, at least here at the edge of the millennium, as to be to some extent invisible, functioning as though natural and necessary to the pursuit of excellence. We are after all educated from kindergarten onwards to move within the rhythms of a particular kind of rationality. We may be partly doomed to the triviality, fragmentation, and worldlessness to which we are early groomed. Yet as the example of John Cobb shows, this is no excuse. We do not lack the freedom to

make significant dents in the academic structures that at once
bind us and reward us with our privilege. This privilege in its no-
blest form is called academic freedom. But what is it, if it is itself
forged within the terms of such constraint?

III. ENLIGHTENING LIBERALISM

The concept of academic freedom emerges within the context
of the Enlightenment, as the gradual liberation of theory, and so of
course of theoreticians, from the overt heteronomies imposed by
the state and especially the state church. "Freedom" in the sense
inherited from the Enlightenment seems to be a combination of
two negatives: the freedom from obstacles to individual choice,
and the freedom from sensory particulars. The first, primarily political, conception characterizes the European tradition of liberalism and individualism. It refers to an absence of coercion or
constraint, in which one is not prevented by the will of any authority or person from acting as one would choose to act. John Stu-
art Mill's "On Liberty" is a manifesto of this liberal,
individualistic concept of freedom. This freedom of individual
choice becomes the justifier for *laissez-faire* capitalism. The second, primarily philosophical conception focuses on the freedom of
the individual subject from the vicissitudes of time and sensory
experience. It finds systematic development in Kant's *Critique of
Judgment*. It differs from classical idealism's mental transcendence
of finitude by situating the universal structures of objective truth
within the autonomy of a subject. The freedom of this subject depends upon its own severance from those parts of itself that are
bound by time-conditions. Academic freedom may be considered a
specific institutional excrescence of these interrelated emphases
upon an autonomous individual liberty, structural and subjective.

The liberty of the liberal arts provides the pedagogical heart-
beat of the emancipatory project of what is called bourgeois liberalism. The point of that label is to expose the class interest
inherent in the intended universalism of the liberal democratic
principle. We cannot healthfully outgrow this criticism. Modernity
has been shaped by the dialectic between intellectual, political,
and economic liberalism, and the revolutionary movements that
have repudiated its ideology. Marx systematized the idea that bourgeois rationality, in its appeal to timeless truth and simultaneously to universal democratic emancipation, is in fact masking
its own time- and class-bound interests. The purity of the

philosophal desire to "understand" was exposed as a systematic evasion of change, because change would undermine the privilege, indeed the academic freedom, of those with the leisure for mere theory. The Marxist theory of economic and class justice entered history as the great counterplayer to bourgeois individualism. Liberation from concrete systems of oppression has since been understood in tension with, if not always in contradiction to, Enlightenment liberalism. This opposition is in a sense paralleled by the opposition between "liberal feminists," who are associated especially with the ERA movement and work for equal rights within the liberal democratic terms of free choice, and "radical feminists," who surely do not shun those rights but who focus on the irremediable oppressiveness of the system as such. Interestingly, among the latter, only a few would identify themselves as "Marxist feminists," because most feminists learned early that the Marxist insistence on class before gender as a category of oppression was itself an ideological strategy for the maintenance of patriarchal privilege.

One thing at least is clear: Inasmuch as middle-class academics (male or female, perhaps even African American or white) do not continually struggle with the ideological prestructuring of our own situations, cooptation is an applicable judgment. A certain Marxist suspicion remains quite helpful within any North American academy. But Marxism itself is a great intellectual system assimilated from the outset to university-trained minds, the context of universities, and even university classrooms. (One may reflect on the current crisis of the Communist world as resulting from a fallacy of misplaced concreteness: to apply such a highly abstract scheme literally and immediately to concrete social reality required such totalitarian devices as "the dictatorship of the proletariat.")

That anticapitalist ideology has been taught so widely within the classrooms of capitalism does imply some degree of good faith within the pluralistic commitments of academic liberalism. But it also suggests that we need not limit ourselves to the terms of a dialectic that is in many senses an insider's debate. Liberalism and antiliberal socialism are the two looming faces of late modernity and, I would add, of late patriarchy. As Cobb has worked out systematically in his recent work on economics, these two world systems have shared deep assumptions about the human place on earth.[1] These are presuppositions, indeed ideologies, that have rendered the prospect of a decent earth-future devastatingly uncertain.

These ideologies express themselves preeminently in the dogmas that development and growth are intrinsically good, that national economical health is measured by the GNP, that nonhuman nature is there for the good of "mankind" and is in itself a mere mechanism. The fact that Marxist materialism sets human beings on a continuum with this nature might have, but has not, contributed to wiser ecological policies. This is perhaps attributable to the economic reductionism of its class theory, and at the same time to the problems inherent—from the viewpoint of any organic philosophy of nature—in the metaphor of "nature the machine." As has been often argued, this attitude toward nature correlates with traditional attitudes toward woman (as less mental, spiritual, subjective, active, and so on). It is therefore not surprising that, despite promising early manifestos and gestures, both liberal individual-rights theory and Marxist economic-rights theory have failed to keep their promises to women. Moreover, in sync with their defensive masculinism, both systems have spawned military systems so formidable as to have attained utter futility. While we may be breathing the easier air of the new detente (itself apparently still relying on the charisma of one Soviet citizen), we are also breathing in the cumulating toxicity of unrelenting nuclear testing and waste.

We are at a point in history where the terms must shift. History itself has already shifted them. At this moment most of the Communist world is veering precariously but resolutely into a staggering panoply of liberalizations. Yet at the same time England and the United States, mainstays of old liberal democracy, have sustained a conservative transformation of such magnitude that we must now giggle nervously about the "L-word." In the light of both developments, is it suitable for progressive theologians to join rhetorically with the forces of antiliberalism? Ought not the church-related thinker in particular, who is well aware of the political force that has gathered under the banner of an evangelical Christian antiliberalism (which is in neofundamentalist literature almost indistinguishable from antifeminism), beware of dismissing too blithely the terms of the tradition of biblical criticism and religious and cultural pluralism that the Enlightenment makes possible?

Nonetheless, when it comes to analyzing the circumstances of our own accountability as white North American academics, our critique must direct itself primarily to the structure of ideological disingenuousness transmitted by our own cherished freedom. While I seek no alignment with movements labeling themselves antiliberal or postliberal, I am not arguing for a tender reconciliation with bourgeois liberalism. Rather I am suggesting (in limited agreement with Jürgen Habermas) that it is dangerously ahistorical and abstract to pit progressive thought in any Manichean sense against the Enlightenment tradition. That tradition, with its full inventory of ideological self-deceptions, remains the *sine qua non* for a genuinely emancipatory theory of practice, and practice of theory, within the Western university. Inasmuch as we rely for our economic and social location upon academic structure, we willy-nilly make use of the relatively open space we find there. It is then best to avoid the bad faith of supposing that by criticizing its terms we have therefore transcended it. Emancipatory wisdom may require a certain transliberal pragmatism.

IV. FREEDOM AND COMPETITION

What is emancipatory? I here rely on Beverly Harrison's definition: " 'Emancipatory practice' is precisely an ongoing struggle against structures of oppression and toward realization of the conditions for alternative social relations that enable nonexploitative relations to occur."[2] While the first clause sounds the necessary note of negation, but as negation of negation, not as mere freedom from any constraint, the second clause of this definition prevents the relapse into a merely negative freedom. Moreover, while Harrison's focus is rightly on exploitative relations between human groups, her ethic readily extends to "ecojustice" and the exposé of exploitative relations to nature, which result from interhuman activities of domination and competition. Let us consider such emancipatory practice the activity, indeed the activation, of emancipatory wisdom.

As suggested at the outset, such emancipatory practice cannot occur with conviction or consistency within the present terms of academic liberalism. Why not? More precisely, what is it about academic freedom that inhibits the realization, in theory and practice, of alternative social relations? I characterized the liberty of the Enlightenment in terms of two negative freedoms, freedom from external obstacles and freedom from spatiotemporal conditions, and I have suggested that the Marxist critique is necessary but not sufficient as an analysis of the problem because of its own implication in ecologically damaging economics, unrepentant patriarchal militarism, and the reduction of persons to functions of an abstract economism.

The individualistic anthropology of the freedom from constraint certainly forms the basis for the economics of all mainstream economics departments and business schools in the United States. But the fact that any particular department can insulate itself from interchange with others, in which alternative theories might present significant challenges to, for example, economic theory, is itself a function of the same view of freedom. It translates into academic life as *laissez-faire* pluralism. Different disciplines or departments do their own thing, establish their own corporate structures of internal competition and loyalty, compete with each other for prestige and funding, and see what goes on in other areas of "competence" as someone else's business. The academic "enterprise" almost visibly enervates the imaginative capacity of younger scholars, reduces debate to the construction of one's own "winning" arguments, and reduces critique to self-defense. Where one might expect the bonds of common interest rather than mere Hobbsian bonds of self-interest within at least one's own discipline or subdiscipline, turf wars predominate, and difference appears as intolerable as likeness. The shocking difficulty of creating community even within a departmental faculty reflects more than the problem of narcissistic personalities. The narcissism is itself a symptom of a cultural system, uncritically reproduced in the university, in which performance and production are valued over creativity and community. Most writing is quite explicitly motivated by the demands of the academic marketplace, structured by the economic incentives of tenure and promotion. It is accordingly insipid, stifling any inclinations to poetry or to prophecy. One is instead to struggle endlessly within the terms of the given orthodoxy. Thus at any level, in Whitehead's words, "the training which produces skill is so very apt to stifle imaginative zest."[3] Given the need to build one's academic capital, there are rarely enough time, energy, and resources left for efforts that would build communal collaboration within, across, and beyond academic boundaries. Individuals—often busy writing anti-individualistic essays such as the present one—find themselves thrown back on their own dubious "freedom."

I hope it is clear that I am not arguing that competition should always be avoided or harmony always sought, or that projects that suit my taste for world-conscious creativity cannot "succeed." We must remember that much of the special privilege implicit in academic freedom, allowing such unique advantages as tenure,[4] sabbatical, and extraordinary flexibility of schedule, in fact recalls a pre-bourgeois, monastic-aristocratic hierarchy. (Thus

Margaret Thatcher, admirable at least in the unflinching consistency of her capitalism, could abolish tenure by playing on middle-class resentment.) I am, however, suggesting that the free space that academic institutions do often provide within Western democracies is at once sustained and contaminated by the tropes of a questionable anthropology. The competitive politics of the freedom from constraint, that is, the freedom from the other, merges at this point with the metaphysics of the autonomous ego. The two dimensions of negative freedom together form what we can call the anthropology of disengagement.

V. INDIFFERENT AND ATEMPORAL FREEDOM

The liberalism of the Enlightenment gives rational and political form to the metaphysical freedom of indifference. The freedom to choose *a* over *b* is defined as freedom of the essentially autonomous individual from heteronomous constraint. It is based on the ontology of the insular individual and "his" aggregations. This separative self has been unmasked as a self-isolating ego by both Whiteheadian and feminist forms of communitarianism. In this they adhere to the traditional Christian diatribe against the *curvatio en se* as the original sin; but unlike the classic understanding of sin, they do not identify "self" and its passion for freedom with the insular ego. Although there is much in the discourse of autonomy that we would not wish to relinquish, its ontological gesture cuts against the claims of emancipative praxis. These claims ground individual difference in the matrix of relationships, requiring of us that our creativity should not base itself upon exploitation.

Being "different" is the supreme value of free-market competition. Yet systemic individualism tends, as we see illustrated in the mushrooming corporate homogenization of our environments, to sabotage the very value of difference that it seems to promote. There is less celebration of the difference of the other than there is a growing indifference to the other. Insensitivity, or lack of empathy, does not define metaphysical indifference, which refers to neutral choices. Nor can either of these meanings be identified with the "indifferent truth" aspired to by the Enlightenment. But within the systemic operations of Western individualism, these three meanings of indifference take on a shared meaning. None can enhance noncompetitive, nonseparative, and nonhierarchical relations of difference. They are three modalities of the anthropology of disengagement.

It is not surprising, therefore, that in the university liberal pluralism fails to yield the overflowing richness of community one might expect. Traditional academic pluralism lends itself either to questionable universalizations of particular perspectives or to the more current reaction, well criticized by Cobb theologically, of a relativist subjectivism. Both spin around within the terms of the freedom of indifference. The cycle of objectivism (now usually relegated to self-designated sciences) and subjectivism (usually a phenomenon of the liberal "arts") presents the spectacle of the academic dog chasing its tail. In theology the liberal reaction against universal truth claims is especially complex. It directs itself not only at the scientism of the university heritage but also at the authoritarianism and parochialism of traditional Christianity. But, paradoxically, the relativism of liberal freedom tends to create a subjective stance as disengaged as that of the classical sciences. Theological traditionalists, by contrast, do not suffer from the liabilities of the freedom of indifference; it is perhaps for this reason that they have been gaining power—usually outside and against university-related theological centers—in a value-thirsty society.

Both objectivism and subjectivism have roots in the second negative freedom of the Enlightenment, which I above associated with Kant. Fighting an incipient relativism of his time, Kant managed to retrieve a foundation for both science and morality by planting them in an objectively, that is universally, prestructured subject. On the basis of the mechanistic science of his time, he could not reconcile the "law of freedom" with the "laws of nature." To save freedom, he concluded that "no other way remains than to ascribe the existence of a thing, so far as it is determinable in time, and therefore also its causality according to the law of *natural necessity*, to *appearance alone*, and to ascribe *freedom* to precisely *the same being as a thing in itself*."[5] To be a *Ding an sich* meant for Kant to be free of "experience," understood as hopelessly sensuous and world-bound (and so more "feminine," because for him the ladies were at best aesthetic, never fully ethical, subjects). This way of thinking, although it represented a major breakthrough within its own context, indicates the nature of the profound schism within the academic world and within academics.

With Kant, the subjectivity of the free and rational mind steps right out of time. From the vantage point of theological history this step is nothing novel. But in its new secularizing form it takes modernity, for all its antiecclesial animus, right with it. So whatever positions may evolve within the university with respect to time, history, and the material world, our thought-patterns and our life-styles are marked by this antitemporal freedom. The academic institution maintains the deep structure of a dichotomy between the rational subject, who transcends spatiotemporal conditions, and the nonrational world of nature, which is the object of "his" thought, including "his" body and therefore most of "his" emotions (and above all "hers"). This dichotomy takes such embodied forms as the predominant "talking-head" personality of most academic men and, I fear, women, modeling for students an unwhole relation to our own experiences, bodies, and passions. But it also takes the form of the insulation of the university from the cries of the earth and its suffering bodies. Value-free science and humanistic relativism both unfold, unable to challenge each other, within the well-padded, neo-monastic structure of this disengaged rationality. But while departments of science, economics, and business do produce many of the minds who control the body of the world, the humanities, and the theological work embedded within them, tend to relinquish any serious claims on the world beyond the text.

There is obviously an internal connection between the liberal freedom of indifference and the freedom from spatiotemporal conditions. Ironically, Kant's ethics grounds reason in a priority of the practical which means to undermine any egoistic self-interest. Yet both the freedom from constraint and the freedom from sense-experience cultivate the anthropology and the institutions of a disengaged, disembodied, and dominant ego, originally but not necessarily white, male, and well-to-do. Freedom from spatiotemporal conditions not only generates a scholarship that mistakes irrelevance for sophistication; it also makes it unlikely that one will pursue the most important dimension of the freedom from constraint: freedom for just and mutual relationship. The conditions of injustice are unmistakably spatiotemporal, as are other persons. Other beings are encountered in space and time, as bodies. That is, unless the other is so like oneself that one can imagine oneself in "his" shoes and so, graciously, overlook "his" body, one is confronted by the sexual and racial physicality, by the language and gesture, which mark the other as not the same. In other words, although academic freedom thus far protects for many of us the expression of precisely these sorts of thoughts, it also works against their realization. From its roots, it inhibits the wide modes of responsibility bred by a sense of solidarity, in contrast to those cultivated upon the steeps of Kantian duty. From the vantage point of emancipatory practice, "solidarity is accountability."[6]

Theory unfolded upon the turf of liberal individualism will tend to practice this individualism, whatever its conceptual claims. It does not enhance our sense of ourselves as the acountable, gendered, colored, socially located animal subjects we are. It is also unlikely to foster the wisdom out of which a new global sensibility, at once spiritual and political, can crystallize. Theory articulated in this individualistic context rarely even pretends to seek wisdom at all, because wisdom requires time for perceiving, circumambulating, hearing, intuiting, attending, becoming. From the vantage point of an academic economy in which knowledge is produced and exchanged in a competitive marketplace, the quest for wisdom will appear at best nostalgic, at worst reactionary. Such theory will tend to defer indefinitely any intentional practice, thus enclosing itself within its own systems, even when those systems include the extended study of Marx from a Marxist perspective. All this because the relation of theory to practice within the university will be forced into conformity with the dualism of thinking of a nontemporal subject's "applying" ideas to an external, temporal world.

VI. THEOLOGY AND CHURCH

Several questions remain. What specifically of theological work in relation to the university? Is there an alternative conception of freedom that can serve us in our actual academic situations and not just in an ideal community, which does not exist? Do process and feminist theology shed light on the situation and its alternative?

I have been assuming that theology is an academic and therefore university-related discipline. (Inasmuch as it is not, it remains, at least within the North American context, probably parochial and authoritarian, posing an altogether different set of problems.) When it is theology as distinguished from the study of religion, it is nonetheless profoundly determined by the Enlightenment and its institutional outgrowths. But it understands itself as having at the same time an accountability to another community, designated as "church." For myself, teaching at once in a university-embedded school of theology and a graduate school, the difference represented by the relation to the church is important, extending beyond the responsibility to educate professional church leaders. This difference cannot be summarized by the difference between "faith" and "reason."[7]

For me the importance of the theological "difference" is best suggested by its reference to ecclesiology and soteriology. Theology's symbiosis with the churches, however problematic for women this has remained, has at least guaranteed some level of commitment to an organized community praxis and leadership, one with some genuinely democratic features and some engagement to a unique global network. As long as it does not succumb to its own past temptations to seek escape from spatiotemporal conditions, theology does permit an anthropology of persons in community seeking the whole and holistic salvation of themselves and the world. Something needs to be radically changed in order for us—the whole of us—to be saved. That is the evident condition of the world now. Theology has a certain textual and traditional license to move directly in the concrete, the relational, the embodied, and the transformational, speaking more than before in the preacademic tones of its prophetic and wisdom traditions, in a way rarely possible among other academic disciplines.

This movement beyond the atemporal abstraction is especially evident in its quest for a new paradigm that takes with utmost seriousness the concepts of freedom presented by the liberation movements and their rapidly deepening and expanding theological literatures. At the same time the new paradigm, critical of the monovocal absolutes of traditional church and university truth, will be radically pluralistic: It will advocate as a basic intellectual and theological criterion not a pluralism of indifference based on mere liberal tolerance, but the skill for actively taking in otherness. (This is the radicalism of Cobb's move "beyond dialogue" to a method of mutual transformation.) It will seek to construct its relative truth-claims upon a ground of consciousness of global interdependence and engaged praxis on behalf of what the World Council of Churches is calling "Justice, Peace and the Integrity of Creation."

VII. PROCESS AND FEMINISM

Feminism has been my central experience of liberation, and process my most systematic acquaintance with pluralism and ecocentric cosmology. These two sets of texts and communities have offered me my primary academic methods, subjects, and perspectives, and have allowed my relation to the university, as to the church, to remain refreshingly askew. While both had achieved a certain respectability by the time I became economically dependent upon the university, both are deeply at odds with the dualistic individualism and accompanying academic field-specialism built into the system.

Yet to compare process theology with feminism, even with feminist theology, implicates us in a certain sense in a category mistake. Process thought seeks interdisciplinary, intercultural, and interreligious encounter as a method for breaking down the dualistic worldview of modernity. But in so doing its history, its intentions, and its means remain those of a philosophical theology. While especially in its Claremont life it has spawned an organized, active, and community-encouraging movement—unlike any other philosophical theology—it remains very much an academic affair. Feminism is a movement with an immensely broader base in society, whose original and sustaining impulses are political, social, psychological, and economic, as well as educational. Feminist theology, although it is far more widely canonized at present in seminary and university curricula than is process theology, is nonetheless always only the theoretical component of a sociocultural and ecclesial movement. It bears constantly in its texts the marks of its praxis, its temporality, its female bodies. Both movements have provided for me orientation and community, but the feminist experience has more than any other adult influence forged my consciousness as a personal and political being.

Process thought was always there, in the mental-textual space, as a matrix of concepts allowing me to understand the social and spatiotemporal event-character of individuality, and thus to stabilize, as for a cumulative effect, a theoretical alternative to standard university worldviews. I believe process thought, especially as voice and as relation in John Cobb, accounts for much of whatever conceptual clarity I have, for example in my analysis of connections between patriarchal history, worldview, and the present state of the world. No doubt this is—and here my self-suspicion of cooptation must kick into gear—a matter of a doubly inside job: using male-forged academic abstractions for exposing the phallacies of misplaced concreteness rampant in patriarchy and its educational towers. But more than this: it was Cobb who gently (with a well-timed sentence or two) challenged me to take on a more boldly constructive theme, and then to let that be as strongly and overtly feminist as I would. It is unfortunate that I needed male permission; it is not surprising (I had never had a female professor); and it is fortunate that I got it. So I think of Cobb as something of a double agent for liberation, holding open university space in which new visions can breathe into life.

But I gradually, and none to soon, became aware of how I set up feminism and process thought as a sort of preestablished harmony, a low-conflict contrast; of how difficult it was for me to engage in serious critique of process thought, because my feminism was already developed in its terms; and of how mythically overblown, how naive as to the interaction of experience and text, is the normal claim of so many, including process feminists, that process theology "just fit with what I already felt about life." I could soon, though not immediately, discern the danger of an overtheorized approach to worldview, as characteristic of the bourgeois intellectual male. This is precisely the sense in which even the best of theory articulated within the space of academic freedom tends to recapitulate the separation of the mind from the world. Here even the marvelous Whiteheadian alternative to a universe of discrete minds and mechanical bodies becomes problematic, because it offers a purely mental solution to the problem of dualism. If one only "sees" through the lens of an adequately coherent and consistent system, things are already fine: They are ontologically always, at every instant, reconciling their contradictions, achieving enjoyment, satisfaction, and at least two modes of immortality. I am not prepared to argue that these categories, when understood within their context, are wrong, only that the tendency to settle conflict at the level of metaphysics, even such a temporalizing metaphysics as Whitehead's, inadvertently sustains atemporal habits of thought. I know well in myself the way I carried the Whiteheadian categoreal scheme about in my mind as a kind of grid to which I would deliberately refer not just to get my bearing but to get my answers. In Whitehead and most of his disciples, process thought does not wrestle with the ambiguities of its own situation and its own privilege, or, with brief sweeping allusions to Western history, with the structural and cumulative disbalances of its actual world. Although certainly not without insight into the depth of suffering or the reality of evil, Whitehead tends to view "the problem" almost invariably as one of philosophical misunderstandings.

I could take the opportunity to develop further criticisms of Whiteheadian thought. For instance, the solution of dualism by importing a dyad, indeed one named after the problematic opposition of mentality and physicality, into the constitution of every actuality, must be questioned. Of course it has the merit of avoiding reductive or idealist solutions. But doesn't it simply remove the problem to an entity who has disappeared too quickly to be discerned in any comparable detail in our experience? When Whitehead's suggestions on God's primordial nature are developed into the almost mechanical delivery every instant of an explicit "initial aim," my credulity is strained. I don't experience the possibilities presenting themselves to us as very willful, nor the wisdom sometimes revealed as we grasp them as quite so directive. From a feminist point of view, one must be wary of the many guises by which traditional patriarchal dualisms and theisms modulate themselves to become attractive to the modern, and now even the postmodern, mind. They may present fresh faces of an old liberal in-difference. Inasmuch as this does occur in Whiteheadian thought, the preestablished harmony between academic theology and the anthropology of disengagement will reiterate itself.[8]

In good faith, however, I could pursue no dismissively toned critique. These are questions addressed primarily to my own gullibility. Feminism itself has taught me to leave "the anxiety of influence" to sons slaying their mentor-fathers. Moreover, process thought, while embedded in the abstractionism of liberal humanism, has shown power to transcend the self-deceptions of academic individualism. By virtue of its interdisciplinary and democratic energy, it has, as we see in the work of John Cobb, David Griffin, and the Center for Process Studies, actually fostered a set of influences highly conducive to political transformation; that is, to the transformation of process thought itself to a transliberal movement in solidarity with all movements for justice; and to the transformation of institutional settings and institutionalized minds into openings for emancipative wisdom. To be historical means to recognize actual historical effects. To be a historically grounded feminist means to be suspicious not only of our dependencies on male text, institutions, and teachers, but also of the separatist romance.

With its incomparably broader and richer social matrix, the feminist experience of organization, networking, and praxis has allowed us to turn the liberal arts and the theological school into something different from what they were. But when we work in the university we fall prey to its self-enclosed and competitive freedom (although, I suspect, not quite so much as do women and men who are not feminists). The inevitability of cooptation is perhaps no excuse for cooptation. But process thought has taught me to think in terms of degrees, not absolute qualitative differences or strict Kantian imperatives. Separatism, the belief sometimes

espoused by radical feminists that they could operate in independence of significant male influence, suffers not only from an ahistorical sense of self-production, but also from the illusion of a pure
feminist integrity. Such claims, as far as I can tell, tend to take the
form of highly abstract, self-righteous and competitive discourses,
defenses, and turf wars resembling the worst of the patriarchal university. In this it succumbs, according to the irony of all self-
righteousness, to what it fears: in this case, cooptation. Like
traditional academia, feminist competition for political correct-
ness neither fosters conversation with other women (especially
with women of color), nor generates the widening gyre of networks
needed for the work of saving the world. As Sharon Welch puts it,
"it is tragic when our empowerment defeats us—empowered to
name reality, yet encouraged by the standards of academic work to
phrase our concerns in a way that makes it difficult for women
outside the academy to hear us."[9]

But my characterization of separatism is merely a caricature
of a temptation that haunts but rarely possesses theological feminists. The feminist understanding of emancipatory practice has
irrevocably altered the criteria of good scholarship. Feminist theology, Christian and Jewish, with its connections to ritual and communal experiment, to African-American womanist, post-Christian
and goddess spirituality, as well as to male-authored liberation theology, may represent the most exciting current development of a
pluralistic freedom. Thus the general struggle for a new theological
paradigm and in particular the process development of its own political potential have much to gain from feminism. Feminism, on
the other hand, can certainly do without any explicit recourse to
process theology. Yet part of the wisdom of the emerging feminist
maturity inheres in its nondefensive but critical engagement in
the slowly interconnecting global network of social movements; it
is these movements which perhaps pose the most hopeful alternatives to apocalypse.[10] The basic concerns and rhythms of process
theology have turned it into one such alternative, or rather source
and method for the inspiration, direct and indirect, of such alternatives. By dint of its ecclesial and communitarian inclinations and its interdisciplinary commitments, it cannot without
at least some bad conscience collapse into the characteristic complacency of its social location. It moves in the direction that
feminism has always trod, of that which the Chilean "barefoot
economist" Manfred Max Neef, working from a theory and practice sharing deep affinities with Cobb's economic project, has
called "transdisciplinarity."[11]

VIII. CONCLUSION

In conclusion, let me again evoke the name of Wisdom. With its affinities to Classical and Renaissance as well as Hebrew ideals, the image helps us to straddle the academic and ecclesial worlds to which theology accounts. Academic stress can virtually eliminate the energetic time or psychological space needed for the pursuit of wisdom. (Stress corresponds to the "anxiety" which "will quickly leave you" if you seek Wisdom.) Wisdom, at least as practiced in indigenous religions and in the biblical tradition, is irredeemably implicated in the sensuous, the communal, the experiential, the metanoic, the unpredictable, the imaginal, the practical. John Cobb says that "it takes time to be." I have experienced him as an educator, a guide, an author, who *lets* be. This practice is in accord with his commitment to noncoercive means of efficacy: in contrast to the control of matter by mind, of object by subject. Wisdom means taking the time that it takes to become. This is not to defer action—although activism itself often forfeits wisdom—but to hold it consciously in its feedback loop with theory, or more precisely, imaginative vision. But for process theology, time is not a matter of quantity but of relationship: between self and not-self, between now and not-now. Knowledge has as its object the components of relationship. Wisdom raises consciousness, in the act, of relationship itself. Relationship is neither outside of time and space, nor someplace statically within them, as within vessels. Combining Whitehead with present political concern for particularity, we might say that wisdom knows relation to be not simply but socially located. But the social embraces the cosmological.

Why wisdom? I mention wisdom, rather than, say, the less inflatable "understanding," for two reasons. The first is that John Cobb has brought it, or rather her, up. In his more recent thinking about his christocentric pluralism (his catholic christocentric theology, to be precise), he expresses regret that the Fourth Gospel did not use the concept of Sophia rather than Logos.[12] He proposes that we begin to speak of Wisdom rather than Word. His preference derives mainly from incarnational and cosmological considerations. He does not always mention the feminist option for Wisdom. Sophia (*Hochma*) is the only clear female image of a divine creative principle in the Bible. Elisabeth Schüssler Fiorenza, among others, has argued that Jesus was a prophet of Sophia-Wisdom, the original Q tradition of which the Johannine prologue is a masculinizing rendition.[13]

When systematically linked, as it was biblically, to principles of social justice for the vulnerable and the poor, the quest for wisdom avoids the pitfalls of spiritual individualism and becomes the source of an emancipated and emancipatory imagination. When emancipatory wisdom gets conveyed in and around the academy, it smacks of subversion. But it also alters the form and function of the academy, taking advantage of the free spaces to open up the world, the world as we and our students bring it with us and as we and our students bring ourselves to bear upon it.

Under present global circumstances emancipatory wisdom will not, I suspect, be able in the foreseeable future to alter the university structure fundamentally. It is unrealistic to think that the universities could survive as the social structure for the education of the nation's young if they were to enter into direct antithesis to state purposes. The dramatic cutbacks of the 1980s already served as punitive warnings. As has also proved to be the case among the once mainline churches, internal class, race, and gender imbalances do much of the maintenance work for the *status quo*. When the subversive influences continue to exercise their wisdom, making churches and academies into free spaces rather than insularities, the self-regulating mechanisms of the free-market economy take over, and loss of students and members combine with economic distress to threaten the emancipatory initiatives.

However, the effectiveness of groups and movements within university and university-related settings does not depend upon their becoming the new mainstream. Moreover, economic threats do not necessarily prove lethal. In many ways—the case of the environment most notably, and probably of the world debt crisis next—there is a growing social awareness of the need for imaginative alternatives. The *kairos* is certainly here, as a point of crisis and opportunity. The academy will look foolish not only to its progressive critics but to its own consumer public if it does not begin to pool its resources to come up with strategies and visions for a viable future. We may find our arguments for inter- and transdisciplinary work falling upon ears more willing to hear.

At any rate, emancipatory practice and its wisdom require us to move with self-criticizing but not self-paralyzing awareness within the context of university-related theological practice. Let me suggest in closing the following list of Wisdom-criteria for work that does not collapse into the old routines of academic freedom: (1) This work will be interdisciplinary and transdisciplinary both in content and context. (2) It will practice a freedom not of indifference but of difference, experimenting in liberation from the tendency to re-create the traditional imbalances of text and power regarding gender, race, class, sex, culture. (3) It will thus grant hermeneutical privilege (which does not mean uncritical or un-conditional truth-status) to those traditionally subjected to bias, as a means of its own liberation as well as theirs. (4) It will involve a freedom not from the conditions of space, time, and relationship but a sensuous freedom (erotic, in Whitehead's sense) that takes time and takes place, that opens the senses, that opens up the presence of history and the physical cosmos, and that therefore teaches awareness of our own inevitable bias and simultaneously trust in the deliverance of our experience in relation. (5) It will value "imaginative zest" over the normal educational emphases on mastery, control, and repetition, because the energy of image is the interiorization of the sensuous. (6) It will move, because of its pluralism and its passion for justice, away from (even White-headian) orthodoxies and towards orthopraxis as the experiential ground for its truth-claims, indeed for its academic accountability, seeking opportunities to demonstrate the way in which theory grows from and into concrete personal, historical, and global reali-zation. Is it fair to suggest that the undertanding inspired by Sophia-Wisdom is the missing, meditating third in the dyad of theory and practice?

Wisdom calls us to watch for her early, at our own gate. I know of no other major white male theologian who has been watching earlier or more wakefully than John Cobb. This is the philo-sophia of his theology.

NOTES

1. Herman E. Daly and John B. Cobb, Jr., *For the Common Good: Redirecting the Economy Toward Community, the Environment, and a Sustainable Future* (Boston: Beacon Press, 1989).

2. Beverly Wildung Harrison, "Theological Reflection in the Strug-gle for Liberation: A Feminist Perspective," *Making the Connections: Es-says in Feminist Social Ethics* (a collection of Harrison's essays), ed. Carol Robb (Boston: Beacon Press, 1985), 248.

3. Alfred North Whitehead, *Process and Reality*, corrected edition (New York: Free Press, 1978), 338.

4. Interestingly, the Supreme Court has in January 1990 unani-mously ruled against the special shield that universities, as employers,

have retained. The University of Pennsylvania had claimed academic freedom as the basis for its right to secrecy in tenure deliberations; that is, academic freedom had been used as an argument for refusing to let the Equal Employment Opportunity Commission investigate its files to respond to complaints of race and sex discrimination by a woman denied tenure. Although moves of the state against academic freedom can never be greeted unambiguously, this case represents a surprising victory of emancipatory justice against so-called academic freedom. It is the sort of case in which the banner academic freedom protects the interests of an old-boys' network, thus showing rather transparently the white male location of this Enlightenment privilege.

5. Immanuel Kant, *The Critique of Practical Reason and Other Writings in Moral Philosophy*, trans. and ed. L. W. Beck (Chicago: University of Chicago Press, 1949), 170.

6. Harrison, "Theological Reflection," 244.

7. I cannot hypostatize my faith as some separate epistemological variable: it is something like deep trust in the process in which reason, feeling, sensuality and world enter into meaningful relationship. It is a faith that the spirit at work in the process is real and is trustworthy. It is a trust in the wisdom at the heart of things; it is not, however, a confidence that that wisdom will be heard or heeded. This trust comes as readily into conflict with traditional ecclesial understandings as it does with the rationalism of the university.

8. For a useful feminist critique of the embeddedness of process theology in modern liberalism, see Susan B. Thistlethwaite, "Still Crazy After All These Years: A Theological Education Adequate to the Situation of Survivors of Sexual and Domestic Violence," in *Opening Closed Doors: Teaching about Consciousness of Sexual and Domestic Violence*, ed. Carol Adams (San Francisco: Harper & Row, 1990).

9. Sharon Welch, "Ideology and Social Change," in *Weaving the Visions*, ed. Judith Plaskow and Carol Christ (New York: Harper & Row, 1989), 340.

10. I am thinking of the persistence and the promise of a worldwide women's movement, ecological movement, peace movement, and the liberation or democracy movements, all of which show at least the potential for provisional convergence. On the alternative political power of the social movements, see the writings of Richard Falk, for example, *The Promise of World Order: Essays in Normative International Relations* (Philadelphia: Temple University Press, 1987), 22–24.

11. Manfred Max-Neef, "Human Scale Development: An Option for the Future," in *Development Dialogue* 1 (1989): 18. "Transdisciplinarity is an approach that, in an attempt to gain greater understanding, reaches be-

yond the fields outlined by strict disciplines. While the language of one discipline may suffice to *describe* something (an isolated element, for instance), an interdisciplinary effort may be necessary to *explain* something (a relation between elements). By the same token, to *understand* something (a system as interpreted from another system of higher complexity) requires a personal involvement that surpasses disciplinary frontiers, thus making it a transdisciplinary experience."

12. John B. Cobb, Jr., "Toward a Christocentric Catholic Theology," in *Toward a Universal Theology of Religion*, ed. Leonard Swidler (Maryknoll: Orbis, 1987), 88.

13. Elisabeth Schüssler Fiorenza, *In Memory of Her* (New York: Crossroad, 1983,) 130–32.

8

John Cobb's Trinity: Implications for the University

John B. Cobb, Jr., developed a doctrine of God in *A Christian Natural Theology*, an anthropology in *The Structure of Christian Existence*, and then, drawing on both, an innovative christology in *Christ in a Pluralistic Age*. Toward the end of that latter volume he gave some attention to a constructive understanding of the trinity and a doctrine of the Spirit. On the whole, however, he gives no sustained attention to these topics that would bring the discussions of God and Christ into a full process interpretation of the trinity. Rather, the works since the christology have been devoted primarily to interreligious dialogue, ecology, political theology, economics, and education. But Cobb has often stated that the task of the Christian theologian is to give critical reflection on Christian faith, suggesting that creative transformation is particularly necessary for images that deeply form the Christian consciousness. "Trinity" and "Holy Spirit" well qualify as formative Christian images. What are the implications of Cobb's theology for these images?

In some respects, it may be considered far afield to discuss the implications of Cobb's position for a doctrine of the Spirit and the trinity in a volume dedicated to theology and the university, even though the collected essays are written in his honor. I shall argue, however, that Cobb's works on the diverse topics mentioned above, including education, *are* his doctrine of the Spirit, with certain implications for a process interpretation of the trinity. When his views on education are seen in this light, one might be even more explicit in developing the connections between Cobb's theology and an agenda for the university.

The development proceeds first with a summation of Cobb's doctrines of God and Christ, and the implications he suggests for trinitarian thought. Questions are raised relative to the latter that push toward an alternative formulation of the Spirit. This, in turn, refines the position on the trinity. The whole will then be queried in relation to the university's structure and purpose.

I. GOD AND CHRIST

The major task of *A Christian Natural Theology* is to reestablish the viability of developing Christian theology in conversation with philosophy and the sciences, as well as with the religious data of the Christian community. The test case comes in the doctrine of God, for here Christianity faces the problem of establishing that there is indeed a referent for the word "God" beyond linguistic or psychological reductionism. Accordingly, and drawing heavily upon the conceptuality of Alfred North Whitehead, Cobb builds the analysis of experience that leads from existence as actual occasions to a conception of the human person as a responsible being in society. He focuses particularly upon the ground of novelty, especially as novelty takes one beyond the past in the direction of beauty and peace. Following Whitehead, Cobb suggests that peace includes but transcends beauty, with an ultimate breadth and depth that includes all values, becoming a "harmony of harmonies." Such peace is neither achieved at present nor has it been achieved; it rests in no ideal past, and it eludes any immediate attainment. Yet it functions as a lure within the soul toward civilization, toward some ultimacy of community that includes yet transcends all that we have experienced. It defies its own contradiction in our histories, functioning as something within the depth of things that continuously renews hope and energy toward some more pervasively satisfying mode of community. And with this allusive discussion of peace as the ultimate lure toward novelty, Cobb begins his discussion first of Whitehead's, and then of his own, doctrine of God as the source of novelty.

The actual development of the doctrine explores the technical aspects of Whitehead's thought relative to God as the principle of concretion, of limitation, and of order. The arguments are by now familiar to persons acquainted with process philosophy and theology: God's primordial nature is the locus of all possibility, and source of the initial aim whereby the possibilities are adapted to the good of the world, providing at once a principle of limitation and a novel lure toward transcendence of the world's past. Cobb's revision of this doctrine is likewise technical, exploring the insufficiently developed unity of the primordial and consequent natures that comprise the Whiteheadian God, and arguing that God's own feelings of the world through the consequent nature are essential to the relevance of the aim of God for the developing world. This aim is then formulated within God as a propositional feeling, with appetition that it be realized in the becoming world.

Cobb questions how the becoming occasion is capable of prehending the propositional feeling within God, given God's incomplete concrescence according to Whitehead's own scheme. He argues that God should instead be interpreted as a series of actual occasions, analogous to the human soul. This move establishes the propositional feeling to be prehended in a past occasion of God, clearing the way for the new occasion to prehend it as its necessary initial aim.

Cobb has since revised his technical arguments, but the basic concern here is not to summarize Cobb's doctrine of God relative to its philosophical viability within Whitehead's system, but to examine it with regard to the function of God in the world. Through the initial aim, God is creator *with* the world. The "withness" is taken in two senses. First, each entity in the becoming world prehends not only God, but also its entire past. Insofar as the past had intentions toward the future, these intentions can also be propositions for the new occasion, functioning analogously to the initial aim of God. God's aim is one among many, but its distinctive property is that it and it alone is the source whereby the present might transcend the past toward novelty rather than fall captive to the past in terms of sheer repetition. Thus God as creator is associated particularly with the newness of things, and with the creative advance of the world toward more complex forms of order, whether in nature or the human community.

Although God's creativity is exercised in conjunction with the world, and although God is prehended as past by the becoming world, God is nonetheless more appropriately associated with the future. If prehension of God is the route toward transcendence of the past, then God is the source of the world's future. The paradox obtains that while God is prehended because God is in the past of the becoming entity, God is prehended as that which is future relative to the entity. The doctrine of God thus focuses creativity in God through God as the source of the future of the world. Insofar as a becoming occasion's historic past also contains a propulsion toward the new, this past was in its own time also derived from God. All novelty is associated with the primordial nature of God.

The understanding of God as the creative power of the future also entails important considerations concerning the nature of God's power. This power is fundamentally persuasive rather than coercive. Cobb develops this Whiteheadian thesis not only in *A Christian Natural Theology,* but also in *God and the World.* This development ensures not only the freedom of the world, but also the freedom of God. If the nature of existence is to receive influences from the past and to aim toward the future, and creatively to integrate these as one's own novel becoming, then no occasion has the power totally to determine the being of another; freedom is within the essence of that which exists. One is influenced but not determined by that which is prehended. This applies even in the case of coercive force; how the force is received is in some respects, no matter how minute, variable within the affected organism. Relative to God, God is affected by the world through the consequent nature, but this effect is influential rather than determinative. God is free, exercising and experiencing power with others.

What, then, is the character of God for Cobb? Here the fact that Cobb introduced his discussion of God through the notion of peace is fundamental. God—as Creator, as Future, as Free—is the ultimate locus of that peace that is felt as the lure of the world. God is peace, an ultimate inclusiveness of all values in a transcending, transforming, and everlasting beauty. Precisely this notion of the character of God lies behind the notion of God as future; it is a future whose content is reflective of this peace that inheres in every initial aim toward novelty. God as peace is also God as creator; it is the peace of inclusive complexity that functions to draw the world toward more complex forms of order. God as peace is the ultimate form of God as free; it is the power of God's internal creativity whereby God is able to receive the whole world through the consequent nature and to incorporate that world transformatively into God's own actualization, which is to say, peace. The notion of peace is thus central to Cobb's understanding of God.

And what of Christ? Ten years intervene between publication of *A Christian Natural Theology* (*CNT*) and *Christ in a Pluralistic Age* (*CPA*); within that period, two other books were published that are critical to the christology. The first of these is *The Structure of Christian Existence* (*SCE*), where Cobb carefully builds on his earlier work in anthropology. The Whiteheadian conceptuality has already provided him with the dynamics of human existence; this is developed in the second and third chapters of *CNT.* What is needed is to integrate historicity into the anthropology, and this Cobb does in *SCE.* By analyzing the different structures of consciousness exhibited in the various religious communities of the world, he demonstrates the uniqueness of the Christian structure of consciousness, and thus prepares for the fully developed christology that is to come. In fact, since christology presupposes clear doctrines of God and humanity, in one sense *CNT* and *SCE* can both be considered prolegomena to the christology of *CPA.*

But the second book referred to interrupts the projected agenda, radically affecting the form of the christology to come. This book is the little study pamphlet entitled *Is It Too Late? A Theology of Ecology,* which was prepared for the "Faith and Life" series of adult religious education. This book, published in 1972 but written in 1969, merits for Cobb the Kantian phrase of being "shocked from dogmatic slumbers." In it theology takes on a new urgency. Theology is no longer simply the critical reflection upon one's faith for the sake of finding contemporary forms of faith; theology takes on an imperatively prophetic dimension in a milieu in which "the survival of life itself may be at stake" (11). In previous books, there is a deep awareness of the interrelatedness of all life, but in this book that awareness takes on the existential knowledge that the vulnerability of interdependence can lead to planetary death as well as to richer forms of complexity. Process is not necessarily progress, and freedom allows the creative lure toward novelty to be perverted toward destructive ends. The human program, especially as developed by those whose structure of consciousness is formed around the paradoxical individualism of Christianity, is rapidly leading us toward ecological disaster. A radical ethical dimension is introduced into theology. It is no longer simply sufficient to reinterpret faith; one must transform it for the sake of the transformation of the world.

Cobb's consciousness of ethical responsibility conjoined with theology is not in itself new (consider, for example, the chapter "Man as a Responsible Being" in *CNT*), but the urgency of this conjoining is new. Henceforth, theology must underscore one's radical responsibility for the well-being of the world. It is this sensitivity, as much as the careful preparation through *SCE* and *CNT*, that gives *Christ in a Pluralistic Age* its central theme: Christ is an image of creative transformation in the world, with implications for how we build our cities, how we engage in deepening human community through interreligious dialogue, and how we can foster hope within a desperate world.

The christology is deeply continuous with the doctrine of God formulated earlier, particularly in the central notion of peace. God is incarnate in the world through the initial aim, which is itself derived from God's primordial nature—the source of peace—and God's feeling of the world in the consequent nature, which, in integration with the primordial nature, is the actualization of peace. The initial aim draws the world toward relevant forms of peace, which in turn represent a creative transformation of the past toward wider forms of inclusiveness. Jesus of Nazareth becomes the one in history who fully constitutes himself through this initial aim of God, thus becoming the manifestation of God's peace in history. The abstract technical notion of God is clothed with the historical form of love, leading to hope. Jesus is the Christ in history, and Christ is the image of creative transformation.

The effect of Christ is to establish a field of force through which those who identify themselves with Christ become open to the risk of an identity radically informed not only by their own personal and cultural past, but also by the past and the future of others, and hence toward the creation of more diverse modes of community that include the good of others as well as the self. This open identity is not restricted to the human scene; it includes an empathic association with the well-being of the whole created order. This openness of identity is itself the impulse toward acting for inclusive forms of the good, or peace.

Such an identity is fluid, dynamic, relativized. Its only absolute is that the lure toward creative transformation renders all absolutes radically open to question. While at times this value of creative transformation may seem to border on valuation of the new for the sake of the new, to interpret it thus would be a gross distortion of Cobb's position. Peace is the aim of all creative transformation. The particular *form* of peace is always to be questioned, but its questioning is governed by inclusiveness of well-being, which is to say, by peace itself. The amazing hope that is offered by viewing Christ as the principle of creative transformation is not simply that God is at work in human history, working in us, with us, and through us, for the incarnation of peace, but that the peace that so draws us is not illusory. It is grounded in the very nature of God, and is mediated to us in every initial aim.

The ethical force of this christology has many implications, not only for the religious pluralism addressed specifically within the book, but also for cultural pluralism. Consider Cobb's discussion of memory and hope as constitutive of the self. Normally, self-identity is formed through owning a remembered past and through purposes and hopes for the future. Feelings about the self are extended to the various circles of others who share similar memories, and similar hopes: a family, a faith community, a culture. These groups share varying modes of kinship with the self, and are accordingly more or less included in one's notion of well-being. But what if one became open to memories of a past quite different from those of one's kinship groups? Suppose, for example, an American of European ancestry sought to listen to the memories of an American of African ancestry. And suppose that, in turn, the person of African ancestry heard the stories of the Euro-American. A new commonality of shared memory could emerge and, with it, a critical concern for a common future. Community would be enlarged, and new modes of peace made possible. The previous identification of one's past would be creatively transformed to include a more complex history, creating in the process more complex selves, making possible a wider concern for the future, which would translate into forms of action in society that could make the new vision of the future actual.

It follows that the third portion of *CPA* is entitled, "Christ as Hope"; if there is incarnate in the world a force for peace in the Whiteheadian/Cobbian sense described above, then no situation, however dire, dare be deemed final. What is required is that, through the power of the Christ, one release the narrow past in openness to the future. This openness allows an individual or community to constitute itself in conformity to the transforming initial aims of God, the Christ, and so become a force for peace in the world. Peace is as possible as the persuasive power of God.

The doctrine of God, then, concerns the transcendent locus and power of peace; the doctrine of Christ is the application of that peace to the world. Where creative transformation exists, there the Christian discerns the Christ: God's initial aim toward peace immanent in the world. The technical aspects Whitehead used to explicate this understanding are the primordial nature of God (identified extensively by Cobb as the *Logos*) and the initial aims of God for the world.

II. THE SPIRIT

What, then, of the third aspect of God commonly understood in the Christian tradition as the Holy Spirit? Unlike God and Christ, which are given extended treatments, the Spirit receives but little attention. There is, however, a powerful reference to the Spirit in the closing pages of *Is It Too Late?*:

> It [the power of hope] is not to be found somewhere outside the organisms in which it is at work, but it is not to be iden-tified with them either. We can conceive it best as Spirit. It is the belief in this Spirit, the giver of life and love, that is the basis of hope. In spite of all the destructive forces [we] let loose against life on this planet, the Spirit of Life is at work in ever new and unforeseeable ways, countering and circum-venting the obstacles [we] put in its path. In spite of my strong tendencies to complacency and despair, I experience the Spirit in myself as calling forth the realistic hope apart from which there is no hope, and I am confident that what I find in myself is occurring in others also. . . . What makes for life and love and hope is not simply the decision of one indi-vidual or another, but a Spirit that moves us all. (143–44)

In this passage, the identification of Spirit is remarkably sim-ilar to what will be named Christ in *Christ in a Pluralistic Age.* But in the conclusion of that latter work, also, Cobb turns his attention toward the distinctive doctrine of the Spirit, now associ-ating Spirit with "Kingdom of God." He has named the second person of the trinity in a twofold sense: the Logos of God, which is the power of creative transformation but not yet the incarnation of creative transformation, and the Christ, who is the initial aim of God become immanent in the world. He also names Spirit in a twofold sense as the anticipation in history of God's full and final reign (the Kingdom of God), and the fullness of that reign in the consequent nature of God. This follows the traditional distinction between the "economic trinity," or the experience of God in his-tory, and the "immanent trinity," or the inner dynamics of God. Cobb's delineation of the immanent trinity is that the primordial nature is the Logos, giving rise to the Christ as the power for creative transformation in the world, and the consequent nature is the Spirit, or the world as received and creatively transformed within God. There is no real third term in this formulation, unless it be taken to be the fullness of God in what has traditionally been named "Father."

Cobb underscores the tentativeness of his formulations, saying that this trinitarian (and christological) view is very much in process. A difficulty with the formulation as thus far given is that there is no functional distinction between the notion of Christ and Spirit in history. The terms could be interchangeable, as in fact they are in the extended passage quoted above from *Is it Too Late?* There is, or course, a distinction *vis-à-vis* God if they are identified with the primordial and consequent natures respectively, but then the issue is that to call both together the first person of the trinity seems forced; we are really left with a diunity rather than a trinity.

I suggest another way to view the Spirit (and, consequently, trinity) in Cobb's system, one that is somewhat parallel with his christology. Cobb began the christology by recounting André Malraux's history of Western art in its movement from portraying Christ as the transcendent, remote deity, to a more humanized Christ as benevolent king, to a suffering and dying Christ on the cross. The movement continues with the introduction of human scenes into the background of the holy figure, and the gradual movement into the foreground of human activity. There is an increasing personalization and individualization of the human figures, and eventually the disappearance of the Christ-figure altogether. The simply human has come to dominate, but with personal, emotional history now given witness. Cobb argues that the disappearance of the Christ is in fact the progressive work of the Christ, the incarnation of Christ into a principle of creative transformation that works through an interiorized pluralism. The principle calls for the relativization of all its forms in a restless movement ever beyond itself, expressed in our contemporary age in abstract art. The disappearance of "Christ" is the effective work of Christ.

There is a very brief parallel to this story in a fourteenth-century painting not of Jesus, but of the Spirit, in the angelic annunciation to Mary. Indeed, annunciation paintings may well have surpassed paintings of the crucifixion as a favored theme. In nearly all of the paintings, the Holy Spirit is represented as light or in the form of a dove, often hovering between Mary and the angel. But there is a significant exception. Giotto has painted typical annunciations, with the Spirit in the form of a dove. But in one painting the angel bows before the young woman, and where the dove was usually portrayed there is a window looking out onto fourteenth-century Florence. Central in the bordered cityscape is a hospital: the Hospital of the Holy Spirit. The intriguing aspect about the painting is that in extant plans of the Florence of that time, there was indeed a Hospital of the Holy Spirit, but not in the location portrayed by the artist. Giotto intentionally moved the hospital in his painting so that it would be midway between Mary and the angel, in the place commonly assigned iconographically to the Spirit. The Spirit had become incarnate in a work of mercy.

Cobb has never given a fully developed doctrine of the Holy Spirit that goes beyond the few pages in *Christ in a Pluralistic Age*. Rather, since 1975 he has published books such as *Beyond Dialogue, The Liberation of Life* (with Charles Birch), *Process Theology as Political Theology*, and *Christian Identity and Theological Education* (with Joseph C. Hough). But could it not be that these *are* Cobb's doctrine of the Spirit? The doctrine of the Holy Spirit is not to be given in direct theological discussion, but in "works of mercy," or of creative transformation. Like the dove replaced by the hospital, the theology of the Spirit requires implicit portrayal through works directed toward the good—the peace—of the world.

The Spirit facilitates the Christian community's openness to its own transformation. In our day, this can well be portrayed through interaction with other religions, through a new shaping of consciousness toward care for and with the earth, through political responsibility in a crisis-ridden international situation, and through education of church leaders who can facilitate the Christian community's own openness to God's call for creative transformation. This, of course, is the role of Christ in Cobb's christology, while the Spirit is the anticipation in time of the Kingdom of God. But what *is* such an anticipation, if not creative transformation? The two symbols are conflated.

If there is a desire to transform Christian symbols, giving them new meaning and power, would it not be better to give content to "Spirit" that is distinctive while yet consistent with the content of Christ? The unique content traditionally ascribed to the Spirit in Christian history has been that of a unitive, purifying force: The Spirit unites us with Christ and with one another in the formation of a community called "body of Christ." Hence the Spirit is an indwelling presence, witnessing to God through works of love. Cobb's christology suggests a new dynamism that might be infused into the doctrine of the Spirit, with interesting consequences for the notion of the trinity.

Cobb associates the Christ with the initial aim, or the Logos of God become incarnate. We are called, like Jesus, to constitute ourselves according to this aim; that is, to integrate the aim into our own becoming, so that the initial aim becomes our subjective aim. We would then be co-constituted by God's aim for us and our own free response. The means whereby we appropriate the aim is prehension: God feels the aim for us, clothed in an appetition that this aim be realized. When this aim is toward more complex forms of novelty that allow richer modes of community in the world, then the aim is the principle of creative transformation, or the Christ. When we adopt that aim, we are co-constituted by the Christ, and creative transformation is incarnate once again in the world. Thus the aim *and* its incarnation are named the Christ.

In adapting this to a new formulation of Spirit, let us assume that God's appetition is itself creative, so that God does not passively await the nascent entity's prehension, but in fact, along with the world, evokes the new occasion, creating it through launching it on its brief but all-important journey. This is God as transcendent, persuasive creator, creating the world through a word for its good and inviting the world's own creative response. The fullness of God generates this word in recognition of the world's need; it is a particular word, fitted to the world. Thus far this formulation is nearly a reformulation of Cobb's christology; it needs only the stipulation that those aims that result in the world's creative transformation are those that are particularly named Christ. But it stops short of Cobb's christology by saying that aims toward creative transformation in themselves constitute that generative word from God that Christians can name as continuous with that which is seen in the one named Christ in history.

I propose that to speak of God's creatively transforming word is sufficient to name Cobb's "Christ," or principle of creative transformation. This Christ is the word that awaits our response, and not yet the word integrated with that response. But it is a word combining God and world, since it expresses God's aim for us in the light of our condition. Cobb calls it a "propositional feeling" in God, or an "eternal object" from God's primordial envisagement related to the particularities of our circumstances as felt by the consequent nature. God meets our condition, and in this sense the aim has the twofold nature of God primordial and consequent, reflecting God and the world, divinity and humanity.

But if the Spirit is traditionally understood to be "Christ in us," an indwelling force that unites us with God and one another, whose fruits are those things that build up the community, then the Spirit might well be that element of the aim that we allow into our becoming, or the subjective aim insofar as it conforms to the christic aim from God. In traditional (although Eastern rather than Western) language, the Spirit proceeds "from the Father through the Son"; in this process formulation, also, this would be the case, since the Spirit derives from the aim from God's own nature mediated to us through the Christ. Insofar as we instantiate that aim, the Spirit is born in us, becoming one with us in the creation of community. In other words, Christ *offers* creative transformation; the Spirit *is* creative transformation realized in the world.

In this case, of course, the Spirit is not manifest as Spirit per se, but only in "works of mercy," or the unitive work of God with us in history. There is no direct identification of the Spirit, only the indirect witness to the Spirit's presence through acts of creative transformation: openness toward one another involving our deepest identity in interfaith or ecumenical dialogue; open and concerned action for the well-being of the whole of this earth; empathic identification with others, such that their future good is as important as our own; and a will to move toward yet ever more complex modes of community. Under this reading, Cobb's works in these areas *are* his doctrine of the Spirit. But this has radical implications for his doctrine of the trinity.

III. TRINITY

There are interesting analogies between a process formulation of the nature of God and the more traditional formulation of the trinity. Traditionally, the "Father" eternally generates the "Son," and from the two proceeds the "Spirit" (this is Western theology; orthodox theology, as noted, names the "Spirit" as proceeding from the "Father" *through* the "Son"). The "Son" is the logos of God, or God's own self-knowledge, and the "Spirit" is the will or love of God, whereby there is infinite union between "Father" and "Son." The works of God flow from this immanent trinity, or the immanent trinity is the ground of God made manifest as the economic trinity. Creation is analogous to generation, incarnation is analogous to being generated, and redemption is analogous to divine union, being the community-building work within the world.

While each work is chiefly associated with but one member of the trinity, the fullness of God is involved in each of the works. For example, God as "Father" is creator, but, in the work of creating, the "Father" speaks a word (the "Son") and the "Spirit" "broods over the face of the waters" (Gen. 1:2). Through the triune act, creation comes into being.

An analogous Whiteheadian formulation would call for the amorphous realm of possibilities to be likened to the traditional "Father," eternally generating from these possibilities the divine character in the primordial vision, which is analogous to the divine self-knowledge, or immanent trinitarian work of the "Son." God is *always* generating the divine character; apart from such generation there is no God. But while we might make this analogy regarding "Father" and "Son," it is not possible to extend the trinitarian formula so neatly to "Spirit." Traditionally, the immanent work of the Spirit spoke only to the unity between the generative and generated aspects of God, and the Spirit therefore proceeded from "Father" and "Son" together, or from the "Father" through the "Son." In either case, the designation for the work of Spirit was entirely intratrinitarian. Thus while one might be tempted to make a correlation between Spirit and consequent nature, inasmuch as the consequent nature does in fact proceed from the primordial in Whitehead's model, this does not take the full origin of the consequent nature into account. In the process model, the consequent nature derives both from the primordial nature *and* the world. The consequent nature is the received world as God integrates that world with the primordial vision. If the consequent nature be Spirit, then through the Spirit the world is introduced into God. The Spirit proceeds not from "Father" and "Son" alone, but also from the world: Spirit names God *and* the world. The Father eternally generates the Son, and Father and Son, together with the Spirit, generate initial aims for the world. The world, together with the Christ of the initial aims, generates Spirit. Through God's prehension of the world, Spirit unifies with God as Consequent Nature, qualifying the continuing generation of aims for the ever newly becoming world and, consequently, the ever-new generation of the Spirit. The Son is generated by Father alone, but Spirit is generated from the Father through the Son *and* the world.

However, even though a full analogy with the traditional trinity cannot be made, there is a point where the process conceptuality can help the traditional notion. God was traditionally understood to be a single rational nature, with three subsistences within this nature. These subsistences were (at least in the West) not self-conscious beings, but three expressions within the single rationality of God. The word "person" was used to designate each of these three modes of the divine being, and for more than a thousand years that word was sufficient. However, as the word "person" began to assume more fully the notion of a singular self-consciousness in the seventeeth century, the trinitarian notion tended toward either unintelligibility or tritheism. In a sense, the process analogy moves away from tritheism toward the older usage of modes of being within God, without the need to use the problematic word "person." But paradoxically, even as it moves closer to the tradition, it creates the sharp disruption of introducing the world into the inner nature of God. This would be so either on Cobb's own development, whereby "Spirit" is anticipation of the Kingdom of God in history *and* the consequent nature, or on my revision of Cobb, whereby Spirit is the incarnation of God's manifold peace in the world. In my revision, as well as in Cobb's position, the Spirit in the world issues into the world within God, or the consequent nature.

By restricting the naming of Christ to the initial aim, and identifying Spirit as the birth of God in us through our adoption of the aim, a dialectic develops between Christ and Spirit as expressions of the economic trinity, with implications for the immanent trinity. We experience God for us in the call of risk to more complex modes of inclusive well-being, or peace, and in the incarnation of those modes in history. But the call is such that each realized mode is itself open to yet deeper and richer modes. There is a dialectic between Word and Spirit, between call and realization, whereby each continuously gives way to the other. In our experience of this interchange, we not only know the creative power of God, but in naming this power *God* we dare to give ourselves to this dialectic. We experience God as call and presence and call yet again. This means that there is ever a movement of transcendence and immanence to the experience of God with us, and we intuit that the transcendence and immanence in our histories is itself but an intimation of yet another dimension within God's own reality of this dialectic of Word and Spirit. What we experience as the economic trinity bespeaks not only God in history, but God's own self, the immanent trinity.

The parallel movement in God would be God's own inner dialectic of word and spirit, or the manner by which God integrates the feelings of the world into God's own character, or primordial vision. That is, just as we receive the call from God—the initial aim—and are challenged to integrate that call into our becoming, so does God receive influences from the world, and is challenged to integrate the world into God's own becoming. The differences are important: God's preexistent unity makes the world less influential on God than God is on the about-to-unify world; thus God's character of peace determines the integration of the world within God. God's freedom is highlighted, not mitigated, by God's inner dialectic with the world. God integrates the world into God's own transcendence, according to God's own purposes.

If God as Spirit in fact proceeds from God and the world, then a complexity is introduced into God far greater than mere threeness, for the world is many, and God is one, as Whitehead is wont to tell us. But if the world is immanent in God as Spirit, then is not God many and one at the same time? Isn't the very reality of peace as actualized in God a deeply communal image, requiring something like a world immanent and transformed within God for its realization? But if the world is not an abstraction, if the world in fact is all its teeming, buzzing manyness received into the nature of God, then peace is a transforming work in God indeed, and a reality for which trinity is but a thin word, albeit the best the tradition offers. The very word, "trinity," is itself creatively transformed to become a symbol of a vastly inclusive God who somehow incorporates the received world into the divine being. So transformed, trinity names God not as three, but God as Peace, God as the transcendent/immanent redemption of the world.

Perhaps what we have is an economic trinity, by which God is experienced as gift, call, and responsibility for the future, as indwelling, empowering, community in the present, and as the deeper, pervasive sense of ultimacy and therefore ground of trust and hope. There is a trinitarian modalism in our experience, hence the economic trinity. But when it comes to the immanent trinity, the ascriptions of a specific threeness, whether Father–Son–Holy Spirit or Logos–Kingdom of God–fullness of God, are too reductionistic for the reality we intend. Trinity is a symbol drawn from time, but surpassed by eternity. God is a deep complexity, source of the world's future both as it comes to us as call, and as we go to it as destiny. For this God receives the world. Thus we use the name trinity equivocally of God: In time, the economic trinity is experienced in three modes, and these three modes refer to the one complex God who generates these three modes in our histories. But in God's own time, trinity is symbolic of God's own threefold movement into an everlastingly deeper complexity that surpasses all number. God eternally generates the divine character, from which, in conjunction with feelings of the world, God generates purposes for the world which are themselves the potentiality of Spirit. Insofar as the world incarnates these purposes, Spirit is born in the world, and therefore received into the divine character, everlastingly completing the divine being through the redemption of the world. The immanent trinity is rooted in this threefold action, but yields a complex unity beyond number. God is the deep reality of creative transformation: Peace.

IV. AND THE UNIVERSITY

I have suggested that Cobb's works on education form part of his implicit doctrine of the Spirit, with implications for the trinity. I have also suggested that the notion of the trinity might offer insight as to the structure and purpose of the university. The problem of the university is not unlike the problem of the trinity: How are the distinctions (of persons or disciplines) to be kept from destroying the unity? If the notion of the trinity has been plagued by the threat of tritheism, the reality of the university is plagued by the threat of becoming a multiversity with no cohesive core.

If we look at Cobb's writings on education as one manifestation of a doctrine of the Spirit, then the guiding norm for education is Peace. Theologically, of course, this notion is grounded in the nature and purposes of God, but ordinarily this grounding is implicit rather than explicit in application. In our explicit treatment here, Peace calls for a widening of identity beyond narrow self-interest. Cobb's insights into the unique problems of education call for a more complex inclusiveness to our educational structures. The sharp distinctions that mirror the rigid individualism fostered in Western, Christian culture must give way to an acknowledged interdependence of disciplines. The "memory" of each discipline must be conditioned by the "memories" of the others, toward the end of a responsible exercise toward Peace. No discipline can ever be an end in itself; rather, disciplines are to be honed for the sake of a whole that is greater than each discipline alone. Each discipline is to contribute to community.

But while this might be a laudable goal, its actualization is challenged by the independence rather than interdependence of the disciplines. Here the relation of Spirit to trinity, and the notion of trinity itself, might be illuminating. Spirit moves from the unity of God to the enrichment of the diverse world and back again to the enrichment of the unity of God. The movement is a dialectic between diversity and unity, everlastingly culminating in an ever more complex unity. Could there be fruitfulness in exploring a parallel movement on the part of the university in its varieties of service to ever-widening constituencies in its world, service that facilitates and enriches the university's own complex unity? The possibility can be elaborated by looking again at the trinitarian model of interdependence.

The trinity is a model of interdependence in that a shared rational nature is manifest in a variety of ways, but each of those ways is integrally related to the others. The university is given to a deepening understanding of all facets of the world and of the human spirit. Clearly, there must be distinctions, such as methodologies and materials unique to single disciplines, but there must also be structures whereby the implications of each discipline are related to all the others. Currently these structures are primarily administrative: A president or provost presides over the institution as a whole. But this model does not sufficiently address the interrelationship of the disciplines, such that each is challenged and enriched by the others.

The nonhierarchical model of the trinity is suggestive. Here each "person" has unique origins that correlate with a particular work, but nonetheless all three are engaged in every work. The immanent trinity yields the economic trinity. Analogously, the needed structure of interrelationship in the university must be located at the functional academic level, with professors and students engaged in interdisciplinary approaches to single issues. Learning from the model of the trinity, those issues might well revolve around a work in the world, so that the university becomes a resource in addressing contemporary problems. The university, embedded as it is within the fabric of the wider society, participates in all the problems of society, be they political, economic, cultural, or ecological. That contextual interrelationship might become the structural opportunity for fostering internal interrelationships among the disciplines. This indicates that the interrelationship of the disciplines is fundamentally realized in the application of those disciplines. As professors and students from a variety of disciplines join to deal with a particular problem in society, the interdependence of the disciplines will become apparent. The university will realize itself as *uni*versity as its purposes reach beyond itself into the needs of the wider world.

There would be a threefold benefit should the university institutionalize a program whereby the various disciplines were regularly involved in speaking to concrete issues in the world. Relative to the disciplines, the process of working with others to address a problem would confront each with the limitations of its own approach, and the implications of other approaches for itself.

A point of transcendence would be gained for self-critique, as each discipline would be enriched and challenged by other forms of knowledge. Relative to the problem situation, the multifaceted approach provided by a number of disciplines working in interrelationship may yield novel routes for meliorating or correcting the issues. Relative to the university as a whole, its continuous engagement in a multidisciplinary way with the problems of its society and world emphasizes its responsibility beyond itself, as well as to itself. In the process, of course, the university experiences its own inherent unity.

Again, following the trinitarian model, God's work in the world proceeds in conjunction with the world. Educators and administrators are not to assume a stance of determining among themselves what the good of society might be, and imposing it upon society. On the contrary, just as the isolation of disciplines from one another must give way within our schools, even so the separations among professionals, and between professionals and those involved in other modes of work, must be transcended. The university must be one partner with others in dialogue and action toward richer modes of community.

The obstacles that work against community are great. We are far more likely, if the present course of history is to continue, to be coteries of various ethnicities, values, and interests whose only commonality is that we each seek our own perpetuation over-against the others. In the process, we all neglect the good of this sustaining earth. The creative transformation needed is awesome. The role of the university is to see itself a participant in this work of creative transformation, contributing its own resources toward the peace of the world as a community of interrelated communities, each striving for the enrichment of all. But it can only do so when it models the very peace toward which it strives, when it owns itself as truly *uni*versity, and not multiversity. The intentional interrelationship of disciplines must model peace, and promote peace.

This goal of peace has never been fully realized in history. The trinitarian understanding suggests, however, that this peace is grounded in the very nature of God, who offers us particular modes of peace suited to that which is really achievable in our own time. Insofar as we in our several callings strive toward this goal, quietly and without attention to itself will occur the dynamic work of Spirit, witnessing to the source of all peace in our histories: the God who calls us.

III. HISTORICAL-DESCRIPTIVE ANALYSES

9

Total Abyss and Theological Rebirth: The Crisis of University Theology

I. THE END OF THEOLOGY

While it is commonly recognized that John B. Cobb, Jr., has been a university theologian since the very beginning of his work and career, it is not commonly understood that this is a rare achievement and role in our world. It is rare because it demands either an integral relation or a correlation between reason and revelation, or what were once known as nature and grace. The very fact that either the correlation or the integral opposition between nature and grace, or reason and revelation, has become virtually unspeakable to us is mute testimony to the vast erosion that has occurred in theology, and occurred with an incredible rapidity. There is little if any real point of contact between contemporary theological language and the dominant theological language of less than two generations ago. So far-reaching has this transformation been that we would have to look to the very beginning of Christian theology to discover a genuine analogy to the contemporary situation of theology. The root question facing us is

169

the very possibility of theology, which is to say the possibility of the coinherence as opposed to the brute and literal contradiction of faith and understanding. Certainly Cobb is and remains a unique voyager among us, and this despite the fact that his work has had such an extraordinary influence, an influence that itself raises the question of whether there is truly a crisis today of university theology and of theology itself.

An all-too-simple way of resolving this question would be to note the minimal influence of Whitehead today: it is seemingly confined primarily to a small group of liberal Protestant American theologians, and this in face of the all-too-obvious truth that Whitehead is the only major modern philosopher who even offered the possibility of the integration of the realms of nature and grace, of creation and revelation. True, Whitehead is a very difficult thinker, but he is no more difficult than Hegel, and unlike Hegel he was capable of writing in a clear and richly rhetorical style. Nevertheless, Whitehead is largely unheard today, and for the most part wholly ignored by theologians. He is ignored, I suspect, because of his profound commitment to both a comprehensive and a unitary thinking, a commitment equally if not even more deeply present in Hegel but significantly absent in twentieth-century Hegelianism. What we have lost is a cosmos or universe, a totality or whole transcending our ultimate divisions between nature and humanity and between nature and grace. This totality was present in the premodern world but has apparently been irretrievably lost in our own. So it is that a chasm now lies between our world and the historical world of theology; even our theological masters still retained a memory of what was once actually manifest as Christendom but is now present only in our libraries and museums.

An equally obvious way of pressing our question would be to note the chasm now lying between the world of church, synagogue, temple, and seminary, and the world of contemporary culture and the contemporary university. All too ironically, the rapid expansion of religious studies in the university has gone hand in hand with the rapid retreat of the seminary from our intellectual and cultural worlds, a retreat that began over twenty years ago and is now challenged only by a radically new Catholicism. Theology itself can barely maintain its existence as a university discipline today, and its future is deeply in question, not least because there are so few younger scholars and thinkers who are even interested in theological questions. Biblical scholarship itself is perhaps the clearest example of this. It is almost impossible to detect the presence of theological thinking in current biblical scholarship except in its most conservative expressions, whereas a generation ago the richest theological thinking in America was occurring in biblical scholarship, as witness Bultmannianism. Younger scholars in all fields of study today appear to be oblivious to theological traditions or heritages of any kind. One should not be surprised at this, if only because no real mediation is now occurring between our world and the worlds of our theological past, whether Christian or non-Christian.

An earlier generation could assume that religious or theological thinking is in some sense truly, even if not literally, universal. Now that assumption is profoundly in question, because of both our contemporary religious worlds and our contemporary thinking and scholarship. Older theologians are simply dismayed to see how contemporary fundamentalism is so impervious to any kind of theological thinking, but so likewise are we dismayed to see how religious questions can be intricately analyzed in much contemporary scholarship without any apparent awareness of their theological dimension. The question of God or of ultimate liberation has not simply been phenomenologically bracketed in contemporary thinking; it would appear to have disappeared altogether. Nothing more dramatically illustrates this than the transplantation of Deconstruction to America. In its Parisian form, deconstruction was deeply even if obscurely theological, but in its American form, which quantitatively eclipses its French source, Deconstruction as such is atheological, even in those Yale critics whom we know to be deeply theological. Likewise, Wittgenstein is ceasing to be a philosophical influence, and with the demise of Marxism and Freudianism we are losing our primary modern intellectual opponents. With that loss there is quite possibly occurring the erosion of the very life and vitality of the religious question in the modern world. As Blake knew, "opposition is true friendship," and religion in being uncontested is thereby ignored, at least in its intrinsically religious dimension.

Of course, the erosion of the theological realm is not simply a theological disappearance. We are seemingly living through the end of ethics, the end of philosophy, the end of literature, the end of theater, the end of painting, indeed, the apparent ending of a whole world of culture, and this not only in America, but in the world as a whole. And yet, although Barth, Buber, and Tillich are no more historically distant from us than are Joyce, Heidegger, and Picasso, we find it all too difficult and unreal to immerse our-selves in our theological masters, whereas masters in other realms continue to affect us as living masters. True, our theological mas-ters were not of the stature of these other masters, but neverthe-less they were our masters, and now they seemingly are so no longer. Perhaps the ever-increasing disappearance of the discipline of theology is not only the disappearance of theological masters, of models of theological discourse, but the erosion of a real theologi-cal language, and with it the erosion of the very possibility of theological statement or speech. We must face the question of whether we are now theologically speechless, and, if so, what this might mean, or whether it can have any real meaning at all. In-deed, it is possible that the apparent disappearance of theology is the disappearance of a real impediment to faith, the disappearance of a deep categorical error, the error of integrally associating think-ing and faith.

II. PAUL AND THE ADVENT OF THEOLOGY

At this point the question of Paul becomes inescapable, at least for the Christian theologian. Paul was not only the first Christian writer; he was the creator of Christian theology, a cre-ator whose depth and originality was such that we shall never be able fully to understand him. All too naturally, innumerable think-ers have identified Paul as the creator of Christianity, and, as false as this may be historically, it is undeniable that he effected a deep movement away from a primitive, or literally apostolic, Chris-tianity. There is good reason to believe that this was most funda-mentally done by his *thinking*, which was apparently the first comprehensive and systematic thinking to arise in Christianity. The deep break that this thinking effected with primitive Christi-anity not only necessitated the movement of Christianity away from Judaism but also the movement of Christianity into an alien and intrinsically "other" world, a world that may be thought of as the intrinsic opposite of the Jewish world, and hence the intrinsic opposite of everything that a primitive Christian could know as life and faith. The apostolic leaders of the early Church did not oppose Paul simply because of a narrow legalism or ritualism; such an illusion has no doubt been forever destroyed by recent scholarship. We must thus face the historical truth that Paul was profoundly opposed by the primitive Church because of the very nature and identity of his faith and witness.

Nothing is more original or radical in Paul than his understanding of Christ, a Christ who is not only the end of the Law but who in some decisive sense is the fullness of the Godhead, and that not only in the resurrection but in the crucifixion as well. Indeed, as discovered and demonstrated by Bultmann himself, the crucifixion and resurrection of Christ are not two events for Paul, but rather one ultimate event, and that event is not only the sole source of salvation but the sole source and ground of faith as well. We might well imagine that nothing could have been more offensive to the faith and teaching of the primitive Church than the identification of resurrection and crucifixion: even if this was realized in a far different manner in the Johannine tradition, it nevertheless marks a gulf between the Pauline and the Johannine traditions, on the one hand, and the faith of the Jewish Christian community, on the other. This gulf is a decisive sign of the incredible diversity of the New Testament, a diversity that reflects deep conflict and discord in the early Christian world and that is found nowhere else in the origin of a great religious tradition. Yet Christianity is the only religious tradition to have begun with a deep movement from one historical world to another, a movement that profoundly transformed Christianity itself, thus making possible the birth of a catholic or universal Christianity.

Certainly one source of this movement was the advent of theological thinking, an advent that occurred not only in Paul and "John" but also in Philo and, at the other end of the world, in the birth of Mahayana Buddhism. The very advent of theological thinking was a revolutionary event; even if it was resisted by Hellenistic Judaism, it effected a profound metamorphosis of Buddhism and Christianity alike, a metamorphosis making possible the universalization of each tradition. Moreover, both Buddhist and Christian theology began with a profound assault upon the logic and conceptual thinking of their respective historical and cultural worlds, an assault effecting a deep negation of the very ground of those worlds, an assault apart from which neither theology could either establish or realize itself. At no other point is there such a firm link between Nagarjuna and Paul; this ultimate negation makes possible both Paul's identification of crucifixion and resurrection and Nagarjuna's identification of samsara and nirvana. If this is a negative and dialectical thinking, it is nonetheless thinking itself, a thinking that was as revolutionary as any other thinking in the world. We need not wonder that Pauline thinking did not enter the center of the Church until Augustine; it is a thinking that is incomprehensible apart from a transformation of the very ground and logic of Greek philosophy, just as Mad-hyamika thinking is incomprehensible apart from a transforma-tion of classical Indian logic and philosophy.

Now such a purely negative thinking is by no means to be identified with a simple absence of thinking. Precisely such think-ing effects a deep transformation of a religious world, a transforma-tion that would surely be impossible if a purely passive inactivity were present. We might well identify such thinking as meditative thinking, but it is thinking nonetheless, and is so even if it can only establish itself by negating every positive category it encoun-ters. Such a purely negative thinking does not occur in a historical or cultural vacuum. We can now see that the classical world had already come to an end in its deepest ground, and that the founda-tion of the Roman Empire was not truly a new beginning but only the beginning of the end of the ancient world. That end was a basis of Paul's thinking. This basis was present not only in Paul's in-tense and comprehensive apocalypticism, but even in his appre-hension of the totality of sin and death. This totality is inseparable from Paul's faith in the ultimate victory of Christ; that victory voids every presence within the old aeon. This voiding is finally identical with resurrection itself, so that crucifixion and resurrec-tion are, indeed, one event.

Just as the Mahayana Buddhist knows samsara as nirvana, so both Pauline and Johannine Christians know crucifixion as resur-rection, and as a resurrection that is inseparable from the totality of darkness and death. That totality of darkness, however, is not only a negative totality, but a totality that is positive and negative at once; its very realization of the totality of death releases and makes real a radically new potentiality, a potentiality that is un-real apart from the voiding of a manifest and established world. Thus it is Paul, the most negative visionary in the history of Is-rael, who theologically made possible the universalization of Israel in Christianity. This universalization would be a driving force in Christianity for two thousand years, and was destined to uproot and transform every positive identity within its own horizon and world. Dialectically, ending is beginning, and absolute ending is absolute beginning—a beginning that occurred in Buddhism and Christianity alike, and that is inseparable from a total erasure. That erasure is the actualization of nirvana or resurrection, a res-urrection that is historically real for the Christian in the voiding of the ancient world.

Even if the advent of theology did not effect that voiding, it nevertheless embodies it. This embodiment is present in the profoundly paradoxical identity of its original language. That language is present for all to see in the Fourth Gospel and the letters of Paul, just as it is even more purely present in the parabolic language of Jesus, which only now is being recovered from the synoptic gospels. As offensive and paradoxical as this language unquestionably is, it is nevertheless a language of incredible power, wholly transcending the power of poetic and philosophical language. This was the treasure that theology was given in its very birth. Even if the history of theology has largely been the dispersal and disguising of this treasure, theology itself has no justification whatsoever once it loses contact with this primal power.

This would appear to be exactly what has happened in our own time, in the very wake of what was once thought to be a theological renaissance. We live in a world in which there is no power whatsoever in contemporary theology, and in which even religious scholarship can proceed as though theological thinking and understanding simply did not exist.

III. THE RISE OF ATHEOLOGICAL THINKING

While it is true that ours is a time of loss, and of deep and profound loss, nowhere else is that loss so literal as it is in the theological realm. This loss is so total that its absence seemingly passes unnoticed. Only in our time has a truly atheological thinking established itself, and most manifestly so among "professors" of religion; our academic world has succeeded in creating a field of religion in which everything exists except the very center and ground of religion itself. This is not unlike that dominant contemporary literary scholarship in which the critic or scholar becomes the author of the text, except for the all-too-significant fact that in our religious scholarship the text disappears as a religious or sacred text, and nowhere more so than in the world of biblical scholarship.

So it is that a sea change has occurred in a single generation, and this was the very generation in which the university replaced the seminary or the divinity school as the primary site of religious scholarship (and perhaps in the not-too-distant future it will be the sole site of such scholarship).

Nothing is more important in assessing this situation than a historical perspective, and we might note that evidence of the presence of atheism in Christendom is not found until the seventeenth century, and not until 1793 (in Blake's *America*) are we given our first modern vision of the death of God. Christendom was most profoundly disrupted by the French Revolution, so that thereafter not only did the Church cease to play a central role in our history, but ever more pervasively our culture and society became dissociated from a Christian ground. Nevertheless, not until the twentieth century did the great body of humanity become alienated from a religious ground, so alienated that for the first time in history the practice and profession of religion has become confined to an ever-shrinking minority of human beings.

This is the situation in which the religious scholar has become a curator, having the same involvement with his or her specialty as an art historian, which is to say that the subject matter must be locked into an all-too-distant historical and human realm. We know all too well that anything that is deeply and truly religious could not possibly be present in our world, a world that has undergone what Eliade termed a "Second fall," a fall in which religion and God have simply been forgotten. At most, we have been given religious visions of an absolute abyss, an abyss totally beyond the possibility of the presence of any kind of light. It could even be said that never before in history have there been such pure and total images of an abyss that is solely an abyss, an abyss whose very presence precludes the possibility of light.

IV. THE PARALLEL BETWEEN OUR TIME AND THE TIMES OF PAUL AND AUGUSTINE

Yet is not something strangely like this the world Paul encountered beyond the synagogue and temple? Do we not hear echoes of such a world in the first chapter of Romans, a world that appears to have been as fully nihilistic as our own and that seems to have been divorced from any possible center or ground? Nor is such a perspective confined to apocalyptic seers: We find its counterpart in the *Aeneid*, in which Virgil unveiled a new world that was wholly uprooted from the moral and religious traditions of the ancient world. In this world the gods are humanly and interiorly absent, and justice and order are preserved by force and violence alone. Almost immediately the *Aeneid* was recognized, and by Augustus himself, as the founding epic of the Roman Empire.

Augustine and Dante could look upon the foundation of the Roman Empire as the necessary counterpart to the foundation of the Catholic Church. And if the Great or Catholic Church was far more deeply a consequence of the Hellenistic and Roman worlds than of the Jewish world, this was the very Church in which Paul disappeared as a real presence until the late fourth century, and in which a suffering or crucified Christ is virtually absent in Christian iconography. What most characterizes the patristic Church, and most distinguishes it from every other major religious body in history, is a passionate longing for immortality, an absolute obsession with Eternity. Perhaps we can understand this obsession as the consequence of the loss of a human world, a loss more profoundly present in the Church than elsewhere, a loss that moved into the very center of theological thinking with the advent of Augustine.

Such a loss is a necessary ground for the birth of self-consciousness, a birth that occurs in Paul but is not renewed until Augustine; it is then renewed with such power as to inaugurate the historical world of self-consciousness, which is ending only in our own day. Just as there is no evidence for the presence of self-consciousness in the ancient world, so there is no evidence of an interior consciousness in that world that is wholly interior, and no evidence of a deep, interior conflict or agon that the Christian, and the Christian alone, has experienced as total guilt and despair. That despair is surely a consequence of the advent of Christianity. Even if it has a counterpart in a profoundly Buddhist sorrow, that sorrow can be known by the Buddhist to be ultimately an illusion that is a consequence of an illusory selfhood. The Christian, by contrast, knows a guilt and despair that are inseparable from the very presence and activity of the individual will.

If Augustine discovered that will, or rediscovered it by way of his discovery of Paul, that discovery was perhaps the primary ground of his theological thinking, and that thinking was as immense and overwhelming in its historical impact as any other thinking in history. Here is theological power in its clearest and most decisive form, a form we recognize if only because it is so absent from our world. This absence goes far beyond what we have known as the diminution of poetic and philosophical power. Augustine was arguably the most influential thinker in the history of Christendom, which gives us some sense of the real power of theology and also of the possibilities of theology. This is especially the case when theology is understood as a fundamental mode of discovery itself, and of a discovery which is foundational in the deepest sense. Yet Augustine's discovery was a rediscovery of Scripture itself, by way of a realization of Scripture in a new world. This new world was a consequence of the disappearance of an old world, and became itself by way of the discovery of Scripture, a discovery that is itself the consequence of the birth of a new world.

Perhaps the most disastrous consequence for theology of the disintegration of Christendom was the retreat of theological thinking from the actuality of history, a retreat most purely effected by Kierkegaard, although fully prepared for by pietism and Schleiermacher. This retreat went far beyond an Augustinian dichotomy between the City of God and the City of Man, if only because in the wake of the end of Christendom faith appeared to have no relationship whatsoever to historical actuality. One of the many ironies of this withdrawal was that, even at this time, the biblical tradition was known to be unique among the religious traditions of the world in being so fully grounded in historical actuality. If a radically new historical understanding of the Bible was the most immediate ground of the modern theological crisis, that crisis eventually resulted in a pure theology of the Word that totally isolated the Word of God from the historical realm. Nothing is more revealing of the consequences of this theological movement than a comparison of Augustinianism with an all-too-modern theology of the Word. Augustinianism finally and deeply realized a new future and a new world, whereas modern theology has realized only the ending of itself, and therewith the epiphany of an absolutely isolated and solitary faith.

Yet it may well be that our theological ending has not yet fully realized itself, and that a dark age waits us through which we must still pass. Just as Augustinianism was reborn by way of a passage through the Dark Ages, a comparable rebirth might well await theology today.

V. A REBIRTH OF THEOLOGICAL THINKING

One ground for such a possible rebirth would be a Pauline and Augustinian passage through the end of history, which was then realized by way of a movement through the end of ancient history, and which is perhaps now being realized by way of a movement through the end of Christendom. If this movement was launched by Hegel, Kierkegaard, Marx, and Nietzsche, it has not yet been consummated theologically, mainly because theology remains determined to seek a haven for faith in the ravages of a collapsing world. Such a haven was denied both Paul and Augustine, at least insofar as faith realizes a human or interior form, and was therefore denied by their thinking. They knew all too profoundly the chaotic abyss that is human existence. This abyss goes far beyond the darkness of Greek tragedy, and interiorly beyond it, because it is the abyss of the purely negative will. Even though that abyss only appeared as a consequence of the ending of the ancient world, it is at the center of our horizon as a consequence of the ending of our world. Although a Kierkegaard could name that abyss, and it has been envisioned again and again in the modern imagination, that abyss continues to elude theological understanding, primarily because it continues to remain impossible to correlate our abyss with its own "other" or ending.

Such is precisely the correlation that made possible both a Pauline and an Augustinian theology. That correlation was most manifestly present in the Pauline identification of crucifixion and resurrection, and in the Augustinian correlation of predestination and freedom, or of the enslavement and the freedom of the will, which is nothing less than a theological realization of the *coincidentia oppositorum* of the totality of sin and the totality of grace. Nothing is more primal in Pauline and Augustinian theological thinking than the integral correlation of sin and grace, of old aeon and new aeon, of slavery and freedom, making possible a sin that can be known only through grace and a grace that can be known only through sin. This very correlation, however, created a whole new world of understanding and experience. Only by passing through the depths of that abyss at the center of their worlds did Pauline and Augustinian thinking succeed in naming and understanding the grace that is given in the Christian name of Christ, a grace that is empty and unreal apart from the totality of sin and death, and yet a grace that radically and totally transforms that sin and death so that death itself becomes life and sin itself becomes grace.

This correlation is not present in modern theology, unless it is approached in Barth's doctrine of election, which understands predestination to be the predestination of Christ alone to damnation. This damnation is the election or salvation of all, and yet a damnation that here simply disappears in resurrection. There is no such disappearance in Pauline and Augustinian thinking, because those theologies were deeply grounded not only in their own worlds but also in the actuality of world itself. That actuality has vanished in modern theology; even if it was deeply present in Kierkegaard, that presence must become absence in a theology directed to the edification of the Church. No form of Kierkegaardian theology could realize itself as a Church theology, just as no genuine theology could fail to be centered in the darkness of total abyss. Only when there is seemingly no way of correlating that darkness with the light of grace does the apparent necessity arise for a theology of grace alone, and thus is born yet another Gnostic Christ of glory. (Perhaps Harnack was not far wrong when he wrote his book on Marcion in response to what he judged to be the rebirth of Gnosticism in the early Barth.)

At no other point does Christian theology stand so in need of the horizon of Buddhism, a horizon in which emptiness and fullness immediately and fully pass into and through one another, and in which the fullness of emptiness is unreal apart from the universal negativity of all and everything. Yet something very like this negativity is present in Pauline and Augustinian thinking. Even if it fails to share the logical rigor and consistency of Buddhist thinking, it nevertheless effects a total negation that might be considered a Western parallel to Buddhist thinking. It effects this parallel even in establishing its own negative thinking, an interior and inverse or doubled thinking that understands interiority or self-consciousness itself as the pure negativity of the old Adam, the sinful will. Yet that is precisely the way by which the totality of the presence of grace is recognized, a totality that is no less comprehensive in Pauline and Augustinian thinking than in a Buddhist Emptiness, even if the understanding of that totality in Christian theology has never reached or even approached the purity and wholeness it has realized in Buddhist thinking. Accordingly, there is a deep potential present in Christian thinking which, from our perspective, is absent in Buddhist thinking. This potential promises a much deeper or purer abyss in Christian thinking, an abyss whose very totality might echo or evoke the totality of grace.

If Siddhartha Gautama was the first thinker in history to realize a truly and fully individual and interior way or path, then Paul was the first thinker or writer in history to realize the freedom of the will, which is possible only through grace and which can be known only in knowing the very bondage of the will. Indeed, it is precisely in knowing and realizing that total bondage that we become open to the presence and the reality of grace. Because the Pauline cagegory of "old aeon" comprehends everything we know as history, this grace voids the positivity or essentiality of all historical presence, so that all such presence becomes absence when history is apprehended as old aeon. Then that very absence is the sign and the seal of the total presence of grace, a grace that can only be present in the total emptiness of history, and that can only be known through the total self-alienation of the purely negative will, a will whose very inversion or doubling is the consequence of the presence of a total grace. That is the resurrection that is only real for us when we are crucified with Christ. It is a grace that disappears as grace when resurrection is resurrection alone.

While resurrection has multiple meanings in the letters of Paul, including various shadings of Gnostic meaning (as most fully manifest in the fifteenth chapter of the First Letter to the Corinthians), the most purely and uniquely Pauline meaning unveils resurrection as dialectically identical with crucifixion, so that it is wholly illusory apart from the passion and death of the Crucified God. This resurrection can be known only in death, in the death of the Crucified God, and by way of a renewal or *anamnesis* of that death. So it is that the death of Christ is not Christ's alone but is at the very center of the life of grace. This life is the renewal of ultimate death as life itself. This life now for the first time can make manifest the freedom of the will, a freedom that must inevitably know itself as the source of sin and thereby realize itself as a life that is death and darkness. The life of grace is life and death at once: a life realizing a love that had never been known or manifest before, and a death realizing a total guilt that now appears for the first time in history. While that guilt is borne by the Crucified Christ, it never appears apart from the Crucified Christ, because only the ending of guilt makes possible its own internal and interior actualization.

The very passage through the abyss of ending, of ultimate ending, makes possible the actualization of total grace, a grace that the Christian knows in the Crucified Christ and that we may surmise to be present in Śunyata, or absolute Emptiness. But a Christian passage through that abyss is also and even thereby a passage through the end of history, an ending that was a primal ground of Pauline and Augustinian thinking and that is now calling us in the context of the end of the cycle of Christian history. If we can apprehend a true parallel between the ending of ancient history and the ending of modern history, and not only a parallel but also an *anamnesis* or renewal, then that renewal is the rebirth not only of an ultimate darkness and chaos but also of a death that is life and death at once, and of an ending that is ending and beginning at once. Interiorly and essentially, such an ending could only be an ending of everything that we know as given and manifest, and therewith an ending of everything that is our own, of everything that we can recognize as being for us or to us in consciousness and experience, and thus of everything presenting itself with a human face or voice.

Yet our origin is in a history whose very beginning was an interior realization of total darkness and chaos, which itself was the consequence of an ultimate ending. This ending was not only the ending of the ancient world but, and infinitely more deeply, the death of the Godhead itself in the Crucifixion. If that crucifixion could be known by the Pauline and the Johannine Christian as resurrection, that resurrection nevertheless occurs in the heart of darkness. It occurs not as the literal ending of death and chaos but as a new life, which is realized only through the finality of death, because death itself is now realized as life—as an eternal life that is the intrinsic and essential "other" of eternal death. Nothing is more fundamental theologically than an apprehension of a resurrection that is crucifixion and resurrection at once. Even if this apprehension is present in the New Testament, it is virtually absent in the great body of Christian theology, despite the fact that an eternal life that is inseparable from an eternal death is deeply present in the Christian imaginative tradition, and most clearly so in the Christian epic tradition. But just as modern theology evolved by way of divorcing itself from the actuality of history, so likewise it evolved by distancing itself from the imagination, above all the Christian imagination.

Need we wonder that theology has become so unreal in our world, even unreal to the believer—who seemingly can believe only by way of the absence of theological thinking? Might then the dissolution of theology be judged to be a triumph of theology itself, a dissolution that is the disappearance of a deep categorical error, the error of integrally associating thinking and faith? Should we say nothing at all about faith, and thus say nothing whatsoever about the content or center of faith, a center that can be spoken in the language of faith and only in this language, thereby precluding the possibility of all merely human languages? This, of course, would be to identify faith with silence, a silence that is most fully and purely embodied in Buddhism but that may well be the last hope of the Christian world. True, this would be a new silence in the Christian world, a silence simply miraculous in the context of that world, and so miraculous as to be wholly invisible and inaudible to all who are innocent of such faith. Is this the silence of the authentic theologians of our world: a silence not even tempted to speak of faith, a silence that is, indeed, the truest guardian of and witness to faith?

If so, we could perhaps look upon the ending of theology in our university and cultural worlds as correlative with the advent or realization of pure faith, so that the seemingly infinite distance between the world of thinking and the world of faith would at bottom be their integral harmonization, allowing each to be fully and only itself. A brave new world may already be present in our midst, a new world most manifestly present in the dissolution of religious and theological thinking, and therewith a world liberated from the internal and interior presence of chaos and abyss. Even if such a new world would be infinitely distant from what we can know as the Bible, that knowledge as knowledge is, from this perspective, wholly distant from faith and thus from the Bible as the Word of God. Such a Word of God could also have no point of contact with what we have known as the actuality of theological thinking, a thinking that is inseparable from chaos and abyss, and a thinking that, if it were now to continue, would inevitably center upon darkness and chaos as it has never done before. Or, at the very least, it would recover its Pauline, its Johannine, and its Augustinian roots as never before, and would open theology to the absolute abyss that we know now to be present. This abyss alone gives promise of anything that we can know theologically or imaginatively as resurrection.

Nothing more manifestly characterizes the deepest expressions of modern literature and painting than the epiphany of a total abyss; even if that abyss is only an abyss, it is precisely therein that the triumphs of the twentieth-century imagination have most deeply realized their overwhelming power. But is this not also true of the greatest triumphs of prophetic faith and of mystical vision throughout the history of religions? Surely this is true of the biblical prophetic tradition, and of the renewals of that tradition in Augustine, Eckhart, Luther, Blake, and Kierkegaard, just as it is also true of both Theravada and Mahayana Buddhism. Moreover, the very occurrence of these triumphs occurred in historical worlds that were undergoing profound transformations, historical worlds in which an old world was coming to an end and a new world was aborning. Even if such new worlds were unnameable at the time of their dawning, they nevertheless were present, although invisible and inaudible as such in their initial realizations. While the prophetic revolution was both occasioned by and culminated in historical catastrophe for Israel, it nonetheless realized the birth of Judaism, Christianity, and Islam. Each of those births ushered in truly new historical worlds that went far beyond anything manifestly present in their beginnings.

Paul could know the totality of history as old aeon as the consequence of the triumph of the crucifixion and resurrection of Christ. Accordingly, Paul could know history as an abyss that is total precisely because it is immediately coming to an end. That very ending is the triumph of grace, a total grace, even if the epiphany of that totality is inseparable from the epiphany of a total, chaotic darkness that is most immediately and actually present within, and only manifestly present within those who know a total grace. So it is that a knowledge of the total presence of a total abyss is a decisive sign of a knowledge of the total presence of total grace, a grace whose actualization is inseparable from the actualization of abyss, even as the eternal life of resurrection is inseparable from the eternal death of crucifixion. Such a *coincidentia oppositorum* of eternal life and eternal death is certainly not confined to Paul, and is found in a far purer form in Theravada and Mahayana Buddhism alike, but it is unique to Paul among ancient visionaries insofar as it is so intimately conjoined with a cosmic totality. This totality is both ending and beginning; the triumph of the new aeon is inseparable from the end of the world.

Now we can see that Paul was a witness to the ending of the ancient world. This witnessing is a primal basis of Paul's theological thinking itself, which is to say a primal basis of the very birth of Christian theological thinking. This ending demands to be renewed today, and has already, in fact, been renewed in our deepest posthistorical thinkers and visionaries, such as Nietzsche and Joyce. Theology can only continue to ignore this ending by refusing its own rebirth. Such a rebirth may well be an impossibility (as all hope may be an illusion in our world), but nonetheless it cannot become manifest as an impossibility until it is realized as such, and that cannot occur as long as there is no real theological movement towards rebirth. Perhaps that is the root of our theological impotence and passivity, an interior even if unconscious recognition that there is no possibility of theological rebirth, and that it is only in an inactive and wholly lifeless form that theology can preserve itself in our world.

No one has more decisively opposed such a retreat than John B. Cobb, Jr., and if his efforts are doomed to failure, then our theological world has little if any hope, unless we were to reverse Cobb's vocation by becoming mere curators of an archaeological past.

10

Theology and Rhetoric in the University

I. THE REDISCOVERY OF RHETORIC

In the medieval European university there was no question that theology was central. As the place of theology came to be questioned, its dialogue partner until very recently was philosophy. Philosophy was to provide the comprehensive vision of reality within which the various disciplines found their places. If theology was to belong in the university, it would justify its place through its relation to philosophy. The assumption was that philosophy brought into order what all people could know, while theology ordered the special knowledge of Scripture, or of Scripture and tradition. As time passed, much philosophy came to have little interest in the insights of theology. Partly in response to this secularizing of philosophy, theologians were led to work hard at philosophy of religion, in order to provide a general frame in which to place the special tradition of their faith (which, for universities in Europe and America was, of course, predominantly the Christian faith, although Jewish thinkers also played an important part in this effort).

More recent times have seen a shift in the role played by philosophy. The analytic philosophy so prevalent in Britain and America has no place for a vision of the whole such as was the aim of the older philosophy. Within limits, the same can be said of the newer neopragmatism. The hermeneutic philosophy of Continental universities is a powerful tool for interpreting religious tradition, and Jewish and Christian hermeneutics have been deeply influential in its formation. Of itself, however, it has little to say about the relation of theology to other intellectual activities in the university, and in some of its forms it has been divisive in the university in that it has been sharply negative to "scientific" inquiry. That opposition is one of the signs of the dissection of the university into unrelated disciplines, so marked a feature of contemporary intellectual life.

One response to this situation is to try to do better what philosophy used to do. I shall return to this. But a striking feature of humane studies today is the renewed interest in rhetoric as an activity in which we all engage and that can provide a common mode of communication among different kinds of inquiry. Because rhetoric has always been an important companion to theology, especially in reflection about preaching, it is worth looking at the new interest in rhetoric as a possible unifying factor in the university.

Rhetoric, of course, has a long history, but in the earlier part of this century it was overshadowed by poetics; that is, attention was focused on form, on relations within a work of art, as in the New Criticism. Fruitful as the focus on form was in many ways, it represented one aspect of the fragmentation of intellectual life into separate and at best only weakly related areas. A critic like Kenneth Burke, who through his long career insisted on taking a literary work as an action, was often misunderstood or simply neglected.

The university scene is very different today. The rediscovery of rhetoric (and even often of the Sophists, who, in our tradition, originally formulated the goals of rhetoric) is a way of indicating that a text cannot be understood simply in terms of its ideas or even in terms of its formal structure, but must also be seen in relation to its audience, in terms of what it can do.

Chaim Perelman and Lucie Olbrechts-Tyteca's *A New Rhetoric* was a pathbreaking work in the modern appreciation of rhetoric.[1] Perelman and Olbrechts-Tyteca present their work as opposed to Descartes's kind of reasoning aimed at attaining certainty.[2] Their work, along with others, has encouraged interpreters in a wide range of subjects to look favorably on reasoning from probabilities and on taking the effect on the audience as a major factor in interpretation. We may term *A New Rhetoric* a mediating work. It builds on and expands the categories of the ancient rhetoricians, though moving beyond them in its concern wider than that with the spoken word and in its explicit focus on the structure of argumentation, on how arguments are persuasive. By implication, this approach raises the political question of the pragmatic effect of a statement or of a work as a whole. But this book does not engage in the polemic against traditional philosophy that is often associated with a new interest in rhetoric. Others have made more radical claims for rhetoric, asserting that metaphysics is no longer possible, that the assumed referential aspect of language is illusory (because language refers only to other linguistic elements), and that rhetoric is thus at last freed from philosophy.

The various approaches to rhetoric overlap, and the implications for the place of theology in the university vary with the way in which rhetoric is interpreted. All forms of rhetoric agree that action of some kind is implied in communication, and those who are interested in theology will rejoice that we are moving toward an emphasis on thinking as a form of action or on the action that is intended as a result of thinking. At the same time, the long-standing suspicion of rhetoric as manipulative and as ethically relative must also be taken into account. For the sake of simplicity I shall examine three uses of rhetoric within the university: (1) rhetoric as a form of communication within the university; (2) the rhetoric of discovery; and (3) the rhetoric of social change.

II. THE RHETORIC OF COMMUNICATION

To turn to rhetoric as communication within the university is to acknowledge that the different disciplines cannot comprehend one another in their specialized vocabularies and ways of thinking. "Front-line" work can be understood only by those with years of specialized and sharply-focused training in a particular field, whether it be deconstruction, particle physics, or macroeconomics. Because we cannot comprehend one another's specialized and most rigorous ways of thinking, we must learn to be more self-consciously reflective about the more general, rhetorical modes of communication by which we can, in a measure, understand one another.[3]

As a working hypothesis, such an emphasis on rhetoric is content to assume that what is being done in the various special disciplines at the edge of discovery is well worth doing, that the university justifies itself by its various probings into new knowledge. This emphasis also accepts as inescapable the density and incomprehensibility of the various specialized models of understanding to those who have not learned them thoroughly by apprenticeship within the discipline. Similarly, the function of the university in society is assumed to be viable in its general present form. A university alert to communicative rhetoric would indeed be more effective in society, both because the wider world would be better able to know what the university was about, and because the public would beat the path to the university's door to learn the rhetorical ways of communicating that are so effective.

The logic of communication in many disciplines concentrates as narrowly as possible on the "subject matter," and has in many cases moved increasingly toward mathematical symbolization, which minimizes the personal participation of the "sender" and "receiver" of the message. In contrast, a rhetoric of communication within the university will focus both on the audience and on the believability of the speaker. The message will be cast in terms that will make contact with things familiar to the audience; conversely, when we are trying to understand something too recondite to grasp fully, our trust in the speaker will be a factor in the credibility of the message.

The action that will result from this kind of rhetoric is the building of community, the growth of a university. Work in the specific disciplines will be stronger and more important as the new work takes account of its relation to other fields (the "interdisciplinary" motif); the university will also be stronger as the wider society understands better what it is about. The building of community presupposes a common stock of values, without which the trust that is an essential ingredient in this kind of rhetorical understanding could not take place. The human values and traits that communicative rhetoric presupposes lie at the conscious level; no deep probing of the unconscious is necessary.

Wayne C. Booth is an eloquent spokesperson for the rhetoric of communication. In a lecture at the University of Chicago (one in a series in which leading specialists interpret their fields to a general university audience), Booth offered vivid examples of the limits of specialized understanding. Many of the points in the previous several paragraphs have been drawn from this essay. Booth cites one economics professor who withdrew a dissertation from a prize competition in the social sciences because he was unwilling for the other members of the committee to judge it; they could not possibly understand its excellence, and were expected to accept it on his say-so. Another example given by Booth is a professor of philosophy who says that no one in his department understands his work, which is comprehensible only to a handful of other specialists scattered across the world.[4]

Although Booth does not expect this situation to change, he does claim that, in the face of the inability to construct an overall theoretical framework for all these activities, we can nonetheless employ rational rhetorical means of communicating. His path into the aspects of value and trust mentioned above was to question his colleagues about how they judge other faculty in such matters as promotion, tenure, and grant awards. He found a widespread consensus that it is possible to make reasonable decisions, which rely on judgments of character, of intellectual style (the "quality of reasoning"), and on some degree of understanding of the technical scholarly work.[5] Judgments of character and of intellectual style are basically rhetorical judgments, depending on the kind of probabilities that Perelman and Olbrechts-Tyteca explore.

Booth is well equipped to develop the position he takes, because one of his major works deals with the problems of understanding within his own special field of literary criticism. In a defense of a limited pluralism, Booth offers a description and critique of several major literary critics, each section followed by a response by the critic in question. The work offers a nice demonstration of the power and limits of understanding. Some of the critics took serious exception to what Booth had taken to be what they were doing, despite his serious effort to represent them fairly. In conclusion he writes, "Vitality, justice, and understanding, accepted as goods-in-themselves in all human life, lead us into pluralism as critics, just as they led each of us, not so long ago, out of our infantile ideocentrism into the recognition of a world built of many centers, irreducible to any one."[6]

As a comment on the structure of the university, this style of communicative rhetoric is initially, at least, conservative. Its aim is to increase understanding, which, as the quotation just above shows, is taken as a fundamental and shared value. From this point of view, theology may join in the conversation if it is already a recognized part of the university. Interestingly, Booth cites "Divinity School professors organizing workshops on practical reason" as a typical fruit of the interchange between the university and society that would result from the implementation of his proposals.[7] This suggestion is in line with Joseph Hough and John Cobb's proposals for a clearer direction in theological education.

They call for a new understanding of the minister's role as "practical theologian."[8] But Booth's communicative rhetoric would not itself supply the identity that such practical reason presupposes— any more than it would supply a self-critical understanding of any of the other "disciplines." We may expect that encounter with the work of other disciplines will encourage critical reflection about one's own, however.

But theology would have a different and important role in a university that took the rhetoric of communication among specialists seriously. What is the grounding of the common values, the "vitality, justice, and understanding"? It has often seemed that no defense of such shared values is necessary, even though in the rhetorical tradition it is widely held that values are not universal.[9] Theology will have an important role to play in clarifying the values and goals of research and its application, as is shown, for instance, by the development of joint programs between schools of theology and business, law, and medical schools.[10] The deeper the pluralism that is admitted into the discussion, the more urgent the need for some clarity about shared, or not shared, values. As minority groups, women, and others not traditionally included in the activity of research come to function in the university, the question of shared values and goals becomes all the more pressing. Christian theology does not have a privileged answer to the questions raised, but its long engagement with this range of questions, and its effort to balance a pragmatic assessment of values with a grounding of values in reality, will make it an important contributor to the discussion of the aims of the university. This discussion will bring into focus the question of the relation between the values of a concrete community, whose self-understanding is expressed in Christian theology, and those of other groups. For the university a consequence will be a real questioning of the presupposed values of the different disciplinary fields, which at the start of the inquiry into communicative rhetoric are simply assumed to be justifiable. Alert theology will be one of the factors challenging traditional disciplinary boundaries and challenging the established values that justify research. Once the question of interaction between the university and the wider society comes into focus, there is bound to be a move beyond asking how better communication within the university can be shared to enable actors in the wider society to do more effectively what they are doing. That leads to the rhetoric of social change, which I shall come to after discussing the rhetoric of discovery.

III. THE RHETORIC OF DISCOVERY

From the point of view of our first style of rhetoric, that of communication, discovery or new insight takes place at the rigorous level of specialized models of research. Of course, the knowledge produced by such inquiry is fallible, and the models that structure it will change with time. The actual creativity that lies behind the new discoveries is not a special focus of attention. Rhetoric itself functions at a second stage, after the discoveries have been made.

Another style of rhetoric reshapes the question of understanding to make rhetoric itself the key element in discovery. Such an approach takes its point of departure from the scene of teaching, rather than from the scene of research. This rhetoric of discovery sets itself in sharp opposition to the model of teaching as transmission of information. Here we follow the model of discovery elaborated by Gregory L. Ulmer in *Applied Grammatology*, although we can only sketch a part of his complex argument.[11]

The basic thesis is that linear thinking, which proceeds along a logical chain of deduction, is able to clarify existing knowledge, but not to open the way to new insight. New insight comes from confronting unexpected, "illogical" juxtapositions. This clue to good teaching is not new. What is new is the radical rhetoric of discovery, which claims to uncover the true roots of creative inquiry.[12]

The rhetoric of discovery develops out of deconstruction, on the one hand, and out of an awareness of the power of nonlinear modes of presentation in film, video, and electronic media, on the other. Its background in deconstruction means that it comes with heavy antimetaphysical freight. The struggle against what is felt to be an imposition of truth from the outside has been a stimulus to a different kind of inquiry. How essential the antimetaphysical perspective is to the fundamental insights of the rhetoric of discovery is a question to be examined.

Two examples of juxtaposition will lead us into the rhetoric of discovery. One is from film. Sergei Eisenstein wrote about the juxtaposition of images in a segment of his film *October* (1927):

> Kornilov's march [the march of the general opposed to the revolution] on Petrograd was under the banner of "in the Name of God and Country." Here we attempted to reveal the religious significance of this episode in a rationalistic way.

A number of religious images, from a magnificent Baroque Christ to an Eskimo idol, were cut together. The conflict in this case was between the concept and the symbolization of God. While idea and image appear to accord completely in the first image shown, the two elements move further from each other with each successive stage. Maintaining the denotation of 'god,' the images increasingly disagree with our concept of God, inevitably leading to individual conclusions about the true nature of all deities. In this case, too, a chain of images attempted to achieve a purely intellectual resolution, resulting from a conflict between a preconception and a gradual discrediting of it in purposeful steps.[13]

For Eisenstein, there is no intrinsic connection among the various god-images; the connection is created by their juxtaposition.[14] Thus a montage of images offers a graphic form of argument.[15] This technique, of course, could equally well be used to express an opposite valuation of the image "god."

A second example is the pun, dear to Jacques Lacan as well as to Jacques Derrida, and important in the theory of Umberto Eco as well. All recognize the important role of James Joyce's *Finnegan's Wake* in opening the contemporary imagination to the working of the pun. Derrida has played particularly with proper names, to show that connections other than those suggested by surface meaning can open the way to new discourse.[16] While the connections suggested by Eisenstein's filmic montage were quite rationally chosen to achieve certain effects, the effect of the pun is far more open-ended or polyvalent. Ulmer describes Eco's interpretation of the pun as follows:

The pun or homophone acquires a new status with respect to the new sensibility, attuned no longer to the expectations of cause and effect, the logic of the excluded middle, but to the pleasure of surprise, in that homophones represent the "bridge of least motivation," thus generating the greatest "information." Eco establishes the epistemological importance of the pun by identifying it as the principal figure of *Finnegan's Wake,* understood itself to be an "epistemological metaphor" of "unlimited semeiosis" (the *apeiron,* in Derrida's terms).[17]

Discovery comes, then, more by unexpected juxtapositions than by logic or even by the leap of metaphorical resemblance. The negative side of this rhetoric is clear enough: It is a protest against the limitations of reasoning from the expected. Our statements are scattered fragments within an unlimited realm of possibility. One can emphasize the infinite formlessness of this unlimited realm, but here the emphasis is on an infinite, or close to infinite, network of interrelationships that exist beyond the small line of relationships brought to light in traditional reasoning.

If we were to specify a source for the flashes of insight that are enabled by this rhetoric of surprise (often of shock), it would be the unconscious, as is made clear in Ulmer's discussion of Lacan. The rhetoric of discovery partly lifts into conscious knowledge what is already patterned in our unconscious in ways not directly accessible to us. While the unconscious is not necessarily a universal ground (different resources may lie in the unconscious of different people), the appeal to something universally shared makes possible a nonelite understanding of the finding of understanding.

The pedagogical rhetoric of discovery is thus not directed to a specialized class. One of Ulmer's hopes is that the new electronic media may cut across the lines of specialization that our universities have created. The language, or art, that confronts the learner and surprises her or him is difficult, as obscure as the writings of Derrida or Lacan! It has to be difficult, because the ordinary has such a strong hold on our vision. But it is not difficult in the sense that it could be grasped only by specialists. On the contrary, these devices are intended to speak both to those with tradition of learning and to those who do not stand in this tradition. Lacan's seminars, which attracted philosophers and other academics as well as students in training as psychoanalysts, offers a model of a teaching style that can be at the front line of its particular kind of discovery, at the same time being open to learners with a wide range of backgrounds.

Ulmer interprets this pedagogy in the following terms, drawing on the work of Geneviève Jacquinot on film communication: "The filmic message is didactic, 'no longer because it transmits a knowledge, but because it permits the elaboration of a knowledge.' This elaboration is undertaken not by the one who teaches but by the one who learns, based on a presentation that provides the raw material for an *inventio*. Pedagogy becomes a process, not a product."[18]

Sometimes the pedagogy of discovery is associated with a predetermined goal for understanding, as in the Eisenstein illustration. Sometimes the field is much more open, as in the illustration of the pun, which does not necessarily predetermine what network of relations will be seen by the learner. The actual use of film and television would offer instances of both styles of presentation. If learning by surprise of juxtaposition were taken to be the only path to understanding, this would eliminate the learning of "classical" tradition, or at least break up the continuity of any such tradition, including the Christian tradition. It appears, however, that one does not have to follow this either-or route. The open learning of juxtaposition and the more channeled route of coming to appreciate a tradition can in fact enrich one another.

What is the relevance of this kind of rhetoric of discovery to theology? If it is taken to be the only path to knowledge, it implies that already-known forms that can be imparted in the traditional way do not contribute to real insight on the part of the student. True as this is in its way, it is not the only truth about knowledge, as noted above. I would prefer to follow at least some hints of Ulmer himself, and regard this kind of rhetoric as one, but not the only, kind of rhetoric that will teach us about theology, or that we can use in theology. We can make the point by referring to a specific rhetorical mode: narrative. The rhetoric of discovery aims to break the expected form of narrative, to move beyond its limiting, exclusionary tendency. By organizing the world, narrative inevitably leaves much out. The current exploration of play and carnival expresses a resistance to this exclusiveness. The rhetoric of discovery is a form of play. But we cannot live without organizing our world, even if we regard (as many do today) our narrative patterns as our own creations. We need to take account of both the surplus of meaning, which cannot be contained in a system, and the reach toward limitation, which traditional narrative embodies.[19] We do not have to follow many contemporary interpreters in thinking of form as purely a human imaginative creation. But the recognition of the place of imaginative surprise, of letting go, and also the place for mythical or narrative finding of place, offers a way of being open to what we have termed the rhetoric of discovery, while keeping a place for the organizing vision that forms a world.

The antinomian rhetoric of discovery has links with themes in negative mysticism, and with recent discussions of the function of the parable. These links suggest the seriousness with which theologians must take this "playful," sometimes subversive, kind of rhetoric. We arrive at a picture of theology, like the language of faith itself, as holding in creative tension the move toward organizing the world (and God in relation to it), and the move toward finding unperceived, and even as yet uncreated, connections that not only awaken the joy of surprise but may also lead to new forms of action. This point leads us to our next section.

IV. THE RHETORIC OF SOCIAL CHANGE

At the height of the Nazi and Fascist domination, the political scientist Carl J. Friedrich remarked to me (I was his student at the time), "We need to enlist more writers like Ignazio Silone." Of course he was referring to the novel, *Bread and Wine*, that eloquent statement of human resistance to totalitarian tyranny. Most literary critics quail at the thought of artists being enlisted for a political cause, or of literature expressly written for political purposes (and with good reason, when one reflects on the pressures on creative artists from governments intent upon allowing only forms of expression that support the official vision). Yet one could not possibly understand Afro-American literature, feminist literature, and Latin American literature without seeing and dealing with their political stances. The theology that comes from these communities is closely interactive with the literature.[20]

The connection between rhetoric and social change is simple enough: Rhetoric is aimed at an effect. The rhetoric of social change understands rhetoric as the exercise of power. If much theology, literature, and academic teaching seem apolitical, that may well mean that their rhetorical effect is to maintain the status quo. Probably to most academics this has seemed to be appropriate and natural, although often the effect of "conserving" has not been perceived as the action it actually is.

An academic rhetoric that makes the dimension of action explicit cannot be developed apart from a decision about the role of the university in society. Frank Lentriccia (whose *Criticism and Social Change*, a comment on the thought of Kenneth Burke, will guide much of what follows in this section) cites John Dewey's distinction between "education as a function of society" and "society as a function of education."[21] The point is that those who like things pretty much as they are make education a function of society, while those who want radical change think of society as a function of education, of education as aiming at major change in society. Lentriccia is impatient with liberals who wish only to tinker with the system; he wants a major realignment of the structures of power in society. But his major point is that all thinking and writing are inextricably interwoven with the structures of power in society. His kind of rhetoric looks to the ways in which language exercises power or is responsive to the power exercised by others. The work of the university is neither a detached "understanding," as in our first type of rhetoric, nor a "discovery" that is sheerly open-ended, as in much at least of the second type. It is instead to be the work of making explicit and criticizing the workings of the society, especially in its aspect of exercising power. As such, both the writing of literature and the criticism of literature (which takes place in the university) are acts of power. As Lentriccia puts his interpretation of the Marxist tradition: "Ideas not only have material effects; they have material circumstances as well."[22]

One of Lentriccia's major points is that a rhetoric of change must learn to speak within the symbol system of the prevailing culture. Simply to stand outside and be negative won't work. He has both the writer and the critic in mind. He quotes Kenneth Burke: "One cannot extend the doctrine of revolutionary thought among the lower middle classes without using middle-class values—just as the Church invariably converted pagans by making the local deities into saints."[23]

From this point of view, the criticism of a representational rhetoric, which thinks of itself as simply presenting the world, is that mere representation does not intend to *do* anything. This is very different from an attempt to show that language is totally enclosed within itself, a posture that is more often associated with a disregard of the possibilities of social change. What the rhetoric of social change leads us to learn is how our ways of expressing ourselves grow out of our social location and either reinforce that situation's structure or exert pressure upon it. Lentriccia writes, interpreting Kenneth Burke: "The literary act remains an act. Whatever the unknown and known forces acting upon and through it, in its manipulation of form the literary act produces force and thereby sets loose effects in the 'present' that Burke understands as a temporal crossing. In the act of writing, one of the key sites where past and present are crossed, the present is experienced as history."[24]

This rhetoric, like our second type, is opposed to a single line of tradition or truth. Like our first, it is aimed at the formation of community, but with the great difference that, while the rhetoric of communication presupposes that purely intellectual obstacles stand in the way of understanding and hence of at least a particular type of community, here community is recognized in its lack, in the failure of our modern capitalist societies to be communities. The vision of community will either be lost or be made actual in a measure by "the active involvement of individuals in the great struggle of persuasion."[25]

There is a somber irony in placing together Lentriccia's socialist (humanist Marxist) vision and conventional rhetoric about the failure of communism. Lentriccia at any rate recognizes that the rhetoric of social change is not self-directing. It must go hand in hand with a social vision.

The stake of Christian theology in this kind of rhetoric is clear. Despite the interweaving of church life into the structures of the status quo, theology has been as actively critical of Western capitalist and colonialist society as has any other style of intellectual activity. However unevenly, it has been responsive to the voices of those who have been excluded from social power. A closer attention to the kinds of persuasion that are being used for and against social change, considered as rhetoric, can be a major contribution to a reflective theology that is concerned with social change.

V. THEOLOGY, PHILOSOPHY, AND RHETORIC

Current discussion about religion in the university often centers on the question whether a focus on "religion" or a focus on "theology" is appropriate for the university. The study of "religion" as a human phenomenon seems a more appropriate focus because this term implies studies that are consonant with what goes on in other fields in the university. The implication is that theology represents a parochial point of view that does not belong in the university.

Certainly religion should be studied by the methods understood under the heading of "religion" as an academic discipline. This means making religious behavior and belief intelligible by types of analysis that have proven useful in fields such as psychology and sociology. Often it will mean understanding religious actions and beliefs in other terms than those used consciously by the believing community. Clearly, too, such an approach will be thoroughly pluralistic, and will not privilege the position of Christianity as was the case even in the university of not so long ago. But along with this way of setting the question, one must ask how exhaustive these descriptions are. There is more going on, and at the least one can say that theology can provide access to part of that more.

For theology to interact fruitfully with the wide range of concerns raised by the styles of rhetoric discussed above, more general questions will arise about the nature of language and reality. These are philosophical questions. Philosophy of religion, and also a broader philosophy, are natural loci for thought about the relation between religion and the university. Those who study theology will be an important part of the stimulus toward a more adequate philosophy, because they will frame questions that demand a broader view than the purely technical questions that much academic philosophy has been content to raise. At the same time, theology has a close affinity with the impetus toward action so central to rhetoric. Despite the fact that much current rhetoric has an antimetaphysical, antiphilosophical bent, rhetoric and philosophy still need each other and must learn to interact fruitfully. Rhetorical studies need the perspectives of theology and philosophy if they are to avoid the skeptical relativity that has been attributed to rhetoric since the days of the Sophists. The effort to supplant philosophy with rhetoric is mistaken, because, as Lentriccia sees so clearly, rhetoric itself does not determine its own ends.

To put the question of theology's stake in the rhetorical discussion in the language of traditional Christian theology: Can one discern a "work of the Holy Spirit" in the functioning of the rhetorics we have sketched? Is the quest for understanding across specialist barriers related to a "lure" that is more than something generated simply within the self-enclosed minds of academics? Is the surprised insight into which one may be shaken by the rhetoric of discovery, with its use of juxtaposition, in any way related to a spirit that leads one beyond oneself? Does the rhetoric of social change express a leading toward a wider humanness than my own group expresses? To answer "yes" to these questions means a difficult rethinking of the relation between the church and the world, and a willingness to see an openness in which the power of God can be and actually is at work, in ways not traditionally developed in the doctrine of the Spirit.

The influence can also go in the other direction: the reflections of theology can reshape the forms in which the above styles of rhetoric grasp their issues. For instance, all of them focus on human interchange as the locus of concern. Nature, including our human relation to nature, is not a focal issue for any of the three rhetorical styles noted above. An encounter with current theology can be salutary for those who set the terms of the rhetorical discussion at precisely this point.

As we reflect about the university as a rhetorical area, we find that the interaction with all this discussion is extremely fruit-

ful for theology, indeed, one can say indispensible, if theologians
are to repond intelligently to the world in which they live. None of
these rhetorics, of course, offers a center for theological reflection;
that center will be the church. But one of the great theological
tasks is to think about how the love of God that is known in
Christ is also seen in the world. As Hough and Cobb put it, "Faith
is confidence in God's loving intention and action in the world
and God's acceptance of the world in loving forgiveness. It is confidence that God is everywhere acting creatively and redemptively
for the world, and it is also belief that God calls us to work with
her here and now."[26] To rethink the engagment with broader understanding, especially as it is challenged by the introduction into
the conversation of partners who have traditionally been excluded,
to rethink the surprise of discovery, to rethink the radical reshap-
ing of the society in which we live, all in a realistic context of God
everywhere acting creatively and redemptively for the world, are
tasks that will engage theology and the university, whatever the
particular institutional structures within which the discussion
takes place may be.

NOTES

1. C. Perelman and L. Olbrechts-Tyteca, *The New Rhetoric: A Trea-
tise on Argumentation* (Notre Dame: University of Notre Dame Press,
1969).

2. Ibid., 1–4.

3. This section of the paper draws extensively on Wayne C. Booth,
"The Idea of a University," in *The Vocation of a Teacher: Rhetorical Occasions 1967–88* (Chicago: University of Chicago Press, 1988), 307–34.

4. Ibid., 316, 313.

5. Ibid., 317–25.

6. Wayne C. Booth, *Critical Understanding: The Powers and Limits
of Pluralism* (Chicago: University of Chicago Press, 1979), 348.

7. Booth, "The Idea of a University," 331.

8. Joseph C. Hough, Jr., and John B. Cobb, Jr., *Christian Identity and
Theological Education* (Chico, Calif.: Scholars Press, 1985), esp. chap. 5.

9. Perelman and Olbrechts-Tyteca, *The New Rhetoric*, 74–79.

10. As at Emory University.

11. Gregory L. Ulmer, *Applied Grammatology: Post(e) Pedagogy from Jacques Derrida to Joseph Beuys* (Baltimore: Johns Hopkins University Press, 1985).

12. Although Ulmer's reflections deal with what are traditionally regarded as the humane studies, there is a parallel worth exploring in Jean-François Lyotard's interpretation of new scientific discovery through an attack upon consensus and through parology, or "breaking the rules." See *The Postmodern Condition: A Report on Knowledge*, trans. Geoff Bennington and Brian Massumie (Minneapolis: University of Minnesota Press, 1984), esp. chaps. 13 and 14.

13. Sergei Eisenstein, *"Film Form" and "The Film Sense,"* trans. Jay Leyda (Cleveland, 1957), quoted in Ulmer, *Applied Grammatology*, 278.

14. Ibid., 282.

15. Ibid., 278.

16. See especially Ulmer, *Applied Grammatology*, chap. 2.

17. Ibid., 309.

18. Ibid., 307.

19. Robert Detweiler, *Breaking the Fall: Religious Readings of Contemporary Fiction* (San Francisco: Harper & Row, 1989), 40.

20. On Afro-American literature and theology, see Cornel West, *Prophetic Fragments* (Grand Rapids: William B. Eerdmans, and Trenton: Africa World Press, 1988); on feminist literature, the point scarcely needs documentation, but see the comments of Elisabeth Schüssler Fiorenza in *Bread Not Stone: The Challenge of Feminist Biblical Interpretation* (Boston: Beacon, 1984); on Latin American theology, see Pablo Richard, ed., *Raíces de la teología Latinoamericana* (San José, Costa Rica: Departmento Ecuménico de Investigaciones, 1985), pt. 4.

21. Frank Lentriccia, *Criticism and Social Change: With a Postcript by Kenneth Burke* (Chicago: University of Chicago Press, 1983), 1.

22. Ibid, 5.

23. Ibid., 33 (citing Burke's "Revolutionary Symbolism in America").

24. Ibid., 139.

25. Ibid., 163.

26. Hough and Cobb, *Christian Identity*, 71–72.

11

Protestant Theology and the Modern Ideal of Knowledge

I. A CHANGE IN THE SETTING OF THEOLOGY

During the past 250 years, much of Protestant Christian theology has taken place in the setting of the modern university. In the sixteenth and seventeenth centuries this was only partially the case. More important, however, is that the university in these centuries was itself an established arm of the church, and theological positions in these universities often were under explicit ecclesiastical authority. The development of the modern university drastically changed the role of the church for the university.

The latter sixteenth century and the century that followed produced the great confessional statements that embodied the doctrinal positions of various church bodies. The length of some of these confessions testifies to the theological reflection engaged in by these church movements in coming to an accepted understanding doctrinally. The chief yield of the seventeenth century in Protestant theology certainly resides in these confessional productions that represent church bodies. They well overshadow the work that was done then by individual thinkers of the era who usually also contributed to these confessional statements. Histories of thought that refer to these theological figures see them as church representatives; that is, they are Lutheran, Reformed, Anglican, and so on. This denominational church specification often goes quite far to indicate the kind of positions they take on most theological issues.

To recite this history even so briefly vividly underscores the difference of the present time in Europe and America from that era in theology. The modern university setting has come to dominate the pursuit of Protestant theological reflection. The most prominent figures almost invariably hold positions in university-related academic institutions; many who are aware of and study their works often do not know the church denominations to which these people belong. Church seminaries usually have courses of instruction that need to be approved by university-related organizations, and the faculty of these seminaries have qualified for their positions by advanced study at university centers for the study of religion and theology that are independent of religious denominations.[1]

It is to be expected that such a transformation of the situation of theology would also bring with it significant changes in the content of theology itself. The issues that became the focus of attention of theological minds were, indeed, strongly influenced by the environment of the university and, consequently, affected theological understanding throughout its scope. Changes in the history of theology, Protestant and otherwise, are not limited to the impact of a university setting; therefore, the problem of how to distinguish changes influenced by the university can become a challenge for an interpreter.

Nevertheless, one of the clearest changes is that of the ideal of knowledge. Certainly there has been no more far-reaching influence in the period of time from the seventeenth to the twentieth century than the advances in scientific knowledge, and the university was the institutional center for the dissemination of scientific thought. Theological discussion of "knowledge" was continually and increasingly affected by modern scientific views of how knowledge is attained.

The most famous view was the philosophy of Immanuel Kant in the late eighteenth century. Kant wanted to restrict the attribution of knowledge to natural science and mathematics because the procedures of these areas allowed public verification and progress. Ethical life, art, religion, philosophy itself and many other arenas stood outside the proper realm of knowledge because they are not amenable to such criteria. Kant was clear about the independent importance of these areas; indeed, he labored to show that they were rational. The title *Religion Within the Limits of Reason Alone* indicates that there is a positive relation of purified religion to human rationality. The compatibility of reason and religion properly understood, however, did not prevent religious matters from being beyond the pale of knowledge.

Now it is, of course, true that this feature of Kant's philosophy can be regarded as merely a definitional matter. If Kant and his followers want to restrict the word *knowledge* in this manner, then theology can utilize other words and linguistic circumlocutions to express the epistemological basis for its subject matter; this has been done by utilizing words such as *feeling, awareness, apprehension, intuition, acquaintance,* and the like. Kant's famous strictures against traditional arguments for the existence of God brought forth many advocates who availed themselves of such terminology in attempting to elaborate a theological discussion of the human mind's conviction of the reality of God.

Kant's philosophy was based in the university, and the theological attempt to respond to his contentions even on this linguistic level was performed by people who did this in the context of the university. However, the impact of modern scientific views on theology is not confined to the matter of the language utilized. We may use this Kantian atmosphere to point us to a further scrutiny of changes that have occurred in theological epistemology as a result of the university setting's mediating a new ideal of knowledge.

II. THE KNOWLEDGE OF GOD IN CALVIN'S *INSTITUTES*

Traditionally in Christian theology, the material discussed under the rubric of the knowledge of God dealt with considerations as to how one knows that God is real. These considerations included matters related both to the existence of God and to God's revealed nature. The discussion in this section focused on these epistemological issues, in contrast with the section on the doctrine of God, which usually elaborated more fully and "logically" God's attributes, triune being, creative act, providential rule, and in some cases a doctrine of predestination. It is in the topic of how one knows that God is real that changes in the ideal of knowledge resulting from the atmosphere of modern science can be seen.

An exceptionally useful book to indicate Protestant thinking on the knowledge of God prior to this ideal of knowledge is John

Calvin's *Institutes of the Christian Religion*. This work is commonly held to be the most influential text in the history of Protestant theology. Calvin's work lifts up the word and category of knowledge; indeed, the phrase "the knowledge of God" appears in the title of two of the four books that compose the *Institutes*. The famous opening sentences of the work say: "True and substantial wisdom consists principally of two parts: the knowledge of God and the knowledge of ourselves. But while these two branches of knowledge are so intimately connected, which of them precedes and produces the other is not easy to discover."[2] Insisting that the knowledge of God and the knowledge of ourselves are mutually implicated in one another, Calvin says that without the knowledge of self a human being cannot grasp God as the true source of power and the goal of fulfillment and happiness; yet without knowledge of God one cannot know the self as it actually is because a human being measures itself by standards that shed only a murky illumination. The standards of purity and perfection that allow us truly and deeply to understand ourselves represent an active and practical knowing of God. Recognition of God "consists more in living experience than in vain and high flown speculation."[3]

Noting the practical or, in more contemporary language, the existential nature of the knowledge of God, Calvin then turns to a sharp distinction for his entire discussion throughout the *Institutes*. There is a knowledge of God the Creator, and there is also a knowledge of God the Redeemer. This distinction serves to specify the very titles of the first two books of the *Institutes*: in doing so Calvin is quite representative of theological writing of the Protestant Reformation generally.

It is important to examine how Calvin understands that people come to this knowledge of God. In respect to knowledge of God the Creator, Calvin finds that there are three different ways of coming to the conviction of the Creator. The initial one that he raises in the *Institutes* is an immediate apprehension of the mind that is found in all peoples. It is a seed of religion that is part of the internal constitution of the human self. Calvin describes this recognition of God by such words as "inscribed," "implanted," and "engraved." Why else, Calvin asks, would human beings go to such ridiculous lengths in worshiping all kinds of low things—wood and stone, animals and monstrous representations—unless these people were inwardly driven by a relation to that exalted source of their nature, the creating God? Calvin is aware that many people strive to forget this immediate suggestion of their nature, but he holds that this furious attempt to repel God can never succeed, because this very sense of divinity is that which makes human beings higher than the animals.[4]

Following this immediate way of knowing God the Creator, Calvin takes up another way, one that is not inscribed in the depths of the soul but is "outside" in the universe visibly displayed. However, while this way of coming to a knowledge of God has an outer character in comparison with the inborn seed of religion, this does not mean that it is entirely outside of the human. Human being has a bodily nature and mental powers that operate with this body, these matters being in continuity with the wider world of which humanity is a part. There is a likeness to God imprinted upon the most beautiful forms of this universe, and God "daily discloses himself in the whole workmanship" evidenced there.[5] There are both aesthetic and inferential dimensions to this knowledge of God that comes from the fashioning of the world. Both dimensions are from the same marks of divine glory that appear in the order and harmonious structure of the universe. But clearly Calvin gives priority to the aesthetic dimension in his discussion. God's powers are represented as in a painting that thereby invites all people to the recognition of the divine being. The most untutored and ignorant persons can appropriate the spectacle of this marvelous theatre. Furthermore, the same order that flashes with the beauty of God's glory and evokes aesthetic response can also be scrutinized by human reason. The careful investigations performed by astronomy, medicine, and other sources provide empirical information that human reasoning uses to infer the divine author. The human body can be an especially illuminating subject in this regard. Besides its beauty, the articulation, symmetry, and function of the body is a composition testifying to the ingenuity of a wisdom that is divine. The various allocations of the ingredients of food digested by the body, enabling the several parts of it to function, for example, is an instance of what Calvin finds as striking evidence of God's skillful ordering.

A third way of knowing God the Creator in the *Institutes* is the testimony rendered by the human conscience and its knowledge of right and wrong. Despite its corruption by sin, something remains in this natural capability as a residue of humanity's original gifts. Through the importance of the moral distinction of what is good and to be followed from what is evil and to be avoided, the human is acquainted with the will of God. "Shall we, indeed, distinguish between right and wrong by that judgment which has been imparted to us, yet will there be no judge in heaven?"[6] Calvin interprets the Ten Commandments of the Old Testament as a vividly explicit statement of a law natural to the human self. The conscience is more obscure and wavering than the scriptural commandments, but respect for the neighbor is variously reflected in human relationships. The works that have regard for people are measured noetically by conscience in reference to God. Convicted by the witness of their own conscience, people can tremble before God's coming judgment. Therefore, along with the immediate sense of divinity and the apprehension of the beautifully fashioned order of the universe, the human conscience also testifies to the reality of God in Calvin's theology.

These three ways of coming to a knowledge of God the Creator are all marked by a serious deficiency: Calvin asserts that all of them are confused by sin. The persuasion of the reality of God that they evidence is still present in the sinful situation, indicated for Calvin by the fact the he finds illustrations for his three ways in writers such as Plato, Aratus, Cicero, and other classical figures who were not familiar with the Bible. As a result of sin, however, these ways of knowing do not bring human beings to their proper goal of salvation. The invasion of sin means that, if this destined goal is to be reached, a knowledge of God must come about that is different from that of knowing God the Creator. As already indicated, Calvin names this new persuasion the knowledge of God the Redeemer; he turns to the second book of the *Institutes* to discuss this subject. A representative statement of this distinction in knowledge is the following: "First in order came that kind of knowledge by which one is permitted to grasp who that God is who founded and governs the universe. Then that other inner knowledge was added, which alone quickens dead souls, whereby God is known not only as the Founder of the universe and the sole Author and ruler of all that is made, but also in the person of the Mediator as the Redeemer."[7] This passage clearly states that in reference to the Redeemer there is a distinct persuasion of God's reality in a new way. In this case, however, the knowing is not only a different way for knowing the same Creator, as had been the case with the first three ways previously discussed, but in this instance the knowing brings human beings acquaintance with a different characterization of the reality of God. By the activity that brings the Mediator, Jesus Christ, one becomes convinced of the actuality of God that is different from the knowledge of the Creator. This knowing takes place in the context of sin's being overcome in some fashion by the fact that souls dead in sin are thereby quickened.

The topic of redemption indicates the place of the Bible, because through the illumination of God's Spirit spectacles of Scripture are provided for human beings to learn of the person of the mediator, as well as to confirm and reveal more fully to them knowledge of God the Creator. Out of the freedom of God's love, or favor, or mercy (Calvin interchanges the terms), God becomes present to humanity in Jesus Christ and the Holy Spirit as Redeemer. Calvin underscores again and again the unmerited grace of this bestowal by God, that it is a gift. One cannot "become wise in God's mysteries except by his gift" because the mysteries of redemption are hidden from human insight.[8] Knowledge of God the Redeemer which comes through Scripture's witness to Christ is not confined to the New Testament. The Old Testament also has resulted from God's descending to the human out of God's free mercy. The inclusion of the Old Testament with the New in this respect is a major concern of Calvin; the second book of the *Institutes*, which deals with knowledge of the Redeemer, contains a lengthy analysis of the continuity and interrelationships of the two testaments. It is the one story presented in the Bible that carries the message of redemption: "The original adoption of the chosen people depended upon the Mediator's grace."[9] The Mediator refers to the eternal Son of God or *Logos*, which exercises God's activity towards us and becomes incarnate in Christ. God's coming redemptively near to the human is always an office of the Mediator, and so the Mediator already is active in the Old Testament. Calvin is not unmindful of many differences between the testaments; we shall not follow his discussion here, but his major point is that God's merciful coming near to human beings is the foundation of both testaments throughout the variety of situations and emphases they contain.

This merciful and free coming near is the major element in Calvin's account of knowledge of God the Redeemer. But Calvin makes a distinction between this free coming in merciful love and another feature of redemption. In order for the human being who stands under the curse and wrath of God because of sin to know God as Redeemer, something else is involved. Along with God's coming near: "The second requirement of our reconciliation with God was this: that man, who by his disobedience had become lost, should by way of remedy counter it with obedience, satisfy God's judgment, and pay the penalties for sin."[10] It is important to note that it is the human who is to provide the remedy: Jesus Christ performs the necessary obedience.

Calvin draws out the distinction between God's free mercy and the satisfaction of the curse and wrath of God in the following manner. Suppose, he says, that persons come to realize that they are sinners and will end up in destruction. They are then told that God voluntarily was gracious toward them out of God's free favor and had delivered them. Such persons "will surely experience and feel something" of God's mercy as the Redeemer, but assurance is lacking. A message of God's free favor alone would present a truncated view of the Redeemer. The needed power to deal with sin is missing. The implication is that apprehension of God's free favor alone can throw a person into contradiction. On the one hand, one is impressed with one's sinful situation—one's conscience leads one to see the curse of God blocking one's path wherever one turns—yet, on the other hand, one is told that one stands in God's free favor. The latter seems to say that one does not really stand under wrath, that what one's conscience tells one is a misperception. Calvin, therefore, elaborates this further requirement by holding that, for one captive under the yoke of sin and the slave of Satan, Christ intercedes as the person's advocate and suffers the punishment that threatens all the sinful because of God's righteous judgment. The assurance of peace with God comes with this depiction of Christ's death because it is there that Christ's obedience is finally effective. Being persuaded of God the Redeemer involves a penetration into the crucifixion.

Because the righteous judgment of God hangs over the death which stands between human beings and their final fulfillment, the representative obedience of Jesus Christ must fight through the awful power of death. In so doing, Christ takes the curse upon himself and thereby crushes, breaks, and scatters its whole force, thereby reaching the goal of victory in the resurrection. The resurrection also enlivens all who in faith receive its efficacy. Knowing God the Redeemer in respect to the representative death of Christ and his breaking the curse of God involves a participation in that death. One feels the cost undergone by the Son of God so that his death "mortifies our earthly members," killing the old man in us, and produces a vivification that corresponds to the benefit of the resurrection's liberation from death. Faith by its very nature looks to a future immortality, but it is not a bare hope, because life-giving righteousness has already been imparted by the death of Christ. Speaking of mortification and vivification, Calvin says: "Both things happen to us by participation in Christ"; mortification includes the dread resulting from the awareness of divine judgment, of being stricken and overthrown, the result being discouragement and despair.[11] Newness of life comes about because Christ imparts strength to believers and quickens them to new spiritual life.[12]

Calvin's account of knowledge of God the Redeemer, then, includes the recognition of both the gift of God's free coming near out of merciful love and the participatory appropriation of Christ's representative death. This indicates that there is a certain complexity about knowledge of the Redeemer. It would not be correct to say that we have independent ways of knowing the reality of God here such as we have examined concerning knowledge of God the Creator. Nevertheless, there is a significant differentiation that cannot be erased or collapsed without misrepresenting this knowledge. There are two elements involved in the one way of knowing the Redeemer, according to Calvin.

When we step back and survey Calvin's discussion of the knowledge of God, we find many distinctions. There is a fundamental contrast between knowing the Creator and knowing the Redeemer, and each of these types of knowledge contains a plural number of ways and elements. The knowledge of God is complex in Calvin's *Institutes*. This does not mean knowing is difficult; rather, it means that a human being is persuaded by a plethora of axes to take account of God. Calvin says of this varied manifestation that "so many burning lamps shine for us." It is instructive to see what happens to all these lamps in later Protestant theology and its reflection of a new understanding of knowledge.

III. THE KNOWLEDGE OF GOD IN MODERN THEOLOGY

The Reformation tradition, of which Calvin is so eloquent a representative, largely defined the treatment of the knowledge of the reality of God in Protestant theology until nearly the beginning of the eighteenth century. At this time theological writers appeared who began to recast the discussion of theological epistemology in a quite substantial manner. The first major shift came through the explicit influence of the emphasis on rationality and science that gained such impressive dominance in many areas of intellectual endeavor at the close of the seventeenth century. The development of scientific knowledge that was transpiring at the time brought with it an emphasis in theology on the understanding that Calvin had named knowledge of God the Creator as derived from the fashioning of the universe.

An especially impressive treatment of this type can be found in the writings of Samuel Clarke (1675–1729) in England. Clarke was an Anglican clergyman and pastor, but he gained wide intellectual attention as an able exponent and interpreter of the scientific views of the universe produced by Isaac Newton. Newton was a university-based thinker at Cambridge, and Clarke is most often remembered now for his correspondence with the philosopher Leibniz in which scientific cosmology was debated. Clarke defended Newton's ideas in these letters. In the eighteenth century, however, it was Clarke's theological works of 1705 and 1706 that brought widespread attention to his work. His books in those years, titled *A Demonstration of the Being and Attributes of God* and *A Discourse Concerning the Unchangeable Obligations of Natural Religion, and the Truth and Certainty of the Christian Revelation*, present the most substantial explanation of the knowledge of God under the aegis of the advances in science. He defined the discussion of the subject for three-quarters of a century in England, as well as influencing French thinkers such as Voltaire.

In the first book cited, the *Demonstration*, Clarke says that his aim is to establish that the atheists do not have reason on their side, "when they would have it be thought, that in the fabric of the world God has left himself wholly without witness."[13] Clarke contends that, quite the contrary, reason can show that God is indeed manifested in the structure of the world. He says that he wants to follow an *a priori* method in his demonstration, but his procedure has very little to do with the manner in which this phrase is now used. He means by *a priori* reasoning an inference from the continuous progression of dependent beings around us that none of them is necessary, having its ground of existence in itself; consequently, the totality of such dependent beings cannot be necessary either. There must be an original cause that has always existed and is, therefore, self-existent. We, therefore, can rationally infer that such a cause is everlasting and that it is not limited but infinite.

Up to this point, Clarke's method is a version of rational inference from cosmological contingency and sounds generally like the method familiar to scholastic thought of the Middle Ages. Clarke takes a different turn here, however, because the atheists, he thinks, agree that a self-existent cause of dependent beings exists, but they interpret it as a principle that is not an intelligent being. For Clarke, the intelligence of this being is what is really at issue. The metaphysical context of the discussion is established by questions of dependence and self-existence, eternal duration and infinity, but the real question at issue must be decided by *a posteriori* arguments, which derive from the observation of experience. Particular beings in the world must be proved to be the effects of an intelligent and knowing cause.[14] Scrutiny of the fabric of the world indicates the variety, order, beauty, and impressive contrivance of all things in the world to their respective ends. Clarke often refers to these characteristics as the "fitness in the relations of things." The intelligent design of the order of the world was widely explored in England during the eighteenth century, and Clarke takes it as virtually self-evident for people of his day. The operation of the eye in human beings and animals, the disposition of the astronomical bodies, fruits and flowers, the arrangement of the leaves of plants, the courage of birds in defending their nests, the instinct of insects and animals, and a wealth of other matters illustrate the contrivance that rationally calls for a divine architect and engineer as its explanation.

A special aspect of the evidence that calls for the intelligence of the original cause of the world is the inexplicable production of organic life from the inorganic realm. New advances in science confirm that inorganic powers have no means of accounting for this higher level.[15] Furthermore, the intelligent powers in humans indicate that it is eminently more reasonable that the cause of dependent beings itself possess this capacity, than that such an effect could result from a cause that lacks intelligence. This is the crucial step in the point of contention with the atheists.

Clarke moves on to examine how the fitness in the relations of things differs from necessity and thus calls for freedom in the intelligent cause. On the basis of this freedom Clarke comes to infinite power, then attempts to show that what we require of goodness results from the order of the relations of things in the world. It becomes clear as Clarke proceeds in the *Demonstration* that everything that is affirmed about God can be ascertained from the constitution, order, and harmony of the universe, including infinite goodness and "all the other moral attributes." Scriptural revelation conveys the same content that Clarke has rationally demonstrated. Jesus Christ presents this truth of God in a manner that Clarke says is suited for people of every capacity and understanding.[16] Calvin had insisted that knowledge of God the Redeemer came about because a new manifestation of God was needed in the context of human sinfulness, and that there was more than one way in which God is known as Creator. But in Clarke's thought, all of Calvin's "burning lamps" have become one great searchlight. All aspects of the knowledge of God have a single source in the rational inference from the order of the world.

The knowledge of God the Creator was not discerned alone from the beautiful harmony of the world in Calvin's *Institutes*.

Later in the eighteenth century a thinker appeared who followed a different route from Clarke's in coming to the conviction of the actuality of God. Immanuel Kant is one of the greatest names in the history of philosophy. Although he was not a Christian theologian by the canons of his own day, he cannot be omitted here because he has had more influence on the subject of Protestant theology's reflection on the knowledge of God than any other single modern thinker. Kant set the issues and sometimes provided the answer for much theology on our subject. By the end of the nineteenth century he had earned the name, "the philosopher of Protestantism." Kant's philosophy of religion is an interpretation of Christianity and he himself espoused a properly "enlightened" faith.

Kant is a proponent of the apprehension of God the Creator that comes through a human being's moral conscience. His position on epistemological matters concerning natural theology are so well known that I will not outline them here. After indicating in his critique of the limits of theoretical reason that the idea of the existence of a perfect being is illegitimately presupposed in ontological and cosmological arguments for God, Kant took up the question of the knowledge of God from the actual character of the world, referred to by him as the physico-theological proof. Clarke's consideration of the structure and order of the universe as pointing to God would be called physico-theology by Kant. After indicating that this kind of argument for God is the oldest kind and is in most accord with the common sense of humanity, so that it would be pointless to attempt to diminish its authority, Kant offers a critique that has been used to do just that. He says that an influence of God from the order of the world actually presupposes the existence of the idea of a perfect being of the already negated ontological and cosmological arguments. In making this point, something quite significant about Kant is disclosed. The reason that the physico-theological argument rests upon the cosmological argument from the contingency of the world is that the harmony of the world only calls for an architect who is limited by the adaptability of his materials. Such a God might be very great and powerful and be admired for his wisdom, but that is not what we mean by "God" in theology, Kant states.[17]

It is quite clear in this passage from the *Critique of Pure Reason* that Kant has his idea of God and that God must be the necessary being who is metaphysically perfect. Because the physico-theological approach works with the empirical and determinate

structure of the world, it cannot establish the contingency of matter itself; rather, it assumes matter as already given. It cannot,
therefore, speak fully of God as Creator. While Kant is probably
right in this assertion, the momentous conclusion that Kant draws
is that, because the physico-theological procedure cannot accomplish the above, it does not give access to the knowledge of God at
all. The way to the knowledge of God is an all-or-nothing matter.
The order and harmony of the world do not provide any basis for
theology.[18]

A conviction of the reality of God must come from a way of
apprehension that can entirely account for God as the Creator and
perfect being. Kant's famous discussion finds this in the area of
practical reason. The consciousness of moral obligation brings human beings in touch with that which transcends the phenomenal
appearances of things in the world. Moral duty reveals the freedom
of the self in the practical realm and points to the rational postulation of a Creator who unites the worldly separation of virtue and
happiness. God is implicitly affirmed in a moral human being's
recognition that the moral law is the touchstone of reality. There
is a practical conviction or persuasion of the actuality of God by
means of moral duty for Kant, and this is the only way in which
human beings can come to the full understanding of God that is
epistemologically required for theology. Kant develops his view
here so that everything in religious faith is assimilated to moral
duty.[19] Kant may disagree sharply with Samuel Clarke on how
God is known, but he likewise tries to have only one of Calvin's
lamps furnish all the light for the knowledge of God.

As we have seen, knowledge of God the Creator in the *Institutes* comes not only through the fashioned order of the external
world and the moral testimony of conscience, but also in that seed
of religion that Calvin refers to as the sense of divinity. Friedrich
Schleiermacher's *Speeches On Religion* and his *magnum opus*,
twenty-two years later, *The Christian Faith*, clearly are in line
with this way of understanding the knowledge of God. Despite the
fact that the two books were produced for diverse audiences and
that Schleiermacher's account of the seed of religion is articulated
in widely divergent styles and terminology, there is a basic view
common to both.

In the *Speeches On Religion* Schleiermacher offers a polemic
against the types of approaches that we have reviewed in the writings of Clarke and Kant. Elaborate inferences from scientific in-
spection of the world and subjugation of religion to the realm of

moral conduct do not do justice to what religion is. Religion has its own province in the human spirit and cannot be made the appendage of other faculties and interests. Like Calvin's sense of divinity, the foundation of religion for Schleiermacher is something immediate.

While Schleiermacher modified certain aspects of his account of religion from 1799 to 1821, this immediacy is a point on which he never wavered. That with which religion has to do is so "close" to us that it resists theoretical observation or being made into a postulation of free activity. Discursive thought and moral doing operate in the world of division into subject and object, whereas religion has an "earlier" home, prior to this division. This prior realm is made known to people through intuition and feeling. The unity of the self as thinking and acting resides in this intuitive feeling. A person is convinced by this feeling that one is the same self in both knowing and doing. Religion has to do with the wholeness and unity of the self. That is its peculiar province. But the self's presence to itself is felt in a particular fashion that contrasts with relative modifications and reciprocal activities in which the self is engaged with the world around it. The self exercises some freedom in its acting upon things of the world, just as the self is partially and relatively dependent upon this world. This reciprocal situation makes one feel the contrast with the unity of the self, a feeling of contrast that is unqualified or sheer in its tonality. Schleiermacher says that this sheer feeling cannot be that of freedom, because then one would be simply bringing oneself and the self's world into being. Rather, the feeling is one of sheer, unqualified dependence. This feeling embraces the entire horizon of the self in all aspects of living. It includes the relative freedom and relative dependence of engagement with the world. Without the reciprocity of relative freedom and dependence, one would not be able to differentiate the sheer feeling of dependence from relative dependence upon the world.[20] But because the self is free, the source of this sheer dependence cannot be the world; rather this religious feeling is that of being in relation to God, the "whence" of the self's unity. The vitality of this feeling measures how religious a person is.

Schleiermacher is, of course, aware that not all people recognize this religious feeling. Still, he maintains, such an immediate self-consciousness is present in all persons, however minimal and imperceptible it may be in some cases. When religious intuitive feeling is minimal, then it lacks strength in a person's self-consciousness. But when the intuitive feeling does relate with strength to the self's reciprocity with the world, then persuasion of the reality of God is present.

Schleiermacher rejects any inference to God from the external universe, and he does not treat moral conscience as delivering an apprehension of God. Furthermore, the sinfulness of humanity takes on the character of an unfinished creation, so that redemption is the completion of creation. The free mercy of God is not appropriate language to use in theology because in the human sphere it is always used for a feeling evoked by the plight of others. Schleiermacher has no knowledge of a new departure by God that would call for such language.[21] Schleiermacher, like Samuel Clarke and Kant before him, has taken one of Calvin's lamps and relied upon that single source for the apprehension of God.

Twentieth-century Protestant theology has been marked by some leading theologians who have given thoroughgoing attention to issues in theological epistemology. The category of revelation received considerable emphasis and redefinition. It is generally agreed that Karl Barth has been the most influential theologian of this century, and no one has explored the import of revelation more thoroughly than he has. Barth attacked much of eighteenth- and nineteenth-century theology because it attempted to place God at the disposal of human beings.[22]

The reason behind this charge is that Barth's focus is on the way of knowing God that Calvin depicted as knowledge of God the Redeemer. The new departure comes from God's free favor and love. The majesty of God can only be known when God condescends to come near to human beings. Revelation means that human knowledge follows God's free choosing to be known. Anything that is known solely by means of human finite powers could not be God. God always has the initiative in relation to the world, and the human knowing of God is no exception.[23]

Barth's thought agrees with Calvin's "knowledge of God the Redeemer" by seeing this cognizance as identical with the name of Jesus Christ. God meets us as one of ourselves in the nearness of a human form.[24] Jesus Christ is the concrete embodiment of God's free coming to the human and the only way God can be known.[25] The knowledge of God takes the form of acknowledgment, that is, the recognition of something beyond us. The essential point is that knowledge of God does not reside in anything inherent in the human itself. Rather, it recognizes the divine choice.

The ways of knowing God the Creator as elaborated by Clarke, Kant, and Schleiermacher sharply contrast with the recognition of God in Barth, but he, nevertheless, has one basic agreement with them. He also has taken one of Calvin's ways of apprehending God and insisted that this way is the only access to God. This lamp sheds a redemptive light, but it still shines all alone.

Calvin had insisted that there are two elements in the knowledge of God the Redeemer: God's coming near to the human out of free mercy and love, and the meritorious obedience of Jesus Christ, which pays for the penalties of sin. The latter element is required to address the self-interpretation of the person standing under the curse of God and all that that entailed, but this second element of knowing does not appear in Barth's account of the knowledge of God's free love. Of course, Barth discourses at length on the obedience of Jesus Christ, but he cannot include the complexity of this knowledge of redemption as described by Calvin; to do so would involve the recognition of a noetic relationship to the Creator prior to the knowledge of God's free grace. Barth has continued Calvin's knowledge of God the Redeemer but without the access to the Creator as a different source.

One Protestant theologian who has written powerfully on the self-interpretation of the person faced with the message of the crucifixion of Jesus Christ is Rudolf Bultmann. Originally a part of the same general theological movement as Barth, Bultmann eventually came to be seen as the great alternative to Barth's resolute neglect of matters dealing with existential questions of the person who is outside of faith. Like Barth, however, he focuses entirely on God the Redeemer in theological knowledge. The Cross of Christ is the sole revelation of God to the world. Unlike Barth, Bultmann is concerned to overcome the falsely objectivizing and sometimes mythological language that has attended Christian interpretations of the Cross.

The fact that proclamation of the Cross of Christ can be understood by a person who encounters it shows that the person had a preunderstanding of that which the proclamation can bestow.[26] The self already had an orientation to what authentic life and fulfillment would be. Consequently, Bultmann can write quite tellingly of human powerlessness that speaks of a divine power, of the demands of the good on the conscience (which make one guilty), and of the future's impingement on the past, giving rise to the question of God's otherness and eternity.[27] But these things do not mediate any valid conviction of the true God, "for God is accessible only to faith responsive to revelation."[28] Revelation is found in the proclamation of the Cross of Christ. Outside of this proclamation people can only speak of the idea of God. They do not encounter God. Faith rejects the idea that God is revealed everywhere in religious people.[29] Christian faith in the revelation of God in Christ "asserts that only on the basis of this revelation does man have a knowledge of God which is not just about *man*, thus involving a *concept* of God, but is about God *himself.*"[30]

Bultmann's use of the idea of God that is important as a pre-understanding is filled with rich reflections for theological epistemology. But he sees such existential probing merely as human questioning, not as material by which one can truly know that God is real. God actually comes to the human in only one way, the proclamation of the Cross of Christ. Bultmann says that he has carried through to its logical conclusion in the field of religious epistemology the Reformation doctrine of justification by faith alone apart from the works of the law.[31] Again, we have a theological leader in Protestant theology who maintains that there is only one way of coming to the knowledge of God.

IV. THE MODERN IDEAL OF KNOWLEDGE

When one surveys the diversity that has marked modern Protestant theology and the several ways in which many leading figures from 1700 to the recent past have held that Christian knowledge of God takes place, there is one very evident observation to be drawn. Clarke, Kant, Schleiermacher, Barth, and Bultmann all continue ways and elements in terms of which Calvin discusses the apprehension of God, but whereas the sixteenth-century theologian combined these approaches in his theological epistemology, the later thinkers each pursue one of Calvin's ways as the only manner in which God is known by human beings. These writers are not merely arbitrarily selected figures, because they have had enormous influence and have been fountainheads of major streams of thought. Certainly there have been important views of this subject that do not agree with their positions. Nevertheless, their influence has been so extensive that the feature of their discussions of the knowledge of God that is held in common indicates a major impetus in modern Protestant theology. They illustrate a pattern that suggests that they all have appropriated an ideal of knowledge that contrasts with that present in pre-eighteenth-century Protestant theology. This pattern reflects an ideal of knowledge that insists that such knowing occurs in a single manner. Only one standpoint or axis of apprehension is valid for the way in which God is known. It has long been a conviction of Judaism and Christianity that God is one. But the modern Protestant theological mind has the powerful tendency to conclude further that the *knowing* of God must also be single.

Along with the increased attention to epistemological matters that modern scientific views pressed upon theological thought, the new ideal of knowledge operating in modern science is a leading candidate for this change that contends for singleness in epistemology. The latter seventeenth century was the scene of a most decisive advance in modern scientific interpretation. The category of lawfulness for the behavior of observed facts quickly became established as a defining feature of scientific knowledge. The work of Isaac Newton with its contention of general lawfulness stands as one of the famous expressions of the new way of thought. Immensely important for the formulation of laws adequate to the investigated phenomena was the canon known as Occam's razor. This famous principle contended for simplicity in interpretation. If there are competing theories that can cover the necessary causes and facts, the one that makes the least elaborate assumptions is to be preferred.[32] For instance, in the rise of the Copernican theory of the universe in the sixteenth century, historians of science indicate that it was not primarily the empirical observations that led to the displacement of the Ptolemaic theory. These observations could also be accounted for by the older interpretation. But the Copernican theory came to be accepted because of its pervading *simplicity*, and this simplicity came to be a formal feature of modern scientific theories.[33] Newton explicitly states this idea: "Nature is pleased with simplicity, and affects not the pomp of superfluous causes."[34]

Abraham Maslow contends that the resulting notion is that "scientific work has two directions or poles or goals: one is toward utter simplicity and condensation, the other toward total comprehensiveness and inclusiveness."[35] While the original formulations and applications of inclusive simplicity were in the fields of natural science, the ideal for knowledge that resulted carried over into other areas of thought. A new ideal of systematic unity resulted for intellectual matters in general. This systematic unity often became a goal for Protestant theology in its university setting. The ideal of inclusive simplicity does not appear to have been a consideration for John Calvin, but by the time of Samuel Clarke and that of Immanuel Kant in the eighteenth century, this new form of intellectual thought is certainly operative. The requirements of systematic unity have attained a new hegemony under the influence of what Maslow calls the "simpleward" direction of interpretation.[36] I contend that the feature of inclusive simplicity that arose in modern science has been a factor in the shape that the theological interpretation of the knowledge of God has taken in the modern era. A systematic presentation in theology of matters dealing with the knowledge of God has been guided by an epistemological ideal shaped by the influence of simplicity. Multifarious causes and ways of knowing have been reduced in the simpleward direction.

Protestant theology has not been the only recipient of such an influence. This influence has been part of an atmosphere that the modern university communicated generally. For theology, however, the change to the modern university setting has been an ambiguous factor. The ideal of simplicity often evoked careful attention to epistemological reflection, and that has meant a considerable gain in the understanding related to the life of faith. In this respect the university setting has been stimulating. Yet in appropriating an ideal of knowledge that is shaped by simplicity in such a manner that only one standpoint or axis of apprehension is valid for the way God is known, I think theology has been unfortunately affected. Comprehensive and systematic unity may not have to lead to the insistence that God is known in only one way, but this simpleward indication of the ideal of knowledge of the era of modern science has often had such a result.

In respect to this issue, the theology of Calvin as found in the *Institutes of the Christian Religion* can be instructive. The human epistemological position in relation to God was plurally defined rather than being single. Calvin elaborated different ways of the knowledge of God, and he held that these ways are mutually supportive and illuminating. He did not find it necessary to elevate any of them to being the true way that is exclusive of all other ways. The knowledge of God in the *Institutes* rests upon distinct manifestations of God which present different aspects of the one God. I hold that Calvin is right in contending that the knowing of God is multifarious, and that Clarke, Kant, Schleiermacher, Barth, and Bultmann are wrong in their epistemology of a single access that is exclusive of others. The point is not that Calvin's discussion exhausts the possibilities of understanding the ways that God may be known, but the principle reflected in his theology is that one may be convinced of the reality of God from a number of standpoints, and that what is manifested about God along one axis of experience can take a significantly different form from that of another axis. Certainly, modern theological thought cannot merely repeat the theology of John Calvin, but it can learn from such past thinkers instructive principles that may guide theological thinking in the present, even in the context of the modern university.

NOTES

1. These general remarks do not attempt to specify important variances between Europe and America due to different political traditions regarding church and state.

2. John Calvin, *Institutes of the Christian Religion*, ed. J. T. McNeil, trans. F. L. Battles (Philadelphia: Westminster, 1960), I, i, 1.

3. Ibid., I, x, 2.

4. Ibid., I, iii, 3.

5. Ibid., I, v, 1.

6. Ibid., I, v, 5.

7. Ibid., I, vi, 1.

8. Ibid. II, ii, 20.

9. Ibid., II, vi, 2.

10. Ibid., II, xii, 3.

11. Ibid., III, xii, 3 and 9.

12. Ibid., II, xvi, 16.

13. Samuel Clarke, *A Demonstration of the Being and Attributes of God* (Stuttgart–Bad Cannstatt: Friedrich Frommen, 1964), 260.

14. Ibid., 103.

15. Ibid., 120.

16. Ibid., 264.

17. Immanuel Kant, *Critique of Pure Reason*, trans. N. K. Smith (London: Macmillan, 1933), 522.

18. Ibid., 523.

19. See Immanuel Kant, *Religion within the Limits of Reason Alone* (New York: Harper, 1960). A more extended discussion of Kant and some of the other figures considered here may be found in my "The Knowledge of the Existence of God," *Dialogue & Alliance* I/1 (1987): 27–40.

20. Friedrich Schleiermacher, *The Christian Faith*, ed. H. R. Mackintosh (Edinburgh: T. & T. Clark, 1928), no. 3, 4, 32, 33.

21. Ibid., no. 85, 1.

22. Karl Barth, *Theology and Church* (New York: Harper & Row, 1962), 202.

23. Karl Barth, *Church Dogmatics* (Edinburgh: T. & T. Clark, 1957), II, 1: 21.

24. *Revelation*, ed. J. Baillie and H. Martin (London: Faber & Faber, 1937), 53.

25. Ibid., 55.

26. Rudolf Bultmann, *Faith and Understanding* (New York: Harper & Row, 1969), 315.

27. Rudolf Bultmann, *Essays Philosophical and Theological* (London: SCM, 1955), 92–97.

28. *Faith and Understanding*, 322.

29. Ibid., 318.

30. *Essays*, 98.

31. *Kerygma and Myth*, ed. H. W. Bartsch (New York: Harper, 1961), 210–11.

32. William M. O'Neil, *Fact and Theory: An Aspect of the Philosophy of Science* (Sydney, Australia: Sydney University Press, 1969), 68; Abraham Maslow, *The Psychology of Science* (New York: Harper & Row, 1966), 93.

33. Henry Margenau, *The Nature of Physical Reality* (New York: McGraw-Hill, 1950), 13; Hans Reichenbach, *Modern Philosophy of Science* (London: Routledge & Kegan Paul, 1959), 123.

34. Isaac Newton, *Mathematical Principles*, trans. F. Cajori (Cambridge: Cambridge University Press, 1934), 398.

35. Maslow, *The Psychology of Science*, 72.

36. Ibid., 101.

IV. APPENDICES

Appendix A

John B. Cobb, Jr.:
A Theological Biography

"Creative transformation" has become the
central notion in the thought of John Cobb. His
own spiritual-intellectual journey can itself be
described as a series of transformations.

GEORGIA PIETISM

John Cobb's parents, John and Theodora, both grew up in
Georgia. They met in the Student Volunteer Movement before
World War I, then went to Japan as missionaries in 1919, where
they served, except during World War II, until 1965. John, Jr., the
youngest of three children, was born February 9, 1925. Except for
returning to Georgia at ages six and fourteen when his parents had
furloughs, he lived in Japan, mainly in Hiroshima and Kobe, until
1940, when all unessential Americans were encouraged to leave.
(He was attending a Canadian school, and Canada was already at
war with Germany, Japan's ally.) Young John, then fifteen, returned
to Georgia to live with his grandmother, finished high school, and
attended a junior college, Emory at Oxford.

Throughout this period, Cobb lived in terms of the Georgia
Protestant pietism he had imbibed with his mother's milk. Feeling
like an outsider in both Japan and Georgia, he experienced his main
sense of community, beyond his family, with God, with whom it

seemed natural to converse. In junior college days, his pietism involved an extremely ascetic dimension; for example, money that might have been spent on candy or bus fare was sent to a mission for lepers in the Sudan. His pietism also contributed to strong moral convictions; he brought blacks to his Georgia church and publicly countered the lies in the anti-Japanese propaganda after Pearl Harbor. The negative effect that his pietistic moralism had on others is suggested in a cartoon in the college annual picturing John with a halo around his head and several more dangling from his arm. It was titled "Spares." He muses: "That my sanctity was only skin deep was illustrated by the rage I felt and expressed at this cartoon—which I must admit was one of the funniest in the annual."

TRANSITION TO MODERNITY

A transitional period began with Cobb's decision, before he had finished junior college and after he had pondered pacifism, to join the United States Army in 1944. Because of his background, he was chosen for the Japanese language program, which was filled mainly with academic-minded Jews and Irish Catholics. For the first time he was in the company of intellectuals, and he became aware of the relativity of his own worldview, learning that others regarded Georgia Protestantism as a phenomenon of interest sociologically but not intellectually. Cobb began an avid reading program which exposed him to the intellectual world of the twentieth century, but this exposure did not undermine his faith, which had rested upon personal experience, not upon fundamentalist convictions.

The one clearly extraordinary experience Cobb has had occurred during this period: "One night I knelt beside my bed for prayer in the most perfunctory way, when suddenly the room seemed filled with a presence of the most blessed sort. For a few brief moments I experienced what I can only describe as joy. It passed, I said thank you, and went to bed." He contrasts this experience with another, when he came to the realization that he preferred to go not into government foreign service but into some kind of Christian ministry. Although this "calling experience" had a suddenness and a clarity about it, he can accept a thoroughly psychological explanation of it. But that experience of blessed presence during prayer "simply gave itself to be understood as the presence of God and as a gift totally disconnected from expectation, merit, or anything else in my own life." This experience is germane to his ongoing ambivalence about the desirability, as well as the reality, of personal immortality: "If it were not for that event, I could only regard literally everlasting life as a curse, but if such life partook of that quality, it would be unmitigated blessing." Coming as it did shortly before Cobb's Chicago years, this experience could perhaps be interpreted as a proleptic confirmation that there was *something* to his pietistic faith—which was about to be demolished.

THE DESTRUCTION OF FAITH

The intellectual stimulation and advice he had received from his army friends led Cobb to enroll in the University of Chicago. He chose an interdepartmental program in which he could study all the objections to Christianity produced by the modern world. He describes the motivation and the effect: "I was determined to expose my faith to the worst the world could offer. Within six months of such exposure my faith was shattered." This shattering was not due to particular *arguments*. Rather, "the vision, perspective, or frame of reference of the modern sensibility simply altered my own vision of reality." This interpretation, from about 1965, reflects two motifs of Cobb's first period of reconstruction: (1) Christian faith has to do centrally with a preconceptual perspective, or "vision of reality," and (2) the distinctively "modern" vision of reality is incompatible with Christian faith.

A central effect of this shattering of faith was upon his prayer life, previously his mainstay: "God, who had been my constant companion and Lord up to that point, simply evaporated, and my prayers bounced back from the ceiling unheard." Even after Cobb's faith had returned intellectually, the previous naturalness of prayer did not. Because of his honesty about his struggle with prayer, many people have found his later writing on the subject refreshingly authentic.[1]

Since Cobb's sense of community and self-identity had primarily involved his relationship to God, the loss of belief was far from a merely intellectual matter. He has always felt kinship with those persons, such as Friedrich Nietzsche and Thomas J. J. Altizer, who portray the "death of God" as a catastrophic event.

A CONTEXT FOR RECONSTRUCTION

After a year, deciding that he needed to turn to some affirmative religious study at the same level of sophistication as the negative study he had been undertaking, Cobb entered the University of Chicago Divinity School:

> My occasional prior contacts with members of its faculty, chiefly Joachim Wach and James Luther Adams, had assured me that they had taken account somehow of the problems that had destroyed my faith, and though I was quite unable to see how, it seemed that I should expose myself to what they had to say.

Again, openness led to transformation, this time a constructive one.

A major influence on him during his divinity school days was Richard McKeon of the philosophy department, who led him to philosophical relativism. He was persuaded by McKeon that numerous systems are each capable of handling the range of philosophical problems quite well from their particular perspectives and that "almost all serious criticisms of major thought-systems are primarily a function of approaching those thought-systems with alien presuppositions."

The other major intellectual influence upon Cobb was Charles Hartshorne. Cobb says, "It was through his teaching that I was once again able to take the idea of God seriously." Hartshorne introduced him to the thought of Whitehead, and a Hartshornean Whiteheadianism has cohabited with philosophic relativism in Cobb's mind ever since.

Cobb was able to begin reconstructing his faith in the context of the divinity school community, which was the first to which he really felt he belonged. In retrospect he sees many weaknesses in his education there. For example, there was little exposure to the new ideas from the Continent (this was 1947–50). But it was a "serious community of inquiry in which," Cobb says, "I felt all possible encouragement to think honestly and clearly and independently. I would not trade that for the finest scholarship, although I greatly admire and envy in others a scholarship I do not share." In this period, "Questions of professional preparation receded far into the background, for I was preoccupied with questions of belief for myself."

Cobb's intellectual reconstruction of faith can be described in terms of several stages. Of course, these stages do not signify abrupt beginnings and endings. Each period of dominant interest usually overlapped the previous one by several years. Also, in most respects, each new understanding of what Christian faith and theology should be in our time did not mean a rejection of the previous phase so much as a relativizing of it.

CHRISTIAN NATURAL THEOLOGY

The first person to bring Whitehead's thought to Chicago was Henry Nelson Wieman. Wieman increasingly favored a strictly "empirical theology" free from all dependence upon dubious speculation, and he tended to stress only that side of Whitehead's thought, whereas Hartshorne stressed the metaphysical side. Confronted with these opposing emphases, Cobb read Whitehead for himself and saw that Hartshorne's stance was closer to Whitehead's own.

The systematic issue still remained: Can faith, and hence theology, do without philosophical speculation? Cobb's doctoral dissertation, titled "The Independence of Christian Faith from Speculative Belief," dealt with Wieman, Schleiermacher, and Tillich, who in various ways argued for such independence. Cobb contended, by means of internal criticism, that such independence is an impossible ideal and that it would accordingly be best to make one's speculations explicit, so that they could be criticized. This relationship between faith and speculative philosophy remained his central concern until the late sixties.

Cobb had to rush through his work at Chicago in order to return to Georgia to take care of his older brother. By returning to Georgia he enabled his mother to return to Japan. Having to take whatever position he could find close to Atlanta, Cobb served seven mountain churches and taught in a junior college. Following his dissertation examination in 1952 (after which Hartshorne said, "He's one smart cookie"), he took a job that Ernest Colwell, former president of the University of Chicago and then vice-president at Emory, had arranged with the outgoing dean of the School of Theology there. Since the faculty in systematic theology had not been consulted and was additionally outraged because of Cobb's Chicago background, he was compelled to sign a statement that he would never teach a course in that field at Emory. Had he remained there, he would have become a full-time member of the philosophy department. As it was, after five years Colwell was invited to become president of the School of Theology at Claremont, and he in turn invited Cobb and James M. Robinson to be the core of the new faculty there. Cobb finally had the opportunity to teach systematic theology. For those of us who have been deeply influenced by Cobb's thought and person, this call has to be viewed providentially.

In this context he published his first book, *Varieties of Protestantism* (1960), in which he argued that the central concerns of each denomination do not necessarily conflict with each other. Many years later he would reach a similar conclusion about Christianity and Buddhism.

Cobb next wrote the book that is still his best piece of scholarship, *Living Options in Protestant Theology: A Survey of Methods* (1962). While continuing the argument of his dissertation that speculative beliefs are unavoidable (and this time he included a critique of Barth's "revelational positivism"), he also argued (against neo-Thomism and Boston Personalism) the impossibility of a strictly "natural" theology, in the sense of one based upon data equally open to all persons regardless of their historical background. For example, the "arguments for the existence of God," as developed by philosophers within the Christian tradition, already presuppose the vision of the world as created—e.g., in the perception of it as "contingent." Combining his two conclusions— that Christian theology presupposes a speculative philosophy serving as a natural theology and that there can be no *neutral* natural theology—Cobb points to the need for a *Christian* philosophy or natural theology. With the qualifier *Christian* we indicate our awareness that even the most abstract speculation is carried out from the standpoint of a *particular* perspective, or vision of reality, which is derived from a historically conditioned "community of faith." There is no such thing as philosophy per se, but only Hellenic philosophy, Christian philosophy, Buddhist philosophy, Humean philosophy, and so on. Cobb continued this argument in *A Christian Natural Theology: Based on the Thought of Alfred North Whitehead* (1965).

His insistence upon the relativizing adjective *Christian* showed the continuing influence of McKeon's relativism and put Cobb at odds with Schubert Ogden and David Tracy,[2] who believe that the only criterion for choosing a philosophical support for the theological task should be its intrinsic excellence, judged on purely philosophical grounds. Cobb maintained that that criterion needed to be supplemented by the philosophy's appropriateness to the Christian vision of reality (since other philosophies might be equally excellent from the viewpoint of people with other visions of reality). He suggested that Whitehead's philosophy is appropriate in this sense, as it embodies the Christian vision of the world as creation. Hence, he could agree with those liberal and neo-orthodox theologians who believed that classical theology's use of Greek philosophy, especially Aristotle, had distorted Christian faith, while arguing that the use of Whitehead's philosophy would not.

Cobb's chief concern was God, and he was primarily interested in Whitehead's philosophy because it provided an intellectually cogent way to affirm the reality of God, including God's efficacy in our lives and in the world in general. But Whitehead's doctrine of God is inextricably bound up with his whole metaphysical system. What he meant by God, and the reasons he had for speaking of God, make no sense apart from his quite novel ideas about what the world is made of and about the nature of human perception. So Cobb's "Christian natural theology" includes the discussion of God's reality and efficacy within a discussion of how the world looks through eyes informed by Whitehead's vision.

Given his empirical bent, it was important to Cobb to stress the experiential rootage of talk about God. Most empiricism, equating perception with *sense* perception, has concluded that there can be no direct experience of God. However, Whitehead portrays sense perception as derivative of a more basic kind of relatedness, called "prehension," in which one directly grasps previous events, which themselves have prehended previous ones. This nonsensory preconscious prehension is at the root of our response to reality and is a kind of response that we share with all other events—from animals, cells, and atoms below to God above.

By portraying all levels of reality as having a basic type of relatedness in common, Whitehead could explain how every level of reality could influence every other level. Hence, he could explain how mind and body could influence each other—always a big mystery to dualists. He could thereby explain how God could influence us (i.e., because we can prehend God) and in fact how God can affect all things in the world (i.e., because all individuals have some ability to prehend the actualities in their environment and because God is present in everything's environment). Cobb points out that this makes a Whiteheadian-based theology strikingly different from the tendency of most modern thought, which has denied the meaningfulness of talk about God or at most has limited God to some sphere of distinctively human experience, such as conscience or language. Whitehead had reopened the possibility for speaking of the world as God's creation and for seeing God, as Holy Spirit, directly and intimately related to every detail of the world process.

God's effect upon the world is not, however, total determination of its events. God's power is persuasive, not coercive. This means that the idea of a good creator and provider is not undermined by the problem of evil—another one of those "objections to Christian faith" Cobb had studied. God acts in the world by providing novel possibilities for its creatures. God's "primordial nature," as Whitehead calls this aspect of God, is God's appetitive envisagement of primordial potentialities. It is only because this reservoir of previously unactualized possibilities is energizing in the world that we can understand how novelty is possible (as in the increasing complexity of the evolutionary process). God acts thus not as another coercive force but as a persuasive lure. By stressing this side of Whitehead's thought, Cobb carries on the main thrust of Wieman, who, without employing the speculative Whiteheadian ideas, looked upon the process of "creative transformation" as God in the world.

Whitehead also portrays God, in turn, as prehending the world and thus having a "consequent nature." With this doctrine, Whitehead rejects the long-standing idea, inherited by the early Christian theologians from Greek thought, that to be divine is to be beyond change and passion in all respects. Whitehead's doctrine that God is affected by the world, as the "fellow sufferer who understands," provides a philosophical way of recovering the biblical notion that what we do "unto the least of these" we do unto God, and for making more sense out of prayer than traditional theism ever did.

This "consequent nature" of God was the side Hartshorne had most stressed. It provided a basis for affirming the meaningfulness of life. Hartshorne has long considered personal or "subjective" immortality highly improbable. Our lives have permanent meaning, even in the light of the eventual death of our planet, because we have "objective immortality," being remembered and cherished everlastingly by God.

This is central to Cobb's own eschatology. He has also stressed that Whitehead's view of the person, according to which the soul is distinct from the brain, does make life after death possible. Perhaps through prehensions of God and other souls the series of experiences could find support beyond the body. Cobb has continued to be open to this possibility and to think about forms of continued existence that would be more a blessing than a curse.[3] But he has never made this an essential part of this theology.

During this period, Cobb understood the essence of Christian faith to be a particular preconceptual "vision of reality." As preconceptual, this vision is tied to no particular set of conceptual beliefs. But it is not merely a noncognitive *blik* which can be neither true nor false; it does say something about the nature of reality and hence can in principle be true. One can argue for its truth by formulating a convincing conceptual system that expresses this vision. Further, since the Christian vision of reality sees the world as *creation*, Cobb disagreed with Bultmann's view that faith could be characterized as a self-understanding and explicated by means of a philosophy, such as that of Heidegger's *Being and Time*, that provided concepts for understanding human existence from within but none for understanding God and other creatures in themselves. Partly because he understood the nature of faith differently, Cobb took issue with the use of linguistic, existentialist, or phenomenological analysis as adequate for explicating Christian faith; thus he disagreed with the dominant schools of philosophy of religion and theology in the fifties and sixties. Only a full-fledged metaphysics can explicate the essence of Christian faith, since it is a vision of reality as a whole, not just of the self.

THE STRUCTURE OF CHRISTIAN EXISTENCE

However, Cobb's engagement with the Heideggerian tradition, partly through the influence of his fellow "transplant" from Emory, James M. Robinson,[4] did have an important effect upon his understanding of Christian faith. He came increasingly to see the essence of faith as a particular "structure of existence," which involves a way of relating to others and a way of structuring the various dimensions of the psyche (body, emotions, reason, will, spirit).[5] The Christian vision of reality, requiring a Christian natural theology for its explication, was still seen as necessary, but more as the necessary support for a particular mode of existing than as the essence of faith itself.[6] This shift could be seen in part as a return, in sophisticated form, to his Methodist pietism, in which being a Christian was more a matter of experience and of living than of believing certain ideas. While expressing his agreement with the Bultmannians that faith is fundamentally a mode of existence, Cobb relativizes their position. He finds their equation of Christian faith and unfaith with authentic and inauthentic existence, understood as two permanent possibilities for human existence, radically unhistorical. He finds it incredible to suppose that the complex structure of modern Westerners, as illuminated in *Being and Time*, emerged full-blown with the first appearance of beings worthy of the name human. In his view, there have been many stages of development between us and our apelike ancestors. Also, he finds it unilluminating to lump together modes of being as diverse as those of an Eastern mystic and a Western "other-directed" individual. Finally, seeing the essence of Christian faith as a *permanent* possibility of human existence implies that it is independent of all changing theological-cosmological ideas. One bad effect of this false belief is that it encourages theologians to think they can ignore the difficult task of relating the Christian vision of reality to the cosmological ideas expressed in the natural sciences.

Cobb employs Whitehead's ideas, in conversation with Erich Neumann, Karl Jaspers, and Lewis Mumford, to develop an evolutionary understanding of the rise of animal, primitive, and then axial existence, which has a plurality of structures. Although there can be successive stages within one tradition, e.g., Hindu and Buddhist, Homeric and Socratic, prophetic and Christian, the various traditions cannot be put into some kind of hierarchy. Buddhist existence is basically different from Christian, not a "preparation" for it or an "inauthentic" actualization of the general axial structure. The authentic-inauthentic language makes sense only *within* a particular structure. For example, "spiritual existence," in which one is radically responsible for one's own structure, has an inauthentic mode (self-preoccupation) and an authentic mode (freedom for genuine concern for the other).

Cobb tried out these ideas while lecturing as a Fulbright professor in Mainz, Germany, in 1965–66, and published them as *The Structure of Christian Existence* (1967).

TRANSITION FROM SCHOLASTICISM
TO THE CALL FORWARD

For Cobb, the major figure at Mainz was Wolfhart Pannenberg.[7] His influence increased Cobb's sense of the importance of eschatological hope for Christian faith.

Another influence in that period was the "death of God" movement, with Cobb's best friend from Chicago days, Thomas Altizer, at the center of attention.

One irony of this movement, from Cobb's perspective, was that it appeared just as he was beginning to be able to talk about God and the effects of God in the world without extreme discomfort. In one sense it had no effect upon him, for it was a rejection of the wholly transcendent God, who had already died for him at Chicago, and of a corresponding theological approach (most of whose leaders had been Barthians) which he had rejected.

But it did have an effect. As Altizer saw, Cobb's response to it, *God and the World* (1969), was a transitional work. In retrospect, Cobb regards his work up through 1965 as "Whiteheadian scholasticism," in which he sought to show how Whitehead's thought could be employed to make sense of most of the concerns of neo-orthodoxy. Partly through the influence of the "death of God" movement, and especially of Altizer, he came to reject this maximalist approach, which relied partly on Whitehead's authority, and to favor speaking about God only from his own authentic convictions, which were coming to center on God as the source of novelty.

The central part of *God and the World* is chapter 2, which focuses on the image of God as "The One Who Calls" us forward. It reflects Cobb's greater appreciation for Wieman—although Cobb rejects Wieman's identification of God and creative transformation, seeing God instead as the *source* of such transformation. This chapter also reflects Cobb's change of focus from God's eternal nature to God's concrete effects at particular times—a change already begun in *The Structure of Christian Existence*, which portrayed God's effects in terms of changing structures of human existence. This chapter also shows Cobb's growing conviction that the theological task is not exhausted by developing an intelligible conceptuality for one's time. People live more by images than concepts; the theologian must participate in the process of shaping helpful images.

Chapter 2 has been the most influential part of this book. However, in chapter 3 Cobb applied the results of his metaphysical and epistemological labors of the previous decades to the questions of God's reality, location, and efficacy. Chapter 2 could not have been written without chapter 3. As Cobb later said: "Images are powerful only when those who hold them believe, consciously or unconsciously, that the images are appropriate to reality."[8]

In the remainder of this essay, I will discuss Cobb's position during the decade and a half from 1969 to 1984 as a single movement, dealing with the issues thematically instead of sequentially. It is true that some of the themes developed later than others, but all of them can be seen as elements in a single emerging stance.

FROM ECOLOGICAL CRISIS TO
ECOLOGICAL-POLITICAL THEOLOGY

The most abrupt and datable transformation in Cobb's thinking came in 1969, as the implications of the ecological crisis hit
him. Reinhold Niebuhr had been one of his heroes; he had been
reading the liberation and political theologians with much concur-
rence. But he had continued to separate his political interests from
his theological work, reflecting the departmental distinction between systematic theology and ethics. He says that only the realization in 1969 "that the whole human race was on a collision
course with disaster shook me out of this dualism."[9]

Between 1970 and 1981 Cobb published two books[10] and fifteen papers on ecological concerns. The incorporation of an ecological stance was in one sense relatively natural. As he came to
see, all the needed elements were already there in Whitehead's
thought and even more explicitly in Hartshorne's. The doctrine
that all actualities have experience and hence intrinsic value
means that a purely anthropocentric ethic, in which other creatures are viewed merely as means for our ends, is inappropriate. A
reverence for all being, especially for all life, is called for. In distinction from Schweitzer's unlivable ethic of *equal* reverence for
all life, process thought allows for gradations of intrinsic value,
corresponding to our sense that some forms of life are intrinsically
more important than others. Further, Whitehead offers an ecological view stating that an individual is not a "substance" which is
what it is prior to its relations. Rather, reality is composed of
events, each of which is a creative synthesis of the elements in its
environment. (Cobb has recently come to refer to process thought
as providing an "ecological model" of reality, which has, among
other things, led him to criticize the departmental approach to education.) Finally, the idea that the ultimate locus of value is God's
experience means that our ethic should consider instrumental as
well as intrinsic value and should endeavor to sustain the entire
biosphere.

Since he now saw inherited Christian faith itself as significantly responsible for our plight—as a consequence of its view
that the earth's only value was as the stage for the divine-human
drama of salvation—Cobb began to think not only of making the
Christian vision of reality intelligible but also of transforming it.

The ecological issue involved political issues to a degree, but
it was not until 1982 that Cobb published a programmatic book
arguing that process theology can and must become a political the-

ology, in which both sociological theory and ecological theory are combined.[11] Process theology must overcome its abstractness and deal with the concrete issues of the day. Process theologians must come to relate their work to the sociopolitical matrix in which they are embedded, not just to the history of ideas. Cobb stresses that Whitehead's thought points to the degree to which our perspective and interests are conditioned, even if not totally determined, by the immediate world out of which we arise.

This move represents a reappropriation of the concerns of what Cobb calls the earlier tradition of "process theology," the sociohistorical school of Shirley Jackson Case and Shailer Mathews, which had dominated Chicago Divinity School prior to the arrival of Wieman and then Hartshorne. Case and Mathews had stressed that theological reflection in the early church had been in the service of the church's social mission and that this should be the case today. Most critics point to this school's optimistic assumptions, but Cobb points out that it also had no adequate way to speak of God. With the former weakness remedied by Reinhold Niebuhr, and the latter by Whitehead and Hartshorne, Cobb believes process theology should return to its earlier understanding of the theological task as that of speaking out of our tradition to the most urgent needs of the day.[12]

This move also represents an agreement—an all-too-belated one, Cobb believes—with the main formal point of liberation and political theologians: the rejection of the theory-application model in favor of a theory-praxis model. The point is that one's theory, or systematic theology, cannot be developed in one context, such as the history of Western ideas, and then "applied" to another context. The theory must be developed out of reflection upon the context one is concerned to transform, or it will probably be irrelevant or even counterproductive.

FROM ESSENCE TO CHRIST AS CREATIVE TRANSFORMATION

Closely related to the rejection of the dualism between theology and ethics is Cobb's rejection of his earlier search for an essence of Christian faith. There is no self-identical core to be found in the various embodiments. Christianity is more like an onion than an apple. Cobb has come to agree with Case and Mathews that the essence of a movement is its history. He clarifies this notion in terms of Whitehead's idea of a "living person," which is not a self-identical substance but a serially ordered society of occasions of experience with a particular kind of order. The self-identity of a person is based not upon an unchanging essence, shared by all the experiences—what does the ninety-year-old man have in common with the one-year-old baby he was?—but upon a particular mode of relatedness from moment to moment. This is a relatedness (called "hybrid physical feelings" by Whitehead) in which one does not keep repeating inherited forms but transforms one's character by incorporating new forms which arise from time to time in response to new situations. For the church to be Christian today is not for it to preserve any particular past form, but to live responsibly and creatively out of its tradition, especially its memory of Jesus.

This change in Cobb's thinking has been accompanied by a change in his christology. Earlier he sought to provide a plausible and conceptually clear account of Jesus' distinctive structure of existence, including his relation to God. He had avoided the term *Christ* as being a source of confusion. Now he has come to speak of Christ as the divine Logos—the primordial nature of God—incarnate in the world.[13] This Logos is the source of all creative transformation in the world. So Christ *is* creative transformation. Due to the unique role creative transformation played in the structure of Jesus' existence, it is appropriate to identify him as *the* Christ. Christ as creative transformation is at work in all things.

Since Christianity is the movement that has made Christ central to it, it is natural that creative transformation has particularly characterized its history. To be faithful to Christ today is to continue this process. We are called to appropriate our Christian history responsibly in relation to the major challenges of the day, such as natural science, the ecological crisis, racism, global economic injustice, the encounter with other religions, the feminist critique of patriarchal religion, the anti-Judaism of historic Christianity, and the threat of nuclear war.

This rejection of essentialist thinking, and of the theology-ethics (theory-application) distinction, has led Cobb to abandon the idea of writing a "systematic theology." He earlier had seen the central theological task as hermeneutical: making the unchanging essence of Christian faith intelligible for contemporaries. Now he sees theology as seeking to transform reality, including Christian faith itself, not as simply interpreting it and then leaving the "relevance" to ethicists and other "practical theologians." Writing a systematic theology would imply that Christianity had an unchanging essence which could be stated in abstraction from the concrete issues of the day.

FEMINISM AND BUDDHISM

Cobb's new view does not mean that truth is not important for its own sake, nor that theology should not deal with perennial issues, such as the problem of evil. Nor does it mean that the concrete issues of the day are to be limited to sociopolitical problems. The feminist critique of patriarchal Christianity and the encounter with other religious traditions are two contemporary challenges that, he believes, require a self-transformation on the part of Christianity.

In relation to feminism he has stressed the fact, already seen by Mary Daly, that the Whiteheadian view of God does not share the stereotypically masculine qualities: God's consequent nature is responsive, and God's activity in the world is persuasion, not unilateral imposition. A Whiteheadian view does not oppose "man" to "nature" but sees humanity as part of the organic web of life. It rejects the self-enclosed, autonomous ego in favor of a relational view of the self which is constituted by its relationships to others. Further reflection has led Cobb to dissatisfaction with his earlier suggestions about Christ and the trinity.[14] He has recently suggested that *Christ* should be identified with the incarnation not only of the second "person" of the trinity (the principle of creative transformation) but also of the whole triune God, so that Christ is responsive as well as creative love. He no longer holds that Christ must be called "he," because the second person of the trinity can be called "Sophia," not only Logos.[15]

Given Cobb's childhood, it is not surprising that he has been concerned about the appropriate missionary stance of Christianity in relation to other religions. He has become active in interreligious dialogue, primarily with Buddhism. He had been dissatisfied with his conclusion in *The Structure of Christian Existence* that Christianity and Buddhism simply confront each other as equal but diametrically opposed structures of existence. Through collaboration with a Buddhist, Cobb came to a new way of seeing the relation: Whitehead and Nagarjuna differ not ontologically but only by differing valuations of the ultimate reality of codependent arising, or the many becoming one, which Buddhists call "emptiness" and Whitehead calls "creativity."[16] The negative evaluation by Nagarjuna and the positive one by Whitehead are related to their attention to the different ultimates of Buddhism and Christianity. The Buddhist focuses on emptiness, which is beyond all forms; the Christian on God, who is the source of forms.[17] On this basis, Cobb has come to see Buddhist atheism and Christian theism as both true. They are complementary approaches to the one inconceivably complex reality. Each side can be enriched by creative transformation of itself by appropriating what the other has seen.[18]

By stressing complementarity Cobb rejects the hitherto dominant approaches. He obviously rejects dismissing other religions as false or as mere preparations for Christianity. He also rejects the notion that all traditions are at bottom identical. That notion can result in subtle Christian imperialism, if other religions are understood in terms of Christian categories of "faith" and "God," or Vedantist imperialism, if it is assumed that the Christian God is finally to be understood as the impersonal infinite.

Cobb's rejection of essence thinking is related to his interest in moving beyond understanding to mutual transformation, since the latter is unlikely to occur when each party assumes it is entrusted with a nonnegotiable essence to protect.

CONCLUDING REMARKS

Cobb's interest in the helpfulness of a Whiteheadian approach to the whole gamut of human concerns has found institutional expression. In 1971 he and Lewis Ford launched a journal, *Process Studies*; in 1973 he and I established the Center for Process Studies, with the support of the School of Theology at Claremont and Claremont Graduate School.

About 1975, when Thomas Altizer and I had to decide on a title for a book we were editing on Cobb's theology,[19] the most appropriate one seemed to be *John Cobb's Theology in Process*; in the intervening years, this theological process has continued.[20] A personal biography could equally well be titled "John Cobb in Process." Anyone looking for a self-identical essence would find little in common with the pietistic prig lampooned as "Spares" by his college classmates. Cobb has developed a warm, forgiving, encouraging, concerned, generous spirit which reflects well upon his new God. These characteristics, his originality and clarity of thought, his self-deprecating sense of humor, and his continued sense of responsibility to his institutions, his fellow creatures, and his God make him beloved by his colleagues and students alike.[21]

NOTES

1. "To Pray or Not to Pray: A Confession," in *Prayer in My Life*, ed. Maxie Dunnam (Nashville: Parthenon, 1974), 83–112; *Praying for Jennifer* (Nashville: Upper Room, 1985).

2. See Tracy's critique and Cobb's reply in *John Cobb's Theology in Process*, ed. David Ray Griffin and Thomas J. J. Altizer (Philadelphia: Westminster, 1977).

3. "What is the Future?" in *Hope and the Future of Man*, ed. Ewert H. Cousins (Philadelphia: Fortress, 1972).

4. Cobb and Robinson edited three books in a series called "New Frontiers in Theology." The first two involved the influence of Heidegger: *The Later Heidegger and Theology* (New York: Harper & Row, 1963) and *The New Hermeneutic* (1964).

5. See "The Intra-Psychic Structure of Christian Existence," *Journal of the American Academy of Religion* 36 (December 1968): 327–39.

6. See "Christian Natural Theology and Christian Existence," *The Christian Century* 82 (3 March 1965): 265–67; reprinted in *Frontline Theology*, ed. Dean G. Peerman (Atlanta: John Knox, 1967).

7. The third of the Cobb-Robinson series, *Theology as History* (New York: Harper & Row, 1967), was devoted to Pannenberg's thought.

8. *Process Theology as Political Theology* (Philadelphia: Westminster, 1982), 72–73.

9. Ibid., x–xi. A good study of Cobb's theology that makes this shift in 1969 central is Paul Custodio Bube, *Ethics in John Cobb's Process Theology* (Atlanta: Scholar's Press, 1988).

10. *Is It Too Late? A Theology of Ecology* (Beverly Hills, Calif.: Bruce Books, 1971); *The Liberation of Life: From the Cell to the Community*, with Charles Birch (Cambridge: Cambridge University Press, 1981).

11. *Process Theology as Political Theology.*

12. "Process Theology and the Doctrine of God," *Bijdragen* 41 (December 1980): 350–67; *Process Theology as Political Theology*, 65; "The Origins of Process Theology," *Meaning, Truth, and God*, ed. Leroy S. Rouner (Notre Dame: Notre Dame Press, 1982), 91–111, esp. 104–10. This latter essay is also especially illuminating for the rejection of "essence" thinking, discussed in the next section.

13. *Christ in a Pluralistic Age* (Philadelphia: Westminster, 1975); *Process Theology: An Introductory Exposition*, with David Ray Griffin (Philadelphia: Westminster, 1976), chap. 6.

14. In *Christ in a Pluralistic Age,* "Postscript," and *Process Theology: An Introductory Exposition,* chap. 8.

15. "Christ Beyond Creative Transformation," *Encountering Jesus,* ed. Stephen T. Davis (Atlanta: John Knox, 1988), 141–78. He also sees this move to a triune incarnation as enabling him to speak of Christ's identity with the poor, their suffering, and the truth they can see but the rich cannot.

16. "Mosha-Dharma and Prehensions: A Comparison of Nagarjuna and Whitehead" (with Ryusei Takeda), *Process Studies* 4/1 (Spring 1974): 26–36.

17. "Buddhist Emptiness and the Christian God," *Journal of the American Academy of Religion* (March 1977): 11–26.

18. *Beyond Dialogue: Toward a Mutual Transformation of Christianity and Buddhism* (Philadelphia: Fortress, 1982).

19. Cobb had previously co-edited *The Theology of Altizer: Critique and Response* (Philadelphia: Westminster, 1971).

20. This theological biography was written in 1983 (for inclusion in *A Handbook of Christian Theologians,* revised and enlarged, ed. Martin E. Marty and Dean G. Peerman, copyright © 1984 by Abingdon Press, reprinted in slightly revised form by permission) and therefore, of course, does not deal with further developments since that year. The three most important aspects have been his book with Joseph Hough on theological education (which has evoked considerable response, including *The Education of the Practical Theologian: Responses to Joseph Hough and John Cobb's Christian Identity and Theological Education,* ed. Don S. Browning, David Polk, and Ian Evison [Atlanta: Scholars Press, 1989]), his continuing work in Buddhist-Christian dialogue (he served as the first president of the Society for Buddhist-Christian Studies, 1987–89, and has co-edited *The Emptying God: A Buddhist-Jewish-Christian Conversation* [1990]), and his work in economics in relation to the ecological crisis (which has culminated in the publication late in 1989 of *For the Common Good: Redirecting the Economy toward Community, the Environment, and a Sustainable Future,* co-authored with economist Herman Daly). Cobb has said that he has no big work on his mind that he has been waiting until retirement to write, and that the book with Daly will have to serve as his *magnum opus.* However, having seen Cobb's genuine openness to the future and his resulting changes of mind in the past, we can reasonably hope that further great works will be brought forth.

21. The unreferenced quotations from Cobb in the early sections of this essay are taken from a brief, unpublished theological autobiography written by Cobb about 1965 for the Pacific Coast Theological Society.

Appendix B

A Bibliography of the Writings of John B. Cobb, Jr.

BOOKS WRITTEN

1. *Varieties of Protestantism*. Philadelphia: Westminster Press, 1960.

2. *Living Options in Protestant Theology*. Philadelphia: Westminster Press, 1962.

3. *A Christian Natural Theology*. Philadelphia: Westminster Press, 1965.

4. *The Structure of Christian Existence*. Philadelphia: Westminster Press, 1967. Also translated into German.

5. *God and the World*. Philadelphia: Westminster Press, 1969. Also translated into German.

6. *Is It Too Late? A Theology of Ecology*. Beverly Hills, Calif.: Bruce Publishing Co., 1972. Also translated into German.

7. *Liberal Christianity at the Crossroads*. Philadelphia: Westminster Press, 1973.

8. *Christ in a Pluralistic Age.* Philadelphia: Westminster Press, 1975.

9. *Process Theology: An Introductory Exposition* (with David Ray Griffin). Philadelphia: Westminster Press, 1976. Also translated into Italian, German, and Japanese.

10. *Theology and Pastoral Care.* Philadelphia: Fortress Press, 1977. Also translated into Dutch.

11. *The Liberation of Life: From the Cell to the Community* (with Charles Birch). Cambridge: Cambridge University Press, 1982. Also translated into Japanese.

12. *Process Theology as Political Theology.* Philadelphia: Westminster Press, 1982.

13. *Beyond Dialogue: Toward a Mutual Transformation of Buddhism and Christianity.* Philadelphia: Fortress Press, 1982. Also translated into French, Japanese, and Korean.

14. *Talking About God: Doing Theology in the Context of Modern Pluralism* (with David Tracy). New York: Seabury Press, 1983.

15. *Christian Identity and Theological Education* (with Joseph C. Hough, Jr.). Chico, Calif.: Scholars Press, 1985.

16. *Praying for Jennifer.* Nashville: Upper Room, 1985.

17. *Biblical Preaching on the Death of Jesus* (with William A. Beardslee, David J. Lull, Russell Pregeant, Theodore J. Weeden, Sr., and Barry A. Woodbridge). Nashville: Abingdon Press, 1989.

18. *For the Common Good: Redirecting the Economy Toward Community, the Environment, and a Sustainable Future* (with Herman E. Daly). Boston: Beacon Press, 1989.

19. *Doubting Thomas: Christology in Story Form.* N.Y.: Crossroad/Continuum, 1990.

BOOKS EDITED

1. *The Later Heidegger and Theology* (with James M. Robinson). New Frontiers in Theology, Vol. I. New York: Harper and Row, 1963. Also translated into German.

2. *The New Hermeneutic* (with James M. Robinson). New Frontiers in Theology, Vol. II. New York: Harper and Row, 1964. Also translated into German.

3. *Theology and History* (with James M. Robinson). New Frontiers in Theology, Vol. III. New York: Harper and Row, 1967. Also translated into German.

4. *The Theology of Altizer: Critique and Response* (with Nicholas Gier). Philadelphia: Westminster Press, 1970.

5. *Mind in Nature: Essays on the Interface of Science and Philosophy* (with David Ray Griffin). Washington, D.C.: University Press of America, 1977.

6. *Process Philosophy and Social Thought* (with Widick Schroeder). Chicago: Center for the Scientific Study of Religion, 1981.

7. *Existence and Actuality: Conversations with Charles Hartshorne* (with Franklin I. Gamwell). Chicago: University of Chicago Press, 1984.

8. *The Emptying God: A Buddhist-Jewish-Christian Conversation* (with Christopher Ives). Maryknoll, N.Y.: Orbis Books, 1990.

ESSAYS

1. "Theological Data and Method," *Journal of Religion* 33 (July 1953), 212–23.

2. "The Possibility of a Universal Normative Ethic," *Ethics* 65 (October 1954), 55–61.

3. "Protestant Theology and Church Life," *Religion in Life* 25 (Winter 1955–56), 65–75.

4. "A Protestant Critique of Philosophy of Religion," *The Southern Philosopher* 5/3 (October 1956), 1–4.

5. "Toward Clarity in Aesthetics," *Philosophy and Phenomenological Research* 18 (December 1957), 169–89.

6. "Some Thoughts on the Meaning of Christ's Death," *Religion in Life* 28 (Spring 1959), 212–22.

7. "A Theological Typology," *Journal of Religion* 39 (July 1959), 183–95.

8. "The Philosophic Grounds of Moral Responsibility: A Comment on Matson and Niebuhr," *Journal of Philosophy* 56 (July 2, 1959), 619–21.

9. "Faith in Faith," *Southern California School of Theology at Claremont Bulletin*, July 1959: 3.

10. "Nihilism, Existentialism, and Whitehead," *Religion in Life* 30 (Autumn 1961), 521–33.

11. "An Ontological Approach to the 'Real Presence' in the Lord's Supper" (with Richard Overman), *Journal of the Inter-Seminary Movement of the Southwest* 1 (1962), 33–47.

12. "The Post-Bultmannian Trend," *Journal of Bible and Religion* 30 (January 1962), 3–11.

13. "Consultation on Hermeneutics" (with Robert Funk), *The Christian Century* 79 (June 20, 1962), 783–84; also in *Drew Gateway* 33 (Spring 1963), 123–26.

14. " 'Perfection Exists': A Critique of Charles Hartshorne," *Religion in Life* 32 (Spring 1963), 294–304.

15. "On Being Post-Christian" (response to Nels Ferré), *Christian Advocate*, June 6, 1963: 13–14.

16. "Is the Later Heidegger Relevant for Theology?" *The Later Heidegger and Theology*, ed. James M. Robinson and John B. Cobb, Jr. (New York: Harper & Row, 1963), 177–97.

17. "From Crisis Theology to the Post-Modern World," *Centennial Review* 8 (Spring 1964), 209–20; also in *Toward a New Christianity: Readings in the Death of God Theology*, ed. Thomas J. J. Altizer (New York: Harcourt, Brace and World, 1967), 241–52; *The Meaning of the Death of God*, ed. Bernard Murchland (New York: Random House, 1967), 138–52; *Radical Theology: Phase Two*, ed. C. W. Christian and Glenn R. Wittig (New York: J. B. Lippincott Company, 1967), 191–205; *Sources of Protestant Theology*, ed. William A. Scott (Beverly Hills, Calif.: Bruce Books, 1971); *Contemporary American Protestant Thought: 1900–1970*, ed. William Robert Miller (Indianapolis: Bobbs-Merrill Company, 1973).

18. "Whitehead's Philosophy and a Christian Doctrine of Man," *Journal of Bible and Religion* 32 (July 1964), 9–20.

19. "Faith and Culture," *The New Hermeneutic*, ed. James M. Robinson and John B. Cobb, Jr. (New York: Harper & Row, 1964), 219–31.

20. "A New Trio Arises in Europe," *Christian Advocate*, July 2, 1964: 7–8; also in *New Theology No. 2*, ed. Martin E. Marty and Dean G. Peerman (New York: The Macmillan Company, 1965), 257–63.

21. "Christian Natural Theology and Christian Existence," *The Christian Century* 82 (March 3, 1965), 265–67; also in *Frontline Theology*, ed. Dean G. Peerman (Atlanta: John Knox Press, 1967), 39–45. German tr., "Natürliche Theologie und christliche Existenz," *Theologie*

in *Umbruch: Der Beitrag Amerikas zur gegenwärtigen Theologie* (Munich: Chr. Kaiser Verlag, 1968).

22. "Teilhard de Chardin: The Great Yes-Sayer," *Christian Advocate,* March 11, 1965: 7–8.

23. "Ontology, History, and Christian Faith," *Religion in Life* 34 (Spring 1965), 270–87.

24. "Christianity and Myth," *Journal of Bible and Religion* 33 (October 1965), 314–20.

25. "The Finality of Christ in a Whiteheadian Perspective," *The Finality of Christ,* ed. Dow Kirkpatrick (Nashville: Abingdon Press, 1966), 122–54.

26. "The Objectivity of God," *Christian Advocate,* March 9, 1967: 7–8.

27. "Can Natural Theology Be Christian?" (response to Langdon Gilkey), *Theology Today* 23 (April 1966), 140–42.

28. "Past, Present, and Future," *Theology as History,* ed. James M. Robinson and John B. Cobb, Jr. (New York: Harper & Row, 1967), 197–220.

29. "Speaking About God," *Religion in Life* 36 (Spring 1967), 28–39.

30. "The Intra-Psychic Structure of Christian Existence," *Journal of the American Academy of Religion* 36 (December 1968), 327–39; also in *To Be a Man,* ed. George Devine (New York: Prentice-Hall, 1969), 24–40.

31. "The Author Responds" (to Claude Welch), *Journal of the American Academy of Religion* 36 (December 1968), 342–44.

32. "The Nature of the Conversion Experience," *On Conversion: Four Views* (Report of the 1967 Theological Consultation of the Methodist Board of Missions), 3–15 (largely identical with item 27).

33. "The Possibility of Theism Today," *The Idea of God: Philosophical Perspectives,* ed. Edward H. Madden, Robert Handy, and Marvin Farber (New York: Charles C. Thomas, 1968), 98–123. "Reply to Commentators," 134–38.

34. "Barth: An Appreciation from the Enemy Camp," *Christian Advocate,* March 20, 1969: 7–8.

35. "The Christian 'Dream'," *The Church Woman* 35 (March–April 1969), 13–15.

36. "Wolfhart Pannenberg's *Jesus—God and Man*" (a review article), *Journal of Religion* 49 (April 1969), 192–201.

37. "Reaction to Henry Nelson Wieman's 'The Promise of a Naturalistic Theology,' " *Action/Reaction* 2 (Winter 1969), 6–7.

38. "Freedom in Whitehead's Philosophy: A Response to Edward Pols," *Southern Journal of Philosophy* 7 (Winter 1969–70), 409–13; also, slightly abridged, in *Explorations in Whitehead's Philosophy*, ed. Lewis S. Ford & George L. Kline (New York: Fordham University Press, 1983), 45–52.

39. "What is Alive and What is Dead in Empirical Theology?" *The Future of Empirical Theology*, ed. Bernard Meland (Chicago: The University of Chicago Press, 1969), 89–101.

40. "A New United Methodist Creed," *Christian Advocate*, January 8, 1970: 7–8.

41. "The Meaning of Salvation," *Mid-stream* 9 (Spring 1970), 127–63. "Response" (to six respondents), 238–58.

42. "A Process Systematic Theology" (essay review of Daniel Day Williams' *The Spirit and the Forms of Love*), *Journal of Religion* 50 (April 1970), 199–206.

43. "Justification by Faith," *Master Sermon Series*, August, 1970: 473–82.

44. "Towards a Displacement of Historicism and Positivism," *Concilium* 7 (September 1970), 33–41. (*Concilium* appears in six languages.)

45. "The Population Explosion and the Rights of the Subhuman World," *IDOC-International: North American Edition* (September 12, 1970), 40–62; abridged in *Dimensions of the Environmental Crisis*, ed. John A. Day, F. F. Fost, and P. Rose (New York: John Wiley & Sons, 1971), 19–32.

46. "The Descent Into Hell" (response to Altizer's book), *Christian Advocate*, October 1, 1970: 7–8.

47. "On Being Grateful" and "A Strange Word," *Meditations for Churchmen in the Seventies* (School of Theology at Claremont, 1971), 10–11.

48. "Ecological Disaster and the Church," *The Christian Century* 87 (October 7, 1970), 1185–87; also as "Out of the Ashes of Disaster," *Resource* 12 (March 1971), 20–23.

49. "A Whiteheadian Christology," *Process Philosophy and Christian Thought*, ed. Delwin Brown, Ralph E. James, Jr., and Gene Reeves (Indianapolis: The Bobbs-Merrill Company, 1971), 382–98.

50. "The World and God," *Process Theology*, ed. Ewert Cousins (Richardson, Tex.: Newman Press, 1971), 153–71 (reprint of Ch. 3 of *God and the World*).

51. "Christian Theism and the Ecological Crisis," *Religious Education* 66 (January–February 1971), 3–8.

52. "The Prospect for Process Studies" (with Lewis Ford), *Process Studies* 1/1 (Spring 1971), 3–8.

53. "Hope on a Dying Planet," *The Cresset,* May 1971: n.p.; also in *Bulletin of the Peace Studies Institute* 34/7 (July 1977), 15–19.

54. "Alfred North Whitehead," *Twelve Makers of Modern Protestant Thought,* revised, ed. George L. Hunt (New York: Association Press, 1971), 129–40.

55. "The 'Whitehead Without God' Debate: The Critique," *Process Studies* 1/2 (Summer 1971), 91–100.

56. "Moltmann's 'Hope' and its Substance," *Christian Advocate,* October 14, 1971: 7–9.

57. "Christian Mission and the Role of Worship," *The New World Outlook* 62 (April 1972), 187–92.

58. "Spirit and Flesh: Dipolarity Versus Dialectic," *Philosophy of Religion and Theology: 1972* (AAR Working Papers), David Ray Griffin, Chairman (American Academy of Religion, 1972), 5–13.

59. "Man in Process," *Concilium* 9 (May 1972), 31–47.

60. "What is the Future?" *Hope and the Future of Man,* ed. Ewert H. Cousins (Philadelphia: Fortress Press, 1972), 1–14; also as "Was ist die Zukunft?" *Evangelische Theologie* 32 (July–August 1972), 372–83.

61. "Opening Paper," *IDOC Seminar* 47 (October 1972), 1–7.

62. "Regional Inclusion and the Extensive Continuum" (debate with Donald Sherburne), *Process Studies* 2/4 (Winter 1972), 277–95.

63. "Natural Causality and Divine Action," *Idealistic Studies* 3 (September 1973), 207–22.

64. "Ecology, Ethics and Theology," *Toward a Steady-State Economy,* ed. Herman E. Daly (San Francisco, Calif.: W. H. Freeman and Company, 1973), 307–20.

65. "A New Christian Existence," *Neues Testament und christliche Existenz,* ed. Hans Dieter Betz and Louise Schottroff (Tübingen: J. C. B. Mohr, 1973), 79–94.

66. "The Local Church and the Environmental Crisis," *The Christian Ministry* 4 (September 1973), 3–7; also in *Foundations* 17 (April–June 1974), 164–72.

67. "Mosha-Dharma and Prehensions: A Comparison of Nagarjuna and Whitehead" (with Ryusei Takeda), *Philosophy of Religion and Theology: 1973* (AAR Working Papers), David Ray Griffin, Chairman (American Academy of Religion, 1973), 179–92; also in abridged and revised form in *Process Studies* 4/1 (Spring 1974), 26–36.

68. "On Making a Difficult Decision" and "For World Peace," *Meditations for Churchmen in the Seventies* III (School of Theology at Claremont, 1974), 5, 21.

69. "The Word Became Flesh," *Update,* November, 1974: 2–3.

70. "To Pray or Not to Pray: A Confession," *Prayer in My Life,* ed. Maxie Dunnam (Nashville, Tenn: Parthenon Press, 1974), 83–112.

71. "The Christian Concern for the Non-Human World," *Anticipation* 16 (March 1974), 23–24.

72. "God's Love, Ecological Survival and the Responsiveness of Nature," *Anticipation* 16 (March 1974), 32–34.

73. "Men and Animals," *The Christian Science Monitor,* May 6, 1974.

74. "The Christian, the Future, and Paolo Soleri," *The Christian Century* 91 (October 30, 1974), 1008–11.

75. "The Authority of the Bible," *Hermeneutics and the Worldliness of Faith: A Festschrift in Memory of Carl Michalson,* ed. Charles Courtney, Olin M. Ivey, and Gordon E. Michalson, *The Drew Gateway* 45/1–3 (1974–75), n.p.

76. "Whatever Happened to Theology?" *Christianity and Crisis* 35 (May 12, 1975), 117–18.

77. "Kingdom Come and the Present Church," *Theological Markings* (a UTS Journal), Spring 1975: 19–28.

78. "Comment on Caraway's Critique," *Encounter* 36 (Spring 1975), 112–14.

79. "For Another Transcendence," *Worldview* 18 (June 1975), 36–37.

80. "Strengthening the Spirit," *Union Seminary Quarterly Review* 30 (Winter-Summer 1975), 130–39.

81. "A Place to Go, a Place to Stand" (advance excerpt from *Christ in a Pluralistic Age*), *Kairos* I (Autumn 1975), 5.

82. "Introduction: Conference on Mahayana Buddhism and Whitehead" (with Jay McDaniel), *Philosophy East and West* 25 (October 1975), 393–405.

83. "Spiritual Discernment in a Whiteheadian Perspective," *Religious Experience and Process Theology*, ed. Harry James Cargas and Bernard M. Lee (New York: Paulist/Newman Press, 1976), 349–67.

84. "Theological Brief," *Christian Theology: A Case Method Approach*, ed. Robert A. Evans and Thomas D. Parker (New York: Harper & Row, 1976), 66–69.

85. "Response to 'The Boston Affirmations'," *Andover Newton Quarterly* 16 (March 1976), 249–50.

86. "The Complexity of the Simple Gospel," *Cross Talk* 51 (March-April-May 1976), n.p.

87. "Can the Church Think Again?" *Occasional Papers* (United Methodist Board of Higher Education and Ministry) 1/12 (August 9, 1976), 1–12; also in abridged form in *The Circuit Rider* (United Methodist Publishing House) 1/2 (November 1976), 18–21.

88. "Response to Ogden and Carpenter," *Process Studies* 6/2 (Summer 1976), 123–29.

89. "A Response to Donald Gray," *Proceedings of the Twenty-First Annual Convention*, The Catholic Society of America, 1976: 41–44.

90. "Christ the Companion" and "Christ Our Life" in *Meditations for the Seventies* (School of Theology at Claremont, 1976), 1, 20.

91. "Buddhist Emptiness and the Christian God," *Journal of the American Academy of Religion* XLV/1 (March 1977), 11–26.

92. Minor contributions to *The Future of Science: 1974 Nobel Conference*, ed. Timothy C. L. Robinson (New York: John Wiley and Sons, 1977), 35, 103, 139–40.

93. "Some Whiteheadian Comments on the Discussion" (32–35, 68–69) and "Concluding Editorial Comments" (147–48), *Mind in Nature: Essays on the Interface of Science and Philosophy*, ed. John B. Cobb, Jr., and David Ray Griffin (Washington, D.C: University Press of America, 1977).

94. "Responses," *John Cobb's Theology in Process*, ed. David Ray Griffin and Thomas J. J. Altizer (Philadelphia: Westminster Press, 1977), 185–92.

95. "Beyond Anthropocentrism in Ethics and Religion," *On the Fifth Day*, ed. Richard Knowles Morris and Michael W. Fox (Washington: Acropolis Books, 1978), 137–53.

96. "A Question for Hans Urs von Balthasar," *Communio* 15/1 (Spring 1978), 53–59.

97. "Buddhism and Christianity as Complementary" and "Buddhism and Christianity: A Dialogue Between Drs. John B. Cobb, Jr., and Seiichi Yagi," *The Northeast Asia Journal of Theology*, March/September, 1978: 31–52.

98. "Conversation about Christianity and Buddhism," transcribed in *Gankai*, September, 1978: 42–49 and October, 1978: 42–52.

99. "Can a Christian be a Buddhist, Too?" *Japanese Religions* 10 (December 1978), 1–20; also in *Dharma and Gospel*, ed. G. W. Houston (Delhi: Sri Satguru Publications, 1984).

100. "Kirisutokyo to Toyoshiso no Deaie," *Crescent*, December, 1978: 44–50.

101. "Christianity and Eastern Wisdom," *Japanese Journal of Religious Studies* 5/4 (December 1978), 285–98.

102. "Comment on Eric C. Meyer's Article on Thomas J. J. Altizer," *Ultimate Reality and Meaning* 1/4 (1978), 299–301.

103. "Spiritual Development—A Wholistic Approach," *Update* 19/9 (October 1978), 5–7.

104. "Introduction: Process Thought and New Testament Exegesis" (with David Lull and Barry Woodbridge), *Journal of the American Academy of Religion* XLVII/1 (March 1979), 21–30.

105. "Prozesstheologie und Umweltfragen" and "Prozesstheologie und die Antwort der Kirche auf die Umweltfragen," *EPD* Dokumentation am Main, 9 April, 1979.

106. "Theology and the Environmental Crisis," *APCE Advocate* 4/1 (May 1979), 1–3.

107. "Christian Existence in a World of Limits," *Environmental Ethics* 1 (Summer 1979), 149–58; also in *Religion and Environmental Crisis*, ed. Eugene C. Hargrove (Athens: University of Georgia Press, 1986), 172–87.

108. "Needed Transformations of the Religious and Scientific Communities," *Proceedings of the First International Conference of Scientists and Religious Leaders on Shaping the Future of Mankind* (Tokyo: Kyo Bun Kwan, 1979), 17–23.

109. "Post-Conference Reflections on Yin and Yang," *Journal of Chinese Philosophy* 6 (1979), 421–26; also as "Process View on Yin and Yang," *Hanism as Korean Mind*, ed. Sang Yil Kim and Young Chan Ro (Los Angeles: Eastern Academy of Sciences, 1984), 45–50.

110. "A Critical View of Inherited Theology: How My Mind Has Changed," *The Christian Century* 20 (February 1980), 194–97.

111. "Response to 'Selected Fiction: Tales I Tell Myself'," *Occasional Papers* (United Methodist Board of Higher Education and Ministry) 33 (June 16, 1980), 1–2.

112. "Can a Buddhist be a Christian Too?" *Japanese Religions* 11/2–3 (September 1980), 35–55.

113. "A Theology of Story: Crossan and Beardslee," *Orientation by Disorientation* (Studies in Literary Criticism and Biblical Literature), ed. Richard A. Spencer (Pittsburgh: The Pickwick Press, 1980), 151–64.

114. "Foreword" to Delwin Brown, *To Set at Liberty* (Maryknoll, N.Y.: Orbis Books, 1980), xi–xiv.

115. "Process Theology and Environmental Issues," *Journal of Religion* 60/4 (October 1980), 440–58.

116. "Theologie im Prozess," *Evangelische Kommentare*, December, 1980; also as "Process Theology and the Need for a New Approach," *The Korean Roots*, October, 1981; and as "Process Theology and an Ecological Model," in *Pacific Theological Review*, Winter, 1982, and in *Cry of the Environment*, ed. Philip N. Joranson and Ken Butigan (Santa Fe: Bear & Co., 1984), 329–36.

117. "Process Theology and the Doctrine of God," *Bijdragen* 41 (December 1980), 350–67.

118. "Three Responses to Neville's *Creativity and God*" (with Charles Hartshorne and Lewis S. Ford), *Process Studies* 10/3–4 (Fall–Winter 1980), 93–109.

119. "Process Theology Lends Clarity to the Christian-Buddhist Dialogue: A Conversation," *Ten Directions* 11/1 (January 1981), 3–10, 13.

120. "Preface" to Paolo Soleri, *The Omega Seed: An Eschatological Hypothesis* (Garden City, N.Y.: Anchor Press/Doubleday, 1981), 13–26.

121. "The Integration of Objective Studies and Practical Theology," *The Iliff Review* XXXVIII/1 (Winter 1981), 51–63; also in *Integration: Objective Studies and Practical Theology* (Report of the 16th Biennial Meeting of the Association of Protestant Education for Ministry), ed. Robert Browning.

122. "Feminism and Process Thought: A Two-Way Relationship," *Feminism and Process Thought*, ed. Sheila Greene Davaney (New York: Edwin Mellen Press, 1981), 32–61.

123. Interview in *Haelan*, Spring, 1981: 16–18.

124. "Explanation and Causation in History and the Social Sciences," *Process Philosophy and Social Thought*, ed. John B. Cobb, Jr., and W.

Widick Schroeder (Chicago: Center for the Scientific Study of Religion, 1981), 3–10.

125. "The Political Implications of Whitehead's Philosophy," *Process Philosophy and Social Thought*, ed. John B. Cobb, Jr., and W. Widick Schroeder (Chicago: Center for the Scientific Study of Religion, 1981), 11–28.

126. "Postscript: The Problem of Evil and the Task of Ministry," *Encountering Evil: Live Options in Theodicy*, ed. Stephen T. Davis (Atlanta: John Knox Press, 1981), 167–76.

127. "The Identity of Christian Spirituality and Global Consciousness," *Tantur Yearbook* 1979–80 (Tantur/Jerusalem: Ecumenical Institute for Theological Research, 1981), 41–56.

128. "Buddhist-Christian Dialogue: Past, Present, and Future" (with Masao Abe and Bruce Long), *Buddhist-Christian Studies* 1 (1981), 13–29.

129. "The Kingdom of God and Pastoral Counseling," *Occasional Papers* (School of Theology at Claremont, 1981), n.p.

130. "Foreword" to Marjorie Suchocki, *God-Christ-Church* (New York: Crossroad Publishing Co., 1982), vii–ix.

131. "La Theologie du Processus et la Doctrine de Dieu," *Revue D'Histoire et de Philosophie Religieuses*, January–March, 1981: 1–21.

132. "The Religions," *Christian Theology: An Introduction to its Traditions and Tasks*, ed. Peter Hodgson and Robert King (Philadelphia: Fortress Press, 1982), 353–76.

133. "The Origins of Process Theology," in *Meaning, Truth, and God* (Boston University Studies in Philosophy and Religion, Vol. 3), ed. Leroy S. Rouner (Notre Dame, Ind.: Notre Dame Press, 1982), 91–111.

134. "Trajectories and Historic Routes," *Semeia* 24 (1982), 89–98.

135. "Man and Nature," *United Theological College Magazine* 1982–83 (Bangalore, India), 32–36.

136. "Theology and Religious Reality," *Bangalore Theological Forum* XIV/3 (1982–83), 157–69.

137. "Response to Christopher Duraisingh," *Bangalore Theological Forum* XIV/3 (1982–83), 188–90.

138. "Authority and Theology in Ecumenical Protestantism," *Theological Education*, Spring, 1983: 33–44.

139. Articles on "Concrescence," "Creationism," and "Panentheism," *The Westminster Dictionary of Christian Theology*, ed. Alan Rich-

ardson and John Bowden (Philadelphia: Westminster Press, 1983), 115–16, 130–31, 423.

140. "The Presence of the Past and the Eucharist," *Process Studies* 13/3 (Fall 1983), 218–31.

141. "Response to Eckel and Thurman," *Buddhist-Christian Studies* 3 (1983), 37–43.

142. "Theology, Perception and Agriculture," *Agricultural Sustainability in a Changing World Order*, ed. Gordon K. Douglass (Boulder, Colo.: Westview Press, 1984), 205–17.

143. "Is the Church Ready to Legislate on Sex?" *Occasional Papers* (United Methodist Board of Higher Education and Ministry) 55 (January 25, 1984), n.p.

144. "Traditional Religions in Japan and Christianity," *Occasional Papers* (School of Theology at Claremont) 5 (March 1984), n.p.

145. "Overcoming Reductionism," *Existence and Actuality*, ed. John B. Cobb, Jr., and Franklin I. Gamwell (Chicago: University of Chicago Press, 1984), 149–64.

146. "The Meaning of Pluralism for Christian Self-Understanding," *Religious Pluralism*, ed. Leroy S. Rouner (Notre Dame, Ind.: University of Notre Dame Press, 1984), 161–79.

147. "Envisioning a Just and Perfect World," *Religious Education* 79/4 (Fall 1984), 483–94.

148. "Whitehead and Natural Philosophy," *Whitehead and the Idea of Progress*, ed. Harold Holz and Ernest Wolf-Gazo (Freiburg/Munich: Verlag Karl Alber, 1984), 137–53.

149. "On Han Philosophy," *Hanism as Korean Mind*, ed. Sang Yil Kim and Young Chan Ro (Los Angeles: Eastern Academy of Human Sciences, 1984), 8–9.

150. "The Ego," *Buddhist-Christian Studies* 4 (1984), 73–83.

151. "Reply to Jürgen Moltmann's 'The Unity of the Triune God'," *St. Vladamir's Theological Quarterly* 28/3 (1984), 173–77.

152. "Theology as Thoughtful Response to the Divine Call," *The Vocation of the Theologian*, ed. Theodore W. Jennings (Philadelphia: Fortress Press, 1985), 104–19.

153. "Is There Moral Responsibility?" *Performing Arts: Mark Taper Forum* 19/4 (April 1985), 10–11.

154. "Whither the UMC?" *Circuit Rider*, May 1985: 10–11.

155. "Co-Creaturehood or Dominion—A Biblical View of God's Earth," *New World Outlook* XLV/9 (June 1985), 8–11.

156. "Theology and the Future: Dialogue with Chan-Hie Kim," *Modern Praxis* 1 (1985), 242–54.

157. "Process Theology and Liberation Theology," *Process Studies* 14/2 (Summer 1985), 124–41.

158. "Does Theology Make a Contribution to Bioethics?" *Theology and Bioethics: Exploring the Foundations and Frontiers*, ed. Earl E. Shelp (Dordrecht: D. Reidl Publishing Co., 1985), 303–07.

159. "Christian Witness in a Pluralistic World," *The Experience of Religious Diversity*, ed. John Hick and Hassan Askari (Brookfield, Vt.: Gower, 1985), 144–62.

160. "Theologie von Aufklärungswissenschaft zu einem globalen christlichen Denken," *Entwurfe der Theologie*, ed. Johannes B. Bauer (Vienna: Styria Verlag, 1985), 15–40.

161. "Whitehead's Later View on Space-Time: A Response to Patrick Hurley," *Physics and the Ultimate Significance of Time*, ed. David Ray Griffin (Albany: State University of New York Press, 1986), 122–23.

162. "Bohm and Time," *Physics and the Ultimate Significance of Time*, ed. David Ray Griffin (Albany: State University of New York Press, 1986), 154–66.

163. "Epilogue," *Buddhist-Christian Dialogue*, ed. Paul Ingram and Frederick J. Streng (Honolulu: University of Hawaii Press, 1986), 231–36.

164. "Models of Theological Unity," *Circuit Rider* 10/4 (April 1986), 4–5.

165. "Claiming the Center," *Criterion* 25/1 (Winter 1986), 2–8.

166. "Bohm's Challenge to Faith in Our Time," *Beyond Mechanism: The Universe in Recent Physics and Catholic Thought*, ed. David L. Schindler (Lanham, Md.: University Press of America, 1986), 38–50.

167. "God in Post-Biblical Christianity," *Encyclopedia of Religion*, ed. Mircea Eliade (New York: Macmillan Publishing Co., 1987), 16: 17–26.

168. "Alfred North Whitehead," *Encyclopedia of Religion*, ed. Mircea Eliade (New York: Macmillan Publishing Co., 1987), 15: 380–81.

169. "Choose Life," *Seasons of Peace*, ed. Beth Richardson (Nashville, Tenn.: Upper Room, 1986), 30–31.

170. "Beyond Political Theology," *Gottes Zukunft, Zukunft der Welt. Festschrift für Jürgen Moltmann*, ed. Herman Denser, Gerhard M.

Martin, Konrad Stock, and Michael Welker (Munich: Chr. Kaiser Verlag, 1986), 457–66.

171. "Antwort an Johann B. Metz und Langdon Gilkey," *Das neue Paradigma von Theologie*, ed. Hans Küng and David Tracy (Munich: Benziger Verlag, 1986), 145–50. Also as "Response to Johann Baptist Metz and Langdon Gilkey," *Paradigm Change in Theology* (New York: Crossroad Publishing Co., 1989), 384–89.

172. "Barth and Barthians: A Critical Appraisal," *How Karl Barth Changed My Mind*, ed. Donald K. McKim (Grand Rapids: Eerdmans, 1986), 172–77.

173. "Christianity, Political Theology, and the Economic Future," *Civil Religion and Political Theology*, ed. Leroy S. Rouner (Notre Dame, Ind.: University of Notre Dame Press, 1986), 207–23.

174. "Christology in Process-Relational Perspective," *Word and Spirit: A Monastic Review* 8 (1986), 79–94.

175. "Theology and Space," *Beyond Spaceship Earth: Environmental Ethics and the Solar System*, ed. Eugene C. Hargrove (San Francisco: Sierra Club Books, 1986), 291–311.

176. "Interview with J. Cobb," *Interviews with Nobel Laureates and Other Eminent Scholars* (Bombay: The Bhatstivedanta Institute, 1986), 22–32.

177. "Response to Wiebe," *Buddhist-Christian Studies* 6 (1986), 151–55.

178. "I Say, 'Keep the Quadrilateral'," *Circuit Rider* 11/5 (May 1987), 4–9.

179. "Response to Loomer," *American Journal of Theology & Philosophy* 8/1–2 (January & May 1987), 52–55. Also published in *The Size of God: The Theology of Bernard Loomer in Context*, ed. William Dean & Larry Axel (Macon, Ga.: Mercer University Press, 1987), 52–58.

180. "Response to S. Mark Heim," *Journal of Ecumenical Studies* 24/1 (Winter 1987), 22–23.

181. "Foreword" to Robert Brizee, *Where in the World is God?* (Nashville: Upper Room, 1987), 9–12.

182. "Global Theology in a Pluralistic Age," *Dharma World* 14 (November/December 1987), 31–37. Also in *The Unitarian Universalist Christian* 43/1 (Spring 1988), 34–45.

183. "Toward a Christocentric Catholic Theology," *Toward a Universal Theology of Religion*, ed. Leonard Swidler (Maryknoll, N.Y.: Orbis Books, 1987), 86–100.

184. "The Buddhist-Christian Dialogue," *Ecumenical Trends* 16/2 (February 1987), 17–19.

185. "Goetz, Creel, and Process Theology," *Christian Century*, January 7–14, 1987: 22–24.

186. "Dialogue Without Common Ground," *Weltoffenheit aus christlichen Glaubens: Fritz Buri zu ehren* (Bern: Verlag Paul Haupt, 1987), 145–54.

187. "Ultimate Reality: A Christian View" (in Japanese), *Annual Report from the Institute of Asian Studies* (Kyoto: Hanazono College, March, 1987), 10–32. Also "Response" (to Maseo Abe's critique), 46–50.

188. "Can You Still Lead?" *The Unitarian Universalist Christian* 42/4 (Winter 1987), 13–15.

189. "The Adequacy of Process Metaphysics for Christian Theology," *Faith and Creativity: Essays in Honor of Eugene H. Peters*, ed. George Nordgulen and George W. Shields (St. Louis, Mo.: CBP Press, 1987), 63–80.

190. "The Resurrection of the Soul," *Harvard Theological Review* 80/2 (1987), 213–27.

191. "Altizer and Christian Theology," *CLIO*, Summer, 1987: 331–44.

192. "Response to Rita Gross," *Buddhist-Christian Studies* 7 (1987), 105–12.

193. "Education and Religious Pluralism," *Daedalus* 117/2 (Spring 1988), 147–50.

194. "Christ Beyond Creative Transformation," *Encountering Jesus*, ed. Stephen T. Davis (Atlanta: John Knox, 1988), 141–78.

195. "Is Theological Pluralism Dead in the UMC?" *Christian Century*, April 6, 1988: 343–47.

196. "A Christian View of Biodiversity," *Biodiversity*, ed. E. O. Wilson (Washington, D.C.: National Academy Press, 1988), 481–85.

197. "Death and Dying: A Christian Perspective in the Context of Buddhist-Christian Dialogue," *Seeds of Peace* 4/2 (May 1988), 12–17.

198. "Wholeness Centered in Spirit," *Spirit-Centered Wholeness*, ed. H. Newton Maloney, Michele Papen-Davids, & Howard Clinebell (Lewiston/Queenston: Edwin Mellen Press, 1988), 225–45.

199. "Ecology, Science, and Religion," *The Reenchantment of Science: Postmodern Proposals*, ed. David Ray Griffin (Albany: State University of New York Press, 1988), 99–113.

200. "Thinking Theologically about Theological Education for the Future," *Theological Education for the Future*, ed. Guy Fitch Lytle (Cincinnati: Forward Movement Publications, 1988), 60–72.

201. "Wirtschaft gegen Gemeinschaft," *Evangelische Kommentare*, August, 1988: 445–50.

202. "Postmodern Social Policy," *Spirituality and Society: Postmodern Visions*, ed. David Ray Griffin (Albany: State University of New York Press, 1988), 99–106.

203. "Minjung Theology and Process Theology," *An Emerging Theology in World Perspective*, ed. Jung Young Lee (Mystic, Conn.: Twenty-Third Publications, 1988), 51–56.

204. "Theology and Economics," *Journal of Theology: United Theological Seminary* XCII (1988), 25–33.

205. "A Theology of Continuing Education," *SACEM: Proceedings at the 1988 Annual Meeting*, n.p.

206. "Theology and Economics," *The Whirlwind Culture: Frontiers in Theology: In Honor of Langdon Gilkey*, ed. Donald W. Musser and Joseph L. Price (Bloomington, Ind.: Meyer Stone Books, 1988), 135–49.

207. "Being Itself and the Existence of God," *Existence of God*, ed. John R. Jacobson and Robert Lloyd Mitchell (Lewiston, N.Y.: Edwin Mellen Press, 1988), 5–19.

208. "Befriending an Amoral Nature," *Zygon* 23/4 (December 1988), 431–36.

209. "Pannenberg and Process Theology," *The Theology of Wolfhart Pannenberg*, ed. Carl E. Braaten and Philip Clayton (Minneapolis: Augsburg, 1988), 54–74.

210. "Ministry in the World: A New Professional Paradigm," *Beyond Clericalism: The Congregation as a Focus for Theological Education*, ed. Joseph C. Hough, Jr., and Barbara Wheeler (Atlanta: Scholars Press, 1988), 23–29.

211. "Theologie in den Vereinigten Staaten: Woher und Wohin," *Evangelische Theologie* 2 (1989), 200–13.

212. "Landing the Whiteheadian Plane in the Field of Economics," *Contemporary Philosophy* XII/9 (May 1989), 16–21.

213. "Deconstruction and Reconstruction of God," *Witness and Existence: Essays in Honor of Schubert M. Ogden*, ed. Philip E. Devenish and George L. Goodwin (Chicago: University of Chicago Press, 1989), 162–76.

214. "The Buddhist-Christian Dialogue Since 1946: The Christian Side," *Religious Issues and Interreligious Dialogues*, ed. Charles Weihsun Fu and Gerhard Spiegler (New York: Greenwood Press, 1989), 571–89.

215. "The Earth and Humanity: A Christian View," *Three Faiths—One God*, ed. John Hick and Edmund S. Meltzer (London: Macmillan, 1989), 113–28.

216. "Ultimate Reality: A Christian View," *Buddhist-Christian Studies* 8 (1988), 51–64.

217. "Foreword" to *Leaving and Returning* by Stephen C. Rowe (Lewisburg: Bucknell University Press, 1989), 9.

218. "Foreword" to *Of God and Pelikans* by Jay McDaniel (Philadelphia: Westminster Press, 1989), 11–12.

219. "Foreword" to *On the Way to God: An Exploration into the Theology of Wolfhart Pannenberg* by David P. Polk (Lanham, Md.: University Press of America, 1989), xi–xii.

220. "Response by John Cobb," *The Education of the Practical Theologian: Responses to Joseph Hough and John Cobb's Christian Identity and Theological Education*, ed. Don S. Browning, David Polk, and Ian Evison (Atlanta: Scholars Press, 1989), 121–29.

221. "A Process Concept of God" (39–51), "Response to Stephen Davis" (56), and "Comment on John Hick" (165–66), *Concepts of the Ultimate*, ed. Linda J. Tessier (London: Macmillan, 1989).

222. "The Bible, the Church, and the Family" (with William A. Beardslee), *Open Hands*, Fall, 1989: 4–5.

223. "Eternal Objects and Archetypes, Past and Depth: A Response to Stanley Hopper," *Archetypal Process: Self and Divine in Whitehead, Jung, and Hillman*, ed. David Ray Griffin (Evanston: Northwestern University Press, 1989), 125–28.

224. "Only One Thing!" and "John's Response to Allan," *Circuit Rider* 14/3 (April 1990), 6–7, 8.

225. "From Individualism to Persons in Community: A Postmodern Economic Theory," *Sacred Interconnections: Postmodern Spirituality, Political Economy, and Art*, ed. David Ray Griffin (Albany: State University of New York Press, 1990), 123–42.

226. "Free Trade Versus Community: Social and Environmental Consequences of Free Trade in a World of Capital Mobility and Overpopulated Regions" (with Herman E. Daly), *Population and Environment* 11/3 (Spring 1990), 175–91.

227. "One Step Further," *CTNS Bulletin* (Center for Theology and the Natural Sciences), Winter, 1990: 1–3.

228. "Research for a Theological Faculty," *Theological Education* XXVI/2 (Spring 1990), 86–105.

229. "Postmodern Christianity in Quest of ˜Eco-Justice," *Insights: The Newsletter of the Chicago Center for Religion and Science,* May, 1990: 9, 11.

230. "On the Deepening of Buddhism," *The Emptying God: A Buddhist-Jewish-Christian Conservation,* ed. John B. Cobb, Jr., and Christopher Ives (Maryknoll, N.Y.: Orbis Books, 1990), 91–101.

231. "Two Types of Postmodernism: Deconstruction and Process," *Theology Today* XLVII/2 (July 1990), 149–58.

BOOK REVIEWS

1. "The Basis of Christian Sociality," *Christian Eschatology and Social Thought,* by Ray C. Petry. *Interpretation* 10 (October 1956), 462–63.

2. "Disturbing Complacency," *Essays in Christology for Karl Barth,* ed. T. H. L. Parker. *Interpretation* 11 (October 1957), 464–66.

3. "The Method of Analysis," *Faith and Knowledge,* by John Hick. *Interpretation* 12 (October 1958), 456–58.

4. *Aesthetics,* ed. E. Wilkinson. *Philosophy and Phenomenological Research* 19 (December 1958), 263–64.

5. *Art and the Human Enterprise,* by Iredell Jenkins. *Philosophy and Phenomenological Research* 20 (September 1959), 129–30.

6. "A Panorama of Theologies," *The Case for Orthodox Theology,* by Edward J. Carnell; *The Case for Theology in Liberal Perspective,* by L. Harold Dewolf; *The Case for a New Reformation Theology,* by William Hordern. *Interpretation* 14 (January 1960), 94–96.

7. "The Problem of Authority," *Holy Writ or Holy Church,* by George H. Tavard. *Interpretation* 14 (July 1960), 358–61.

8. *A Protestant Speaks His Mind,* by Ilion T. Jones. *The Pulpit* 31 (August 1960), 252.

9. *Spirit, Son and Father,* by Henry P. Van Dusen. *The Personalist* 41 (Winter 1960), 107–08.

10. *The Lure for Feeling,* by Mary Wyman. *Religion in Life* 30 (Winter 1960–61), 147–48.

11. *The Language of Faith,* by Samuel Laeuchli. *Christian Advocate,* July 19, 1962: 16.

12. *Intellectual Foundation of Faith*, by Henry Nelson Wieman. *Drew Gateway* 32 (Winter 1962), 107–08.

13. *Church Dogmatics IV/3*, by Karl Barth. *Interpretation* 16 (October 1962), 472–75.

14. *On the Love of God*, by John MacIntyre. *Journal of Religion* 43 (April 1963), 154–55.

15. *The Empirical Theology of Henry Nelson Wieman*, ed. Robert W. Bretall. *Religious Education* 58 (July–August 1963), 405–06.

16. *The Rationality of Faith*, by Carl Michalson. *Christian Advocate*, November 21, 1963: 19–20.

17. *Jesus and Christian Origins*, by Hugh Anderson. *Christian Advocate*, July 30, 1964: 14–15.

18. *History, Sacred and Profane*, by Alan Richardson. *Interpretation* 19 (April 1965), 220–22.

19. *Schleiermacher on Christ and Religion*, by Richard R. Niebuhr. *Religious Education* 60 (May–June 1965), 244–46.

20. *Process and Divinity: The Hartshorne Festschrift*, ed. William Reese and Eugene Freeman. *Journal of Religion* 45 (October 1965), 335–37.

21. *A Handbook of Theological Terms*, by Van Harvey. *Perkins School of Theology Journal* 18 (Winter 1965), 39–40.

22. *Zukunft und Verheissung*, by Gerhard Sauter. *Erasmus* 18/7–8 (1966), 206–07.

23. *The Relevance of Science: Creation and Cosmogony*, by C. F. von Weizsäcker. *Zygon* 1 (March 1966), 111–13.

24. *The Phenomenon of Life*, by Hans Jonas. *Interpretation* 21 (April 1967), 196–200.

25. *History and Hermeneutics*, by Carl E. Braaten. *Journal of Religion* 47 (April 1967), 154–56.

26. *No Other God*, by Gabriel Vahanian. *Religion in Life* 36 (Summer 1967), 295–96.

27. *Worldly Theology*, by Carl Michalson. *Christian Advocate*, October 19, 1967: 15–17.

28. *A Natural Theology for Our Time*, by Charles Hartshorne. *Religious Education* 62 (November–December 1967), 533.

29. *Science, Man and Morals*, by William H. Thorpe. *Journal of the American Academy of Religion* 36 (March 1968), 68–72.

30. *Memory and Hope,* by Dietrich Ritschl. *Religious Education* 63 (March–April 1968), 146–47.

31. *Experience and God,* by John E. Smith. *Religion in Life* 37 (Winter 1968), 617–18.

32. *Process Thought and Christian Faith,* by Norman Pittenger. *Religious Education* 64 (March–April 1969), 148–49.

33. *Revelation as History,* ed. Wolfhart Pannenberg. *Christian Advocate,* May 29, 1969: 16–17.

34. *A Rumor of Angels,* by Peter L. Berger. *Theology Today* 26 (July 1969), 221–22.

35. *Systematic Theology: A Historicist Perspective,* by Gordon D. Kaufman. *Journal of the American Academy of Religion* 38 (June 1970), 219–21.

36. *Philosophy of the Future,* by Ernst Bloch. *Theology Today* 28 (July 1971), 249–52.

37. *Experiential Religion,* by Richard R. Niebuhr. *Interpretation* 27 (January 1973), 100–01.

38. *God the Problem,* by Gordon D. Kaufman. *Review of Books and Religion* 2 (Mid-February 1973), 7.

39. *A House for Hope,* by William A. Beardslee. *Religion in Life* 42 (Spring 1973), 137–38.

40. *The New Consciousness in Science and Religion,* by Harold K. Schilling. *Religious Education* 68 (November–December 1973), 752–56.

41. *A Process Christology,* by David Ray Griffin. *Religion in Life* 43 (Winter 1974), 505–06.

42. *The Becoming of the Church: A Process Theology of the Structure of Christian Experience,* by Bernard M. Lee. *Process Studies* 4/4 (Winter 1974), 303–04.

43. *The Holy Spirit,* by Norman Pittenger. *Religious Education* 70 (May–June 1975), 342–43.

44. *What is Process Theology?,* by Robert Mellert. *Religious Education* 71 (January–February 1976), 101–02.

45. *Thinking About God,* by John Macquarrie. *Journal of Religion* 56 (April 1976), 208–09.

46. *Blessed Rage for Order,* by David Tracy. *The Christian Century* 93 (April 14, 1976), 369–71.

47. *A Nation of Behavers*, by Martin E. Marty. *The Wilson Quarterly*, Autumn 1976: 132.

48. *Bioethical Decision Making: Releasing Religion from the Spiritual*, by Barbara Ann Swyhart. *Process Studies* 6/4 (Winter 1976), 292.

49. *Theology and the Philosophy of Science*, by Wolfhart Pannenberg. *Religious Studies Review* 3/4 (October 1977), 213.

50. *The Recovery of the Person*, by Carlyle Marney. *Religion in Life* 158 (Winter 1979), 505–06.

51. *Beyond Existentialism and Zen*, by George Rupp. *Interpretation* 34 (January 1980), 82–84.

52. *Animal Rights*, by Andrew Linzey. *Environmental Ethics* 2 (Spring 1980), 89–93.

53. *Creativity and God*, by Robert C. Neville. *Theology Today* 37 (October 1980), 374–75.

54. *Becoming and Being: The Doctrine of God in Charles Hartshorne and Karl Barth*, by Colin Gunton. *International Studies in Philosophy* XII/1 (1980), 119–20.

55. *Theology of Nature*, by George S. Hendry. *Zygon* 15/4 (December 1980), 430–36.

56. *Buddhist-Christian Empathy*, by Joseph J. Spae. *The Eastern Buddhist* XIV/1 (Spring 1981), 138–39.

57. *The Analogical Imagination*, by David Tracy. *Religious Studies Review* 7/4 (October 1981), 281–84.

58. *Bent World: A Christian Response to the Environmental Crisis*, by Ron Elsdon. *Environmental Ethics* 4/4 (Winter 1981), 359–62.

59. *After Fundamentalism*, by Bernard Ramm. *TSF Bulletin*, May–June, 1983: 15–16.

60. *Whitehead, Process Philosophy and Education*, by Robert S. Brumbaugh. *Teachers College Record* 85/2 (Winter 1983), 329–31.

61. *Buddhism and American Thinkers*, by Kenneth Inada and Norman Jacobson. *Journal of Religion* 65/3 (July 1985), 455.

62. *God in Process Thought*, by Santiago Sia. *Modern Theology* 3/1 (October 1986), 107–09.

63. *Polity and Praxis: A Program for American Practical Theology*, by Dennis P. McCann and Charles R. Strain. *Journal of Church and State* 29/1 (1987), 139–40.

64. *Christian Theology: An Introduction to its Traditions and Tasks*, by Peter Hodgson and Robert King. *Theological Education* XXIV/1 (Autumn 1987), 144–46.

65. *Animal Sacrifices*, ed. by Tom Regan. *Environmental Ethics* 10/2 (Summer 1988), 181–82.

66. *Hartshorne and the Metaphysics of Animal Rights*, by Daniel A. Dombrowski. *Environmental Ethics* 11/4 (Winter 1989), 373–76.

67. *Community and Alienation: Essays on Process Thought and Public Life*, by Douglas Sturm. *Journal of Church and State* 31/3 (Autumn 1989), 555–56.

68. *Models of God: Theology in an Ecological, Nuclear Age*, by Sallie McFague. *Religious Studies Review* 16/1 (January 1990), 40–42.

69. *Inscriptions and Reflections: Essays in Philosophical Theology*, by Robert P. Scharlemann. *Christian Century*, February 21, 1990: 192–93.

List of Contributors

THOMAS J. J. ALTIZER is author of *The Gospel of Christian Atheism, The Descent into Hell, The Self-Embodiment of God, Total Presence, History as Apocalypse,* and *Genesis and Apocalypse.* He is Professor of Religious Studies at the State University of New York at Stony Brook, New York 11794.

WILLIAM A. BEARDSLEE is author of *Literary Criticism of the New Testament* and *A House for Hope* and co-author of *Varieties of Postmodern Theology* and *Biblical Preaching on the Death of Jesus.* He is Charles Howard Candler Professor of Religion, Emeritus, at Emory University, and is now Director of the Process and Faith Program of the Center for Process Studies, 1325 North College, Claremont, California 91711.

DAVID RAY GRIFFIN is author of *A Process Christology, God, Power, and Evil, God and Religion in the Postmodern World,* and *Evil Revisited,* co-author of *Process Theology, Varieties of Postmodern Theology,* and *Primordial Truth and Postmodern Theology,* and editor of *Physics and the Ultimate Significance of Time* and *The Reenchantment of Science.* He is Professor of Philosophy of Religion and Theology at the School of Theology at Claremont and Claremont Graduate School and Executive Director of the Center for Process Studies, 1325 North College, Claremont, California 91711.

JOSEPH C. HOUGH, JR., is author of *Black Power and White Protestants* and co-author of *Christian Identity and Theological Education* (with John Cobb) and *Beyond Clericalism: The Congregation as a Focus for Theological Education.* After having taught ethics at the School of Theology at Claremont and Claremont Graduate School from 1967 to 1989, during which time he served as Dean of the School of Theology for fourteen years, he is now Dean of the Divinity School at Vanderbilt University, Nashville, Tennessee 37240.

GORDON D. KAUFMAN is author of *Systematic Theology: A Historicist Approach, God the Problem, An Essay on Theological Method, The Theological Imagination,* and *Theology for a Nuclear Age.* A past president of the American Academy of Religion, he is Edward Mallinckrodt, Jr., Professor of Divinity at Harvard Divinity School, Cambridge, Massachusetts 02138.

CATHERINE KELLER is author of *From a Broken Web: Separation, Sexism, and Self,* a forthcoming work on eschatology tentatively entitled *Open Apocalypse: Towards a Feminist Constructive Theology of Relation,* and numerous essays in feminist theology and religious thought. She is Associate Professor of Constructive Theology at The Theological School of Drew University, Madison, New Jersey 07940.

HANS KÜNG is author of *The Church, Infallible? An Inquiry, Justification, On Being a Christian, Freud and the Problem of God, Does God Exist?, Eternal Life?, The Incarnation of God,* and *Theology for the Third Millennium,* and co-author of *Christianity and Chinese Religions.* He is Professor for Ecumenical Theology and Director of the Institute for Ecumenical Research at the University of Tübingen, Waldhäuser Strasse 23, D-7400 Tübingen 1, Germany.

SCHUBERT M. OGDEN is author of *Christ Without Myth, The Reality of God, Faith and Freedom, The Point of Christology,* and *On Theology,* and editor and translator of Rudolf Bultmann's *New Testament and Mythology and other Basic Writings.* He is Director of the Graduate Program in Religious Studies and University Distinguished Professor of Theology at Southern Methodist University, Dallas, Texas 74275.

WOLFHART PANNENBERG is author of *Jesus—God and Man, Theology and the Kingdom of God, Basic Questions in Theology* (4 vols.), *The Apostles' Creed, Theology and the Philosophy of Science, What is Man?, The Church, Ethics, Faith and Reality, The Idea of God and Human Freedom,* and *Metaphysics and the Idea of God.* He is Director of the Institute on Fundamental Theology and Ecumenics and Professor of Systematic Theology on the Protestant Theological Faculty of the University of Munich, Schellingstrasse 3/III, 8000 Munich 40, Germany.

MARJORIE HEWITT SUCHOCKI is author of *God–Christ–Church: A Practical Guide to Process Theology* (now in revised edition), *The End of Evil: Process Eschatology in Historical Con-*

text, numerous articles on feminist and process theology, and a forthcoming book on sin. After serving seven years as Dean of Wesley Theological Seminary, she is now Ingraham Professor of Theology at the School of Theology, Claremont, California 91711.

JACK VERHEYDEN is editor of Friedrich Schleiermacher's *Life of Jesus* and author of several essays in historical and systematic theology. His essay in the present volume is the sketch for a forthcoming book on that topic. He is a member of the Department of Religion at Claremont Graduate School, which he chaired from 1973 to 1985, and Professor of Theology at the School of Theology, Claremont, California 91711.

Index